EVALUATION AND EDUCATION: AT QUARTER CENTURY

EVALUATION AND EDUCATION: AT QUARTER CENTURY

Ninetieth Yearbook of the
National Society for the Study of Education

PART II

Edited by
MILBREY W. MCLAUGHLIN AND D. C. PHILLIPS

Editor for the Society
KENNETH J. REHAGE

Distributed by THE UNIVERSITY OF CHICAGO PRESS • CHICAGO, ILLINOIS

The National Society for the Study of Education

Founded in 1901 as successor to the National Herbart Society, the National Society for the Study of Education has provided a means by which the results of serious study of educational issues could become a basis for informed discussion of those issues. The Society's two-volume yearbooks, now in their ninetieth year of publication, reflect the thoughtful attention given to a wide range of educational problems during those years. In 1971 the Society inaugurated a series of substantial publications on Contemporary Educational Issues to supplement the yearbooks. Each year the Society's publications contain contributions to the literature of education from more than a hundred scholars and practitioners who are doing significant work in their respective fields.

An elected Board of Directors selects the subjects with which volumes in the yearbook series are to deal and appoints committees to oversee the preparation of manuscripts. A special committee created by the Board performs similar functions for the series on Contemporary Educational Issues.

The Society's publications are distributed each year without charge to members in the United States, Canada, and elsewhere throughout the world. The Society welcomes as members all individuals who desire to receive its publications. Information about current dues may be found in the back pages of this volume.

This volume, *Evaluation and Education: At Quarter Century,* is Part II of the Ninetieth Yearbook of the Society. Part I, which is published at the same time, is entitled *The Care and Education of America's Young Children: Obstacles and Opportunities.*

A listing of the Society's publications still available for purchase may be found in the back pages of this volume.

Library of Congress Catalog Number: 90-063418
ISSN: 0077-5762

Published 1991 by
THE NATIONAL SOCIETY FOR THE STUDY OF EDUCATION

5835 Kimbark Avenue, Chicago, Illinois 60637
© 1991 by the National Society for the Study of Education

First Printing, 5,000 Copies

Printed in the United States of America

Contributors to the Yearbook

MILBREY W. MCLAUGHLIN, School of Education, Stanford University, Co-editor
D. C. PHILLIPS, School of Education, Stanford University, Co-editor

MARVIN C. ALKIN, School of Education, University of California, Los Angeles
ROBERT BORUCH, Graduate School of Education, University of Pennsylvania
THOMAS D. COOK, Center for Urban Affairs and Policy Research, Northwestern University
ELLIOT W. EISNER, School of Education, Stanford University
ERNEST R. HOUSE, School of Education, University of Colorado
HENRY M. LEVIN, School of Education, Stanford University
MICHAEL SCRIVEN, Pacific Graduate School of Psychology, Palo Alto, California
ROBERT E. STAKE, Center for Instructional Research and Curriculum Evaluation, University of Illinois, Champaign-Urbana
DANIEL STUFFLEBEAM, Evaluation Center, Western Michigan University
RALPH W. TYLER, School of Education, Stanford University
CAROL H. WEISS, Graduate School of Education, Harvard University

Acknowledgment

As Milbrey W. McLaughlin and D. C. Phillips, editors of this yearbook, point out in their "Preface," the volume marks the twenty-fifth anniversary of "the development of a professional cadre of experts in the evaluation of educational and social programs." The seminal writings of a number of experts in evaluation were enormously influential in shaping the early development of the field of program evaluation. The editors invited several of these authors to revisit the topics of their concern at that time. This volume of essays contains their responses to that invitation.

The National Society for the Study of Evaluation is most grateful to all who have had a part in this interesting enterprise. As the authors reflect upon issues central to program evaluation in the past quarter century, they provide the reader with most interesting and instructive perspectives on an important piece of recent history in education and in evaluation. The Society is especially appreciative of the work of the editors, whose initial proposal for this yearbook was received with great enthusiasm by the Board of Directors. In bringing their work to completion, the editors and the contributors have enabled the Society to produce a distinctive and valuable addition to its yearbook series.

The Society is also indebted to Margaret Early, who assisted in editing some of the chapters of this volume, and to H. Jerome Studer, who prepared the name index.

Editors' Preface

Ever since members of the human race first developed social or political programs, they also have been carrying out evaluations. From the dawn of history down to the present, kings and emperors, prime ministers and presidents, dictators and chairmen, generals and senators, have all wanted to monitor their programs and to receive data about them—whether these programs involved colonial settlement, military conquest and "pacification," wars on poverty, five-year plans for agricultural or industrial development, mass education, and the like. Furthermore, those on whose shoulders fell the task of actually operating or delivering the programs—school principals and teachers, curriculum constructors, agricultural experts, health care professionals, "back room boys" in the military, and so on—also hungered for the feedback that evaluation can give. And yet it was not until 1969 that the first NSSE Yearbook on evaluation appeared (*Educational Evaluation: New Roles, New Means*, edited by Ralph Tyler), and it was a further twenty-one years until the present volume! The moral is simple: Although evaluations have been of enduring interest, until very recently the methodology of evaluation was virtually taken for granted.

It often takes an anniversary to stimulate discussion, examination, meta-inquiry, the weighing of pros and cons, a looking back over the thorny path that has been travelled. And so it is with evaluation. It is about twenty-five years since the passage of the Elementary and Secondary Education Act (ESEA, 1965) in the United States served as catalyst for the development of a professional cadre of experts in the evaluation of educational and social programs. The silver anniversary has stimulated the production of the present volume; and no doubt there will be other publications marking the event. Already published is an *International Encyclopedia of Educational Evaluation*, and the *Educational Researcher* has carried a retrospective piece on evaluation. See Ernest R. House, "Trends in Evaluation," *Educational Researcher* 19 (April 1990): 24-28.

This is not to say that educational evaluation was born only in 1965: clearly this is not the case. During the nineteenth century (and earlier in some corners of the globe), many countries engaged in a flurry of educational activity and started to set up national systems of compulsory education; and from time to time this activity was subjected to scrutiny. But evaluation as an activity in its own right was not paid much systematic attention. In the early years of the twentieth century there were a few pioneering efforts at conceptualizing the nature of the evaluation enterprise; indeed, Ralph Tyler, one of the contributors to the present volume, started publishing on issues of evaluation of student progress as early as 1929. (For an intellectual biography of Tyler, see *Educational Evaluation: Classic Works of Ralph W. Tyler*, ed. George Madaus and Daniel Stufflebeam [Boston: Kluwer, 1989].)

However, 1965 was a watershed. President Johnson's "War on Poverty" focused attention on education, and massive funds were made available. And with the money came the demand for accountability, which slipped over into a demand for evaluation. Events moved quickly, and within a few years several academic groups had been established to study evaluation (or "evaluation research"), there were two learned societies (which later merged), and there were several journals.

Whenever experts are set a challenging new task, it is natural for them to approach it initially in terms of techniques and concepts that worked well in the past. So it is no surprise that those who undertook evaluations in the period around 1965 first approached their work in terms of their experience with social science research and more specifically with psychological, laboratory-style research. The true experiment was the favored evaluation design: careful statement of objectives, followed by rigorous measurement and subsequent statistical analysis of the results, became the usual *modus operandi*. This general approach was given theoretical credibility by the early work of Ralph Tyler, who approached educational evaluation through a keen interest in the measurement of student gains in learning.

But problems quickly emerged. It became clear that programs have many aims—often as many aims as there are stakeholders. Programs have fuzzy borders, so that it is not always plain sailing to determine precisely what the program *was* that required evaluation. Programs have important unintended consequences that cannot always be anticipated in advance. Some programs need formative help rather than "go—no go" assessment. In addition, decision makers, while not irrational, did not seem to display their rationality in the manner that evaluators expected—the factors that make for rationality in politicized contexts were not fully appreciated by the evaluation community in the mid-1960s. It also became clear that true experiments were sometimes like lumbering dinosaurs, wonderful as museum pieces but very hard to work with in real settings. And, perhaps above all, it emerged that evaluations—although required—were often paid scant attention by those who had commissioned them.

In response to these problems, members of the evaluation community rolled up their sleeves and set to work. Books and articles rapidly accumulated in which new insights, new concepts, and new distinctions made headway possible. Alternative approaches to evaluation design were developed; the political decision-making process was studied, as was evaluation's role within it; ways of involving stakeholders were devised; ethical issues were grappled with.

And this brings the discussion around to the present volume. To mark the twenty-fifth anniversary of the emergence of modern educational evaluation, we decided to revisit some of the classic contributions of the past quarter century—contributions to the literature on program evaluation. We extended invitations to the authors to think again about their original topics—the topics they had helped to clarify in their original and ground-breaking works. We asked "Does the original contribution still stand?" "Has anything happened in the ensuing years that would cause you to write the paper or book differently if you were to do it over again today?" "Where does our understanding of evaluation stand today, twenty-five years after the birth of the modern enterprise?" (It is important to note that the focus of our volume is program evaluation; we do not discuss the domains of personnel evaluation or the assessment of educational outcomes.)

Of course, we could not invite all the important authors of the past to join in this task. As editors, we wanted to ensure coverage of a wide range of topics, and we had to adhere to a page limit. These factors necessitated the exclusion of some major figures. Furthermore, several of those we invited to contribute were unable to do so because of other demands of professional life. But we are proud that we were able to recruit so many of these whose earlier work forms the framework within which evaluators work today. Their retrospective examinations not only illuminate the past; even more importantly, they give us a unique glimpse at the issues with which the field of evaluation has to grapple in the years ahead.

The chapters are set out in a topical or thematic order that seems to make sense. Preceding each chapter is a brief statement, written by

Table of Contents

General Statement on Evaluation

Almost half a century ago, in 1942, Ralph Tyler published his extremely influential "General Statement on Evaluation" in the *Journal of Educational Research*. (By that date he had already been publishing for thirteen years, and he was bringing his evaluation of the famous "Eight-Year Study" to a close.) In the following chapter, written in 1990, he makes another general statement on evaluation, based on his rich experience over the intervening years. There are several new issues raised, and there are some changes in emphasis; but readers familiar with his earlier statement will be struck by the continuities. While these continuities are interesting, the changes that have been made in his position all reflect important problems with which the evaluation community has struggled.

Tyler's earliest writings were on issues pertaining to the assessment of student learning, and in 1942 this interest to a large degree influenced his general approach to evaluation. He opened his "general statement" by stressing that the traditional purposes of evaluation—focusing on grading and promotion of students, reporting to parents, and preparing financial reports for boards of education—needed to be broadened. He stated that there were six "purposes of evaluation": to make periodic checks on the effectiveness of educational institutions, "and thus to indicate the points at which improvements in the program are necessary" (a remark that anticipated the later emphasis in the evaluation literature upon formative evaluation); to validate the hypotheses upon which educational programs operate; to provide information of assistance in the effective guidance of individuals; to provide "a certain psychological security" for the school staff, parents, and students—to reassure them that the main objectives of their schools were being attained; to provide a sound basis for public relations; and to help both teachers and pupils clarify their purposes and "see more concretely" the directions in which they were moving.

Tyler went on to uncover six basic assumptions underlying evaluation, which together indicated the "necessity" of basing an evaluation program upon educational objectives; and he argued that these objectives "must be stated in terms of changes in behavior of

1

students." Next, Tyler amplified the general procedure to be followed in the process of evaluation: (1) schools should formulate their objectives, which should be classified into types, and behavioral definitions of these types should be constructed; (2) situations in which students are expected to display these types of behavior should then be defined; (3) promising methods for gathering relevant evidence about each type of objective should be developed and tried, after which the most promising would be selected for further development; and finally, (4) means for interpreting and using the results should be devised.

As a consequence of Tyler's "general statement," a great boost was given to the development of new measurement techniques, and to the recognition by the research community of a wider range of educational objectives than had previously been generally acknowledged.

CHAPTER I

General Statement on Program Evaluation

RALPH W. TYLER

This analysis and discussion of program evaluation is based on my experience with the evaluation of education programs. My observations suggest that these experiences can be generalized to a considerable degree to evaluations of other social programs, such as the Poverty Program of the Great Society in the 1960s.

Purposes for Program Evaluation

There are several purposes for evaluating social programs. Sometimes the evaluation is part of the continual monitoring activity of the institution to ascertain whether a current program is effective and, if not, to redesign it to enhance its effectiveness. Some have identified problems with the present program and seek information about the positive and negative effects of other available programs, together with their initial costs as well as future maintenance costs. Sometimes a program is being developed and piloted in a few contexts. In this connection, evaluations are used to identify aspects of the program that are not producing the results expected. This enables the program constructors to modify the program in an effort to improve its effectiveness.

Program evaluation is also used to identify its differential effects with different populations of students or clients where such differences as ethnic background, social class, education, and income of the family are thought to influence the effectiveness of the program.

Program evaluation is often desired by central teacher centers and other learning resource centers in order to help these centers report to the users estimates of the program's values, limitations, and costs.

Finally, a few institutions and many researchers use program evaluation as part of their procedure in testing the relevance and validity of the principles on which the program is supposedly based.

Principles can be generalized since they have been developed by observations of a variety of practices that revealed similarities among the diversities. Programs as a whole cannot be easily generalized since teachers and other professionals, consciously or unconsciously, modify programs as they interact with students or other clients.

In summary, program evaluation is being used for at least six purposes: (1) to monitor present programs; (2) to select a better available program to replace one now in use that is deemed relatively ineffective; (3) to assist in developing a new program; (4) to identify the differential effects of the program with different populations of students or other clients; (5) to provide estimates of effects and costs in the catalogue of programs listed in consumer resource centers; (6) to test the relevance and validity of the principles upon which the program is based.

Defining the Program

In many cases, programs are not defined. They are merely labeled and these labels mean different things to different persons involved in programs. As an example, in 1945 I was asked by the New York State Commissioner of Education to serve on a committee of three educators to evaluate the outcomes of the New York City experiment with activity schools. This experiment, which had been in progress for eight years, consisted of eighteen elementary schools that were following activity programs and eighteen control schools selected to match the activity schools in the socioeconomic and ethnic composition of the student body. The plan was to compare the achievements of the students in the activity schools with those of the students in the control schools to find out what differences there were, if any. We began our evaluation by asking the school principals what an activity program was. Their answer, in essence, was that an activity program was one recommended by experts at Teachers College, Columbia University and involved children's activities, but they had no precise idea of what an activity program was. We then went to the professors at Teachers College who had recommended activity schools and asked them to describe an activity program. After some discussion, we got a list of fifty-one characteristics of an activity program, including such items as: (1) students participate with their teacher in planning learning activities and (2) students apply what they are learning to their own out-of-school activities.

Using these fifty-one characteristics as a check list, we and our assistants visited all the classrooms in the eighteen activity schools and the eighteen control schools. We found great variation within both the activity schools and the control schools in the extent to which classroom activities involved these fifty-one characteristics. Some of the classrooms in the activity schools had fewer of these characteristics than some of the classrooms in the control schools. To make a meaningful evaluation, we classified all classrooms in the thirty-six schools into three categories: those with 0 to 15 of the characteristics, those with 16-31, and those with 32-51. On this basis we found that the tested, mean achievements of the students in the classrooms having 32-51 of the characteristics were higher than those in the middle category, and those in the middle category were higher than those in the lowest category. Students in carefully defined activity programs were achieving more than those in programs with fewer activity characteristics.

As another illustration of lack of definition, many educators in the 1960s were talking and writing about the desirability of open classrooms. I was asked by the Associate Commissioner in the U. S. Office of Education to make an evaluation of the "open classroom movement." As in the case of the activity schools, I could find no clear definitions of "open classrooms." The idea had come from the reports of the experiences in schools in working class communities in the south of England. These schools reported that their students had changed from passive listening to the teacher and following instructions, to active participation in learning experiences when the classroom doors were thrown open and they could carry on their school activities in the halls and on the playground as well as in the classroom.

Many American schools tried open classrooms, but most of them did not define openness in a way consistent with the conditions for effective learning. A stimulating learning environment is one in which there is a balance between social structure and the structure developed by the student to guide his learning experiences. As John Dewey once said to me, "an environment in which everything is rigidly structured produces slaves; an environment in which there is no structure produces chaotic, whimsical behavior. Learners need an environment in which some things cannot be changed and to which the learners need to adapt their behavior, and other things can be developed by the creative efforts of the learners."

The schools in England reporting the stimulating effect on students of open classrooms enrolled students from working class homes where their behavior was strictly controlled. When given freedom in the school to work out their own plans for learning, these students were excited and actively pursued their school activities within and without the classroom. In my effort to evaluate American open classrooms, I found a parochial school in Nebraska that enrolled students from working class families where at home their behavior was strictly controlled. The freedom provided them by their teachers to plan their learning experiences and to study and work wherever on the campus it seemed appropriate to do so was actively used and greatly appreciated. On the other hand, in this same city, a public school in the slums was trying to follow a program of open classrooms and the school seemed to me to be in chaos. At home, the students had no structure to guide them. Their mothers were overburdened with the responsibilities of making a living and doing the housework. The students came to the school where there was also no structure and they were bewildered and confused. The failure to define clearly an open classroom that would provide a balance for the students between structure in their lives and openness to their creative ideas and activities led to an early demise of the open classroom movement.

Implementation of Programs

Implementation would not be difficult if the new program focused on the same learning objectives as the program with which the teachers had worked earlier, if the new program was based on the same conception of education, if it involved the same kinds of teacher-student interactions and required the same skills of the teachers. This may be illustrated by the selection of a new textbook where the curriculum is not to be changed.

However, if the new program to be implemented focuses on different objectives than did the old program, if it is based on a different conception of education or on different kinds of teacher-student interactions, and if it requires different teaching skills, implementation is more difficult and requires more time. An example of this more complex implementation is that of the adoption of a program in which the focus is on helping students become self-directed problem solvers when the school has previously emphasized memorization of textbook material. This change requires helping teachers and students to develop new conceptions of student learning; new emphasis on giving students responsibility for their own learning; new skills for stimulating, guiding, and rewarding learning; new ways of appraising and recording student progress; and so on. Significant improvements in education usually involve this more complex implementation.

Many schools report that they have adopted new programs although these programs are not actually in operation. In 1933, the famous Eight-Year Study of the Progressive Education Association began. In July, 1934, I was asked to direct a staff to carry on an evaluation of the Eight-Year Study, helping the participating high schools to appraise the progress of their students while they were in the high school, to follow their students into college or employment to see how well they performed in these environments, and to obtain data useful in revising and improving the high school program.

The thirty schools and school systems participating in the study had been selected by a directing committee from a much larger number of applicants on the basis of a proposal submitted by each school describing the program they planned to carry out. Before I visited each of the schools, I read the proposal the school had made describing the program it planned to implement. However, when I visited the schools, only two or three were operating the program described in the proposal. In most cases the proposal had been written by the principal and its contents were not known by the teachers. In two or three schools, however, the faculty had worked with the principal in developing the description of the program they wished to try if they were selected for the study.

I was able to obtain funds to support summer workshops where a team of teachers from each school worked with teachers from the other schools in developing the plans for their program, including plans for implementation. Then, each subsequent summer, teachers from the schools would review the problems of implementation and work out possible solutions so as to achieve actual implementation.

The State of Israel furnishes another example of the problems of implementation. The Knesset, which is Israel's National Parliament, passed an Educational Reform Act in 1968. This statute called for the elimination of school segregation and of student tracking within classes. Most of the leaders in education in Israel were educated in the United States and knew about the U. S. Supreme Court decision declaring school segregation unconstitutional as well as segregation by tracking within classes. So the State of Israel enacted legislation to provide for gradual desegregation. In the first year, thirty schools were to be completely desegregated—within classes as well as within schools. In the second year, an additional thirty-two schools were to be completely desegregated, and so on. Israel is a small country with a school population less than that of Los Angeles, so the number of schools to be desegregated was not large.

In 1970, I was asked by the Israeli Minister of Education to direct a summer training program to teach a selected group of Israelis in educational evaluation. We were to use the sixty-two schools that had been desegregated as a real problem for the students to develop a plan for evaluating the effects of desegregation on the achievement of the students in these schools. However, from my earlier experience, I believed that some of the schools selected for desegregation may not have actually desegregated their student bodies. So the first step I took in the training sessions that summer was to ask the group to go out individually and visit the sixty-two schools to see how many were actually desegregated. They found only two schools that had desegregated their student bodies although the Reform Act called for desegregation in sixty-two schools. This raises the question, "Why are programs claiming to be reforms seldom fully implemented?"

In the United States, the great variability among the thousands of schools makes national or state reforms inappropriate for most schools. For example, segregation was a serious problem in only a minority of schools—those in the large cities of the North and those in most of the southern states. The sweeping charges made by reformers that American high school graduates cannot read are valid for only about 20 percent of high school graduates, mostly in small geographic pockets in large cities and rural areas. When so many educators and parents know that their children are doing well in school, they question the basis for most reform proposals. Because American schools are so varied in student composition, family background, community support, and school effectiveness, it is necessary for each local school to identify its important problems and stimulate discussion and action at the local level. When teachers, parents, and students understand the serious problems in their school, they are more supportive of programs likely to alleviate these problems and I have found that they are then likely to work on actual implementation.

A second problem in implementation of a new program is

providing adequate opportunity for those involved to develop new skills, new understanding, and new attitudes when the new program differs in these respects from the older programs. These opportunities require planning and scheduling because they depend on a supportive environment, which in many cases is not the present school environment. They require some concentration of funds, for incidental expenses are usually inadequate to furnish a concentrated immersion in these new ideas and activities. In some cases, key teachers may benefit from spending a year in a school which offers this environment.

Not only do teachers and students who are to undertake a new program need opportunity for developing the necessary understanding, skills, and attitudes, but also the other persons in the school community need to gain an understanding and appreciation for the necessary changes so that they can be supportive rather than critical of the new behavior of the key teachers. In many cases, the teachers, parents, and students not involved heap criticism, sarcasm, and jest on teachers learning new things. These persons could be supportive of the efforts to develop the program if they understood its real significance. They could strengthen the morale in the total school community.

A third problem in implementing a new program is working out a realistic time schedule with annual or semiannual goals on which to focus efforts. I have found that it usually takes about six or seven years for a complex program to become fully operational as planned. Unexpected difficulties are encountered, some steps in the planning process take longer than anticipated, and other problems may be encountered. Many promising programs are dropped as fads because enough time was not allowed for getting the program into full operation.

In summary, a promising program can be fully implemented if it is seen by the teachers, parents, and students in the local schools as being responsive to their problems, if sufficient opportunities are provided those persons involved in the new program to learn the new understanding, new skills, new attitudes toward students and colleagues, and if sufficient time is scheduled with annual or semiannual goals to furnish a structure for the necessary step-by-step implementation.

Evaluation of Program Outcomes

Usually a program is adopted or developed because it is seen as likely to be more effective or less costly in attaining the outcomes desired, such as an increase in the number of students learning what the school is expected to teach, decrease in the number of persons without jobs, and so on. To ascertain whether these outcomes are being attained requires clear definitions of them.

In the case of learning outcomes, one needs to define both the kind of behavior the student is expected to learn and the contexts in which he is expected to use it. Human behavior does not operate in a vacuum. The environment stimulates certain reactions and in that environment certain reactions are appropriate for constructive responses.

For example, an objective in reading in the primary grades may be "to learn to read fairy tales aloud to entertain the other members of the class and the members of the family at home." An objective in arithmetic may be "to learn to calculate the cost of food each child consumes in a week." An example of an objective at the high school level may be "to learn how to measure the pollution in the air, in the water, and in the soil in the local community and to estimate the accuracy of these measures."

The kind of learning schools seek to help students develop is not the ephemeral kind of behavior demonstrated by a test and forgotten shortly after the test is over. Schools seek a more permanent kind of learning. Students are expected to learn behavior that they internalize, that is, learning that becomes part of their repertoire of behavior to be used whenever appropriate.

These comments suggest the limitations of paper-and-pencil tests given only once or twice a year and the need to consider other ways of evaluation that can substitute for or supplement present testing practices. A valid test of human behavior can be obtained by observing and/or recording samples of the behavior that is evoked by the situation in which this behavior is appropriate. Oral reading behavior can be evoked by asking a child to read a fairy tale to the class. Writing behavior can be evoked by asking students to write for information they need to work out a project in social studies. Where real situations are not easily available for testing, simulations, descriptions, or acting-out scenes like the real situations can be used. A test of learning involves not only the definition of the behavior to

be learned and the selection or development of situations in which this
behavior is evoked but also the development of criteria for appraising
the behavior the students exhibit in response to the situation. To
appraise the behavior in the test situation as correct or incorrect is a
very limited kind of evaluation. If possible, the behavior exhibited by
the student should be appraised in terms of helpfulness to the student
in seeking to improve his performance, and helpful to teachers and
others who seek to help him improve.

In appraising a sample of writing one may use such criteria as
clarity, logical organization, interest, verbosity. In appraising a sample
of student explanations of scientific phenomena one may use such
criteria as appropriate conceptualization, relevant principles chosen,
relevant points used, plausible explanation. In appraising a sample of
student reactions to works of visual arts, one may use such criteria as
perceived patterns of line, mass, and balance, reactions to color,
texture, and the artist's technical skills.

The above criteria when used in appraising samples of student
writing suggest where to focus efforts to improve his or her writing.
Too often, student writing is appraised only in terms of the
mechanics, spelling, conformity to grammatical convention, and
variety of vocabulary. These are the focus of remediation. The criteria
suggested above should be used to guide the continuing improvement
of the student's effectiveness in writing for the various purposes in
which writing could be used in his or her situation.

When the above criteria for evaluating samples of student
explanation of science phenomena are used, it suggests to the student
that one can understand these phenomena by conceiving the natural
world as involving matter and energy that are carrying on processes
guided by principles, and the phenomena can then be understood in
these terms.

The criteria for appraising a sample of student reactions to
products of the visual arts remind the students that these products can
increase the range and depth of their visual perceptions. They may not
have noticed the texture of objects until they studied a painting by
Van Gogh in which the texture was so enhanced that it stood out. In
general, visual artists express their unusual perceptions so clearly that
the viewer can perceive visual characteristics that he or she has failed
to notice in the normal environment. This provides for an increase in
use of visual stimulation and a decrease in boredom that sets in when
the environment is seen as limited in visual stimulation.

When an achievement test is scored only as right or wrong or only with a total mark of excellent, good, fair, poor, or fail, or 90, 80, 70, fail, there is little information to guide the student, teacher, or parent in efforts to improve the student's achievement. But when the student's writing is judged to lack clarity or logical organization or lacking in vocabulary, the focus for efforts to improve his or her writing is indicated. The appraisal obtained by an achievement test should provide information useful in identifying what the student has learned and what he or she has not yet learned, so that further instruction can be based on the assets developed and focused in helping students learn the behavior they have not yet acquired.

It should be clear from the foregoing discussion that the abstract numbers now commonly used in reporting test results are not appropriate for educational purposes. To report that a student is at the 66th percentile on a standard test does not tell what he or she has learned and what he or she has yet to learn. It indicates that the student's score was higher than two-thirds of the students in the norming sample. But education in a democratic society is not a game where there are winners and losers. A democratic society seeks to enable every student to learn to be a self-directed citizen, who works to contribute constructively to that society and to develop fully his potential in the areas in which he is deeply interested. So far as possible, test results should be reported in terms that those involved can understand and be helped in their roles in improving education in our society.

The abstract numbers, percentiles on published tests, standard scores on college admission tests, were developed by psychometricians who sought to translate appraisals of human behavior into terms used in measuring material objects and physical phenomena. They were not designed to help improve learning, and they have not facilitated the efforts of educators to improve education. The desire to compare student achievement led to the development of single abstract numbers as indices of learning in a field, for example, a single number to report achievement in English, or mathematics, or a single number for the grade point average. There are several possible learning objectives in every school subject. Rarely does a student attain these several objectives to an equal degree. It is more helpful to report achievements in each important objective rather than to aggregate the student's varied accomplishments into a single score.

The reports to the lay public, as well as parents are not well understood when abstract numbers are used. Illustrations of significant things done by students are more valid and less likely to be misinterpreted by the public. I know of a community in New England where the high school students devised ways of measuring pollution in that community—pollution of the air, water, and soil. Using a sample of these measures collected over several weeks they wrote a report that they presented to the Town Council and gave to the local newspaper editor. They appeared before the Town Council to speak in favor of legislation to reduce pollution, and they observed and reported on the activities of the lobbyists—pro and con.

Reports of this project made to the general public through the press and through the presentations the students made to the local service clubs were much better understood by the members of the community than the reports of standard test scores. Educators need to report such activities as examples of what students are learning rather than depending on test scores.

The present tests are not based on a comprehensive sample of the behavior that schools are trying to help students learn. Even within a single subject, makers of standard tests find that the variety of objectives and content in different schools, and the limited possibility of presenting test situations on paper, are intractable obstacles to validity. Hence, reports of local scores on these tests are not adequate evidence of the effectiveness of the local schools. If the community is informed about the meaningful projects students are carrying on they can understand and appreciate the work of the schools. They can also understand the problems the school reports in helping some of the students learn this kind of behavior. Program evaluators need to spend more time in finding and developing ways to report the educational achievements of the students in the program.

The evaluation of program effects should be as concrete as possible for each of the outcomes for which the program was designed and also for outcomes that appear to be possible effects, including negative ones. For example, a program in reading in the primary grades that is devoted largely to decoding words may cause students to dislike reading and fail to stimulate their reading of stories not in the text book. This possibility should be tested by evaluating the students' interest in reading. Such an appraisal may be based on children's reports of the voluntary reading, interviews with students about the use of their free time, by interest inventories, and the like. Most programs have some negative effects, which, if known, can often be reduced or eliminated. For example, a program in fourth-grade arithmetic may emphasize computation to the neglect of application to real problems. When such outcomes are identified, the program can be modified by giving a more balanced emphasis in the learning activities.

To summarize, a comprehensive evaluation of the outcomes of an educational program requires clear definitions of the desired patterns of behavior and of other possible outcomes both positive and negative. It then requires the selection or development of test situations that evoke such behavior from the students, and it necessitates the use of relevant and important criteria for appraising the students' reactions in these test situations. Finally, the reporting of these appraisals should be done in terms that can be understood by those who can use the results constructively.

For social programs other than those in education, the rationale is similar. For example, for a program seeking to reduce the number of persons without jobs, there needs to be a definition of "having a job." Does one have a job if he or she is employed temporarily and is soon back on the street? Is it a job to have dead-end work with no opportunity for advancement or a "career"? Many job training programs place participants in jobs that are temporary or dead-end. The participants fail to attain employment in work that permits continued learning and achievement. Developing test situations in job training and placement are experiments with samples of trainees, and the results should be appraised in terms of the definition of desirable jobs.

Evaluation of Costs of Programs

Current reports of program evaluations rarely mention comprehensive studies of the costs of the programs, yet all programs involve initial costs and costs of maintenance. The initial costs are likely to be the cost of initial training of persons for new roles, costs for time used by committees and other groups in study and planning, and costs for such additional persons, equipment, and materials that the program may require.

Maintenance costs may include costs of orienting new persons assigned to the program, costs of periodic evaluation, costs of activities designed to prevent the common deterioration of interest and morale after a program has been in operation for six or seven years, and costs of maintenance and replacement of equipment and materials. Estimates can also be made of innovative ways of reducing costs such as utilizing student interns where the responsibility would enhance the learning of the students. The University of New Mexico reports that, in cooperation with the Albuquerque school system, supervision in the public schools is performed by half-time student interns and the teachers are reporting excellent service from the eager-to-learn interns in school supervision. A thoughtful review of program costs may suggest other ways in which important activities can be performed as part of the education and training functions of the institution.

Selecting a Program

When a program is to be selected from several that are available and seem to be appropriate, each of them should be evaluated as fully as possible and the results compared. Rarely will one program be superior to the others in each of the several desired objectives and in its costs. Hence, the selection will require judgments by the evaluator or an evaluation committee. This judgment should include the matter of practicability in the local situation. Usually an evaluator or an evaluation committee will identify and select a program that may not be highest in the comprehensive evaluation but its evaluation is generally positive and it appears to be most likely to be implemented successfully in the local situation. This is the hoped-for goal of program selection.

A comprehensive program evaluation then requires an understanding of the purpose for which a particular evaluation is undertaken so that the project is designed to obtain information serving these purposes. The need for a clear definition of a program may seem obvious but is often overlooked. Reported programs have sometimes failed to be implemented. A check on implementation is necessary.

The evaluation of program outcomes needs to be guided by clear definitions of outcomes desired and other possible outcomes both positive and negative. To ascertain these effects requires more than conventional testing and reporting. More direct appraisals can be made and reported in terms of criteria useful for the purposes of educational improvement.

Program evaluation involves costs that need to be calculated or estimated from pilot programs before large-scale projects are undertaken. Both initial costs and costs of maintaining the program should be estimated in order to allocate the necessary resources.

In selecting a program, comparisons of outcomes and costs among the available programs can help in making a practicable selection.

The Evaluator's Ethical Code

The foregoing presents a comprehensive conception of program evaluation. It assumes that the evaluator is deeply concerned with developing an honest and objective evaluation of the social program he or she is appraising. However, the evaluator often encounters strong social and political pressures to distort or falsify the results of an evaluation.

Most social programs are proposed and developed by people who become deeply committed to them. The programs are products of their vision and their efforts, often involving enormous personal commitments of time, energy, and other resources. They expect that the evaluation of their programs will prove them to be exceptionally effective. Consciously or unconsciously, they will do all that they can to get strong positive appraisals. Evaluators find it difficult to maintain objectivity and honesty in such contexts.

When a social program is adopted by an institution or agency, many of those who adopt the program believe it is an excellent one that will produce strong, positive results. When the program is adopted, it becomes theirs and their commitments are similar to the commitments of those who developed the program. Evaluators find it difficult to maintain objectivity and honesty in this context.

Although evaluators often encounter such strong political and social pressures, they have a professional responsibility to withstand them. Educational evaluators and appraisers of other social programs are professionals with responsibilities similar to those of the auditors of the financial accounts of institutions and corporations. To distribute a biased evaluation report is a real "white-collar" crime, whether or not it is so defined by law. The improvement of education depends on valid and meaningful evidence. The reports produced by those responsible for an operation are frequently in error, sometimes purposely distributed by the operators, sometimes due to carelessness or ignorance. When I have investigated the public reports on unemployment, housing, and school enrollments, I have often discovered serious errors. Competent, objective, and honest evaluations are essential to guide the continued improvement of schools, colleges, and other social institutions.

The Formative/Summative Distinction

When a new field of investigation opens up, at first it is approached with concepts and methods drawn from older and more familiar domains. These might be completely effective in directing fruitful inquiry, but often they are not and indigenous intellectual tools are required for headway to be made. Evaluation falls into the latter category. Evaluation work was treated initially as a domain of research-oriented social science, but it quickly became apparent that although this was part of the story it was not the whole of it. The evaluator was working under conditions, and on problems, that differed in important ways from those found in the research laboratory. Original conceptual and methodological work was called for.

Among those who had become interested in the problems of evaluation was Michael Scriven, a prominent philosopher of science. As a philosopher, he was well-equipped to make some necessary distinctions and to begin the work of conceptual construction. In 1963, the educational psychologist Lee Cronbach had published a paper, "Course Improvement through Evaluation," in which he argued that evaluation should be aimed more at fostering improvement of programs. Scriven disagreed with this emphasis, and this led him to formulate the now classic formative/summative distinction in his "The Methodology of Evaluation," published in 1967. This forty-five page paper was influential, for in it Scriven drew a variety of distinctions and sketched the beginnings of a coherent account of the evaluation domain. The formative/summative distinction is the one that he revisits in the following chapter.

In his original paper, Scriven did not see formative and summative as being two *types* of evaluation; rather, he conceptualized them as two *roles* that evaluation can play. In the formative role, the evaluator is playing a "constructive" part where the emphasis is on input that will help to improve a program; in the summative role, which Scriven saw as very important and ever-present, the evaluator is determining the worth of the program.

CHAPTER II

Beyond Formative and Summative Evaluation

MICHAEL SCRIVEN

Perhaps the best way to put the formative/summative distinction is due to Robert Stake: when the cook tastes the soup, that's formative evaluation; when the guest tastes it, that's summative evaluation. Is it really necessary to elaborate on something that can be expressed so elegantly? Indeed, is there enough substance in such a simple distinction to carry the weight of any elaborations?

The terms "formative" and "summative" in relation to evaluation first appeared in my 1967 article entitled "The Methodology of Evaluation."[1] After twenty-three years of fairly extensive use of these terms, a number of conceptual problems involving them have emerged, and solving those problems turns out not to be trivial. Some confusions about the original terms persist. To be more precise, some conceptions of them persist or have arisen which I, as the originator of the terms, see as confusions, and in the course of addressing those confusions it became clear that some related distinctions had to be made. Doing this is not merely a matter of terminological tidiness. In many fields—teacher education being one of the most important—mistakes about these distinctions lead to major errors of policy and practice. A number of such errors will be identified in this chapter.

While this chapter presents my best effort to clarify these notions, they have been in use long enough to become common property. Hence the suggestions made here must be considered simply on their own merits as normative analyses of the current concepts. Since I have never reread the original paper, the suggestions may not even provide the best possible analysis of the original distinction. Many suggestions—such as Stake's—and many hundreds of decisions about how to use the terms in later discussions of evaluation examples and practice cannot help but modify a notion with any life in it.[2] Hence,

---

My thanks to James Shaver, Jason Millman, James Sanders, and Daniel Stufflebeam for some very helpful comments on a late draft of this chapter.

the talk here about "errors of interpretation" or "errors" only means "divergences from what seems to be the best analysis" in the eyes of someone who has been thinking about the notions for a considerable time. I will focus here on ten such fallacies (using that term in the sense of "seductive error") while mentioning several others in passing. Examples from education are given some prominence, but workers in educational research are more likely to be struck by the extent of the examples from outside education.

Differences between Formative and Summative Evaluation

The First Fallacy (F1) is the supposition that formative and summative evaluation are *intrinsically different* types of evaluation.

The terms "formative" and "summative" were introduced to illustrate different *roles* for evaluation, which is another kind of difference—exactly the same screwdriver can open crates and turn screws. They are indeed different in fundamental ways; but those differences are almost entirely pragmatic—appropriately enough, for evaluation is a paradigmatically pragmatic subject. The distinctions between them concern the relation of the evaluative information to its environment and use—matters of client and context, as we might say today. There is no essential difference in the properties of the entities themselves, as there is, for example, between causal and correlational claims, or between evaluations of effectiveness and evaluations of efficiency. But there are types of evaluation that tend to be more useful for formative purposes, and types that are more often seen in the summative role, just as one tends to use a bigger screwdriver for opening crates and a smaller one for working on watches—if one can afford two, and has room to carry them both.

To be more specific, formative and summative evaluation are different in the functions they serve and (hence) the destination to which they go. *Formative evaluation* is evaluation designed, done, and intended to support the process of improvement, and normally commissioned or done by, and delivered to, someone who can make improvements. *Summative evaluation* is the rest of evaluation: in terms of intentions, it is evaluation done for, or by, any observers or decision makers (by contrast with developers) who need evaluative conclusions for any other reasons besides development. It may be done by a historian, by a politician, by an agency trying to show fiscal or legal accountability, by a researcher looking for trends or influences, or by someone making decisions on funding or purchasing. Both types of evaluation can adopt different forms or designs, depending on the exact needs of the client or audience and the constraints of the resources and context. The best designs, where alternatives are possible, will often but not always differ for the two purposes.[3]

One might suppose that to say the best designs for the two types of evaluation are often different is to concede most of what people have commonly supposed in thinking the two different. But as we will see, the common confusion is much more serious; it usually involves the inclusion in formative evaluation of types of inquiry that are fundamentally different from evaluation, e.g., explanation or prescription.

The definition of formative evaluation just given is not complicated in itself, but any definition of a process deeply rooted in practice is linked to some of the far-reaching and complex roots of established practice. In the long history of developing artifacts for the maker or the market—artifacts ranging from soup or stone axes to social studies curricula, sculpture, and software—we see the same pattern of phases in formative evaluation, although they have only recently been recognized and named.

Authors and inventors continually evaluate their products in the process of revising them, but we do not normally consider this as part of the process of formative evaluation—although one might call it the zero-level phase. Formative evaluation is thought of as being external to the author or inventor or the work-group that coauthored the product (in its present form). Using current terminology, the phases or stages usually distinguished are: (1) in-house critique by colleagues or other employees not in the development group and by visitors, which is sometimes called "alpha testing"; (2) field trials with hand-holding, i.e., the (preferably but not always) off-site use of typical consumers, in tests supervised and supported by representatives of the development team (this is sometimes called the "hot-house" phase; and in the automobile industry and elsewhere it is referred to as the "focus groups" process); (3) hands-off field trials at remote sites by supposedly typical users working on their own in their usual environment (software developers call these "beta-tests"); and sometimes also (4) full-scale commissioned evaluations by external expert reviewers (the "review preview" phase), in which the reviewer may and should run systematic experiments with end-users. In the light of these processes, or some of them, the product is (or is not) finally revised and released, and summative evaluation begins—for reasons of scholarship, accountability, purchase, refunding, awards, etc.

In practice, stages 2 and 3 are often run together, and 4 is often skipped. Both shortcuts are likely to be costly, as is, for example, the common use of company purchasing agents instead of end-users for the beta-tests, since these moves all violate criteria of external validity for the desired conclusions. More than half the products on the high-tech market—arguably more than 90 percent—exhibit serious defects which could have been easily picked up and corrected by using the four-stage process listed here.[4] About the same figures would apply to programs.[5] The cost of full formative evaluation would, in all these cases, have been minute compared to the costs of not doing it. The latter costs show up in lost sales, in warranty and hot-line service, in bugfix releases and recalls, in lawsuits—and in poor morale in the work group, which leads to retention and hiring problems.

There are three points to note from this. First, although formative is mostly internal (i.e., done by the staff of the originating institution) and summative mostly external, the opposite combinations exist and serve useful purposes, e.g., in good beta-testing and when stage 4 is part of the formative process. So it is incorrect to identify internal with formative and external with summative (a common mistake that is a relative of the First Fallacy). Second, although the primary sense of the terms is as described, changes of context can bring about changes of classification. For example, the published reviews of the first edition of a text, are summative with respect to that edition but they can *function* as formative with respect to the second edition, if the author or editor decides to so use them. Thus, the line between formative and summative can only be drawn by reference to a context. In fact, there are cases where the very same journal reviewers were the ones used by the publisher in a stage 4 procedure as part of the formative evaluation. (They should probably have declined the invitation to do a summative review, unless their advice was ignored.) This example should make clear that since the one can serve the other's purpose, in a different context, there cannot be some sharp internal difference between them. Nor can the distinction rest solely on the question of the intent of the evaluator: a summative reviewer of the first edition did not *intend* to be a formative evaluator of the second edition (he or she may well have argued that there should never be a second edition, and believed that everyone else would agree). Nevertheless, this review may well become part of the formative evaluation process for a second edition. This co-option of summative evaluations into the formative domain is paralleled by cases where formative stage 4 evaluations are, not improperly, released as summative. Third, beta tests can usefully be designed and done exactly *as if* they were summative, but they are in fact formative, because of the context in which they are done. (Here is one point where Russell and Blake diverge. See references cited in footnote 2.)

The power of the context and its interaction with the content—and the limitations on intent as a criterion—becomes still more clear when you consider this question: Is the evaluation of your state of health by your doctor in your regular checkup formative or summative? Suppose the conclusion is that you are suffering from a terminal illness. Can one call that a formative evaluation? It seems paradigmatically summative. Hence one is inclined to say that formative evaluations must be at least capable of being used for improvement. Of course, the design of this evaluation will be the same whether or not it turns up recommendations for improvement.

All one can say is that one *hopes* it will be either favorable or formative. If it's unfavorable, it may be formative or summative. The doctor and you can't be sure whether the evaluation is formative or summative until the examination is concluded, and it is discovered whether the problems are remediable. This example illustrates a general point, which we often forget (partly because we want to), that not all evaluations done in the developmental process, with the hope of identifying ways to improve something, will qualify as formative, because it is not possible to fix every kind of fault. This sometimes happens with teacher evaluation. Thus formative evaluation cannot always be identified by reference to intended function. This counts against what might have been labeled as another in our series of Major Mistakes, the view that function is a (or the) definitive discriminating feature.

The Relative Merit of Formative and Summative Evaluation

One cannot go far with a discussion of the status of the formative/summative distinction today without some reference to the circumstances of its origin. The general sense of a difference between two (or more) kinds of evaluative investigation had been floating around at the commonsense level for some time, as the big evaluation studies of the 1960s started up, and may go back centuries. But it had received little attention because evaluation lacked any legitimacy in science and in the philosophy of science: spending time on a taxonomy of devils seemed frivolous. However, it became clear that one of the leaders in educational research, Lee Cronbach, was arguing for shifting away from what many would now call summative studies toward formative, and also away from comparative evaluation toward evaluation in isolation.[6] These recommendations seemed completely (and equally) inappropriate, and in the course of arguing against the first of them the terms formative evaluation and summative evaluation were coined in an effort to clarify the issue.[7] We're not here focusing on the issue whether evaluation should be comparative, but arguments very like those presented here can be given for the view that comparative evaluation is as crucial as summative.[8] The relevant concern for us is whether the formative and summative distinction is still earning its keep. Cronbach's view as of 1980 was that "these handy terms are not adequate for today's discussion."[9]

Does that mean they should be *discarded, replaced,* or *supplemented?* The tenor of Cronbach's remarks suggests that he prefers the first alternative; certainly, he had no suggestions for replacements. The option explored here is to *supplement* them. Given their usage level it seems unlikely that they are no longer useful, unless they contain some essential flaw not so far noted, or unless there is some more general or more fundamental distinction of which they are simple cases. Survival for twenty years suggests—although certainly it does not prove—that they are not merely the trendy jargon of a period. Some evidence in that direction is that every few years someone who uses them without acknowledgement (not improperly by now, one might say) is greeted with enthusiasm by newcomers who see them as a useful invention.[10]

Cronbach's main problem was that he wanted *summative* evaluation to go away, whatever it was called. In his campaign for that result, one of his assertions represented a second major misconception about formative and summative evaluation. We can use his words in stating the second fallacy:

The Second Fallacy (F2) is the belief that ". . . evaluations are used almost entirely in a formative manner when they *are* used."[11]

This is certainly not true of evaluation in general, although stated here without qualification. The hundred million people who pay to read consumer publications don't do it just for fun, although it is also enjoyable. Their purchases are heavily controlled by what they read, as the market is acutely aware; and what they read is 99 percent summative evaluation. So, in product evaluation, Proposition 1 is false. However, the remark quoted from Cronbach comes from a book on program evaluation; let us suppose that he intended to refer only to that special case, where politics has a powerful influence. But even there the fact remains that the reports from the Office of Technology Assessment and many of the reports from the Congressional Budget Office (or the National Academy of Sciences) are summative evaluations of programs and proposals; are commissioned from these offices by politicians who feel they need them badly enough to have created the offices and put through their budgets every year with bi-partisan support; and are extremely influential in the decisions, as the subcommittee hearings make clear. Even Star Wars, a more expensive program than any in education, is coming up against the results of negative summative evaluation.

In personnel evaluation, serious summative evaluation of applicants and candidates for promotion and retention is usually the major factor in the decisions. It can be argued that in the process of selection for most positions, *only* summative evaluation has any role at all. It may be done badly, but it is summative, not formative, evaluation.[12] Similarly, many programs are programs for the development of products, and all programs use personnel; it is inconceivable that program evaluation not be massively affected by the summative evaluations of those products and personnel. It may take time and politics may confuse the issue, but the summative evaluation has staying power. The way that United States history is taught today in the United States is very largely due to the summative evaluation of the prevailing texts done by a committee of the American Historical Association. "Sesame Street" was legitimated by the Educational Testing Service (ETS) evaluation, although it probably should not have been. The same is true of the IBM Write to Read program; it has been legitimated by an ETS evaluation that appears to be favorable but where the data actually imply a strongly negative evaluation. Summative evaluation is very powerful, rightly or wrongly.

In fact, it should probably be more powerful. Who wants their children taught to read using a method that is only half as effective and no more fun than another program of equal cost? The market supports such programs because it's impossible to get state and federal agencies to take on the political heat of running comparative evaluations of commercial reading products. We do it with pharmaceutical product evaluation; we won't do it with educational product evaluation. Since relatively few drugs relate to life-threatening conditions, this is a clear statement about our relative valuing of health and education.

Cronbach, like many people in program evaluation, has not faced the consistency problem: there can't be one standard for personnel and product evaluation and another for program evaluation. He's a bit late to stop decision makers, such as ourselves, from using summative results in personnel and product evaluation; and there's no way to divorce program evaluation from those. Since the summative evaluation of students is a basic case of personnel evaluation and the summative evaluation of tests, essays, texts, and teachers is about as important, one can hardly make sense of the notion of formative-only, or even formative-mostly, evaluation of educational institutions and programs.

It's difficult to avoid the feeling that Cronbach is pushing for a "kinder, gentler" notion of evaluation. In program evaluation, this can only be done at the expense of the taxpayer and the consumer, and at the expense of innovators with new programs—and defenders of old ones which are being put aside at the whim of fashion. The suggestion, apparently, is that these are not to be adopted (or reinstated) on the basis of merit—which it would take a summative evaluation to discover—but rather kept outside the gates because we have committed to work toward the improvement of those already inside—using formative evaluation. The true merit of the alternatives, or their lack of it, is apparently not to be decisive. This does seem unjust to innovators and conservators, and unfair to consumers, as well as totally inefficient. So the kindly approach, which perhaps comes from the desire not to make students feel badly about themselves because we keep giving them inappropriate comparative ratings, generalizes into misleading students, wasting our limited funds, and weakening our efforts to improve the society.

It is hard to make much of a case for Cronbach's view—or even for the much milder view that formative evaluation is, across the board, even slightly more useful than summative—but it is certainly part of a common response to evaluation, or at least to what are seen as the less friendly aspects of evaluation such as summative evaluation. Possible psychological roots of this will be considered later. A more radical political view would be that the second fallacy is part of the bulwark of rationalizations used to protect the managerial/professional class and other vested interests from the legitimate complaints of the client/customer/critic group.

There has been no lack of attempts to justify this negative attitude toward evaluation with more or less fancy rationalizations. For most of this century the social scientist has appealed to the myth of value-free science to keep evaluation outside the gate. In the years since it sneaked past the guards—with a Congressional pass—Cronbach and many others have made various efforts to keep evaluation in what they see as its place. There was, for example, the untenable distinction between conclusion-oriented and decision-oriented research.[13] On that view, evaluation was seen as decision-oriented, and thus not in the same category as what had previously been thought of as real (conclusion-oriented) research. But the distinction cannot even be made if one recognizes that evaluative conclusions constitute knowledge, knowledge about the worth or merit of things, a kind of knowledge that has always been sought by scholars. For example, much of the conclusion-oriented research for a biography is *necessarily* evaluative; it involves reporting on when and why the subject made good and bad decisions, showed statesmanlike qualities or naivete, etc. Conversely, much decision-oriented research is essentially descriptive (e.g., political polls).[14]

Formative and summative evaluation—and the results of many other kinds of research—are *both* conclusion-oriented and decision-oriented. To be useful, a distinction between the functions of research has to distinguish much more precisely between the *kinds* of decisions or conclusions that are served, and also between the roles of those who receive and use or could use the research results. The definition of formative and summative evaluation provides an example of how a reasonably careful identification of those decisions and roles can provide a reasonably viable and useful distinction.

However, we are not used to the idea that a useful distinction between types of investigation could be based entirely on externalities, on what the logician calls pragmatic rather than syntactic or semantic considerations. Efforts were quickly made to discover the internal differences that many people felt must be there in order to account for the external difference. Perhaps the most frequently encountered candidates are the next two mistakes—suggestions, or sometimes, indeed, assumptions about ways in which formative and summative evaluation are supposed to be intrinsically different.

The Relative Strictness of Formative and Summative Evaluation

The Third Fallacy (F3) is the view that formative evaluation is or can properly be a much more informal process than summative evaluation.

The reason why this view has been widely held[15] perhaps emerges from the recognition of the roots of formative evaluation in what was called the zero-order case of the author critiquing his or her own work. The alpha-testing stage of formative evaluation is also often done in-house and thus has its own authority; it does not have to produce the whole credibility-enhancing apparatus of the external study. Unfortunately, that does not increase the chances that it is valid; the in-house evaluator is usually co-opted in one way or another, typically in the direction of overfavorable evaluations. Doing formative evaluation any less rigorously than a good summative evaluation simply undermines the accuracy of the mid-course corrections, which is all too likely to send the mission in the wrong direction. Put in another way, the formative evaluation should *at least* provide a preview of a summative evaluation, since one of its most useful functions is to be an "early warning system." If it's done informally, it runs a serious risk of creating a false sense of security—or, in the less common case where the informality leads to excessively unfavorable conclusions—unwarranted anxiety. One example of short-changing in informal formative evaluation, one that often leads to disastrous waste of funds, is failing to be serious about the cost dimension in evaluating products under development, and thus failing to realize the problems with the market projections. On many occasions this means the line of development is headed into the dead end of zero sales once the development money runs out, a phenomenon with which everyone involved with government-funded development of educational materials is all too familiar.

The "friendly formative" approach is often accompanied by a related mistake already mentioned—the idea that formative evaluation can be done *entirely* internally and that you only need to go outside for summative. Of course, this makes good sense for the first criticisms of a new project where other members of a work group pick up gross blunders, or even for the alpha-testing. But developers and supervisors continually press this too far. One sees the unfortunate results in educational institutions that never use external examiners; in textbook and software development companies that never get to serious beta-testing (the use of external users to review an almost complete version[16]); and in teacher evaluation where the principal serves in both the formative and summative role. In such cases, you get excellent consistency between the standards and conclusions of the formative and summative evaluations—in itself desirable—but you also get a coauthor reviewing his or her own work, with the expectable lack of objectivity and limited range of viewpoints. One solution worth considering is to use a team of two evaluators, for example, in the case of teacher evaluation, using a principal and a district consultant who is less burdened with personal ties and conflicts. We are on the way to this when a large introductory course is taught by teaching assistants and examined by a committee, but we usually lose the point by having the committee made up of the teaching assistants alone. They have a serious problem of conflict of interest.

Global vs. Analytic Evaluation

Next we come to what is perhaps the most widely held mistaken belief about formative evaluation—and one with very serious consequences in education.

The Fourth Fallacy (F4) is the view that formative evaluation cannot merely consist of an overall rating. It is usually thought that it must contain or imply recommendations for improvement or causal explanations of the performance.

This belief is used to provide an illicit defense against perfectly proper and sometimes essential approaches to teacher evaluation. To explain why F4 is believed, and how to replace it with a related correct proposition, we need to bring in two other distinctions. Together with the original distinction, they make up the major components of a multidimensional conceptual field in which is embedded our commonsensical but complicated practice of evaluation. Setting them out helps us to clarify the meaning of evaluation and improve its practice.

Other terms sometimes used for what is here called "global" evaluation include "holistic," "overall," "macro-evaluation," and "black-box" evaluation. The normal and preferable use of "overall" is somewhat different from the others, as I shall explain shortly. The paradigm example of global evaluation comes from large-scale essay grading in English composition. This can be done globally ("holistically" is the term frequently used there), by quickly reading the whole essay and awarding an overall "impressionistic" grade. Or it can be done analytically by awarding separate ratings to several aspects of the work (originality, organization, mechanics, etc.), these considerations then being combined into an overall grade, either by following a rule or by a judgmental integration. The scoring of the individual answers in the analytic process is guided by a "rubric" or scoring guide related to the particular questions; the rubric may also cover the process of combining the subscores into an overall grade. The analytic approach naturally takes several times as long as the holistic one, and costs in proportion. Of course, it looks more scientific; but research suggests the holistic ratings may be more accurate. Hence the common presupposition that analytic evaluations are preferable must be treated very cautiously. They are certainly more expensive and slower to get, and at least sometimes less accurate.

The analytic approach might, however, be said to be more desirable in that it comes nearer to providing one kind of explanation of the grade. That is, it might be said to "unpack" an overall grade in an illuminating way. In a weak sense of the terms, it can also be said to support or justify the grade, and this is a strong enough sense to mean that, on many occasions, that is exactly why analytic summative evaluation is done. But it is not a causal explanation of the grade, and that is often what a scientific account undertakes to provide.[17] Nor is it a justification in a strong sense, since it merely expands on, rather than provides evidence for, the conclusion. In spite of these caveats, however, it does appear at first sight to be definitely better as a guide to improvement. After all, merely telling you how well you have done does not tell you where to focus an effort at further improvement. Hence it seems plausible that formative evaluation should be analytic evaluation. As we shall see, the matter is not so simple.

First, however, we need to stress the difference between *an analytic approach to evaluation* and *a complete analytic evaluation,* and we need to distinguish two species of analytic evaluation, one of which appears at first sight to be greatly superior to the other for formative purposes.

In this section we have been using the term "overall" in a different way from the other synonyms for "global," consistently with the dictionary's suggestions. An overall evaluation, as we use the term, is simply the bottom line of an evaluation, *however it is reached.* In global evaluation, the overall evaluation is of course the same as the global evaluation. But in analytic evaluation the overall evaluation is what you arrive at after first examining—and usually evaluating—various aspects or parts of whatever you are evaluating *and then combining the results.* In this usage, the overall evaluation is not the same as "the whole evaluation," since that would include the component evaluations.

Analytic Evaluation vs. Fragmentary Evaluation

Analytic evaluation is thus a multistep process of which the last step is the combinatorial step, done judgmentally or by rule, which generates an overall evaluation. Global evaluation is a one-step process, normally a judgmental process, which generates the overall evaluation alone. This difference opens up the possibility, which turns out to be very important in practice, that an analytic evaluation can stop just before the last step. Stopping at that point is in fact often held up as the correct way to do evaluation. The truth is that it is usually just an example of fragmentary evaluation, one species of incomplete evaluation. (Other species of incomplete evaluation are those that, for example, leave out the cost component, or the comparative component.)

To understand why people should imagine that fragmentary evaluation is acceptable, one has to see it in a wider framework. In most cases, it is serving as a halfway house between description and evaluation; it represents a position that is attractive to those with a residual, perhaps unconscious, hankering after the ideal of value-free science. Even amongst professional program evaluators, it is still common to try to avoid adopting any actual evaluation stance, although they still call what they do evaluation. This approach is referred to here as "pseudoevaluative investigation," and it results in a description masquerading as evaluation. It is sometimes rationalized by appeal to the following claim:

The Fifth Fallacy (F5) is the belief that the professional evaluator's duty is to give clients the facts and let them assemble (interpret) these according to their own values or to give them the subevaluations and let them put these together.

The first part of this fallacy creates the curious picture of a professional evaluator doing everything except what is normally called evaluating something. In reality, the situation is even worse. In almost any serious evaluation there have been several explicit subevaluations (e.g., of what are seen as less important issues) done on the way to the last step, so "the facts" usually stem from many previous evaluations. Thus, balking at the last step—the overall evaluation—is rather like deciding you want to be a virgin after the orgy but before the Day of Judgment. The F5 adherent is nearly always guilty of inconsistency as well as misleading advertising.

Even if the last step looks as if it's only presenting facts, and there are no explicit evaluations in the preceding steps, underlying the discovery of those facts would be many layers of full-blooded evaluation (e.g., of the quality of evidence and previous research in the area), since all scholarly endeavor is by definition critical and hence evaluative—the reason why the value-free doctrine is essentially absurd.

The person who balks at the last hurdle is likely to argue that up to that point there is no intrusion in the process of the *personal values* of the client. The defender of something like the Fifth Fallacy (F5) wants to leave it to the client to insert those values into the process. As a matter of fact, it is more than likely you will have had to bring in the client's values—and those of relevant others—several times before getting to this point. But that's not the main weakness in F5.

The main weakness in F5 is that it involves a misunderstanding of the entire nature of professional practice in every practical field— medicine, engineering, architecture, law, accounting. Most of these professionals spend much of their time doing evaluations, e.g., of the client's health, designs, defense, or accounting systems. In all these you have to face the need for *doing complete evaluations keyed to the client's interests*, as opposed to *giving the client the bits and pieces* and leaving him or her to get to the bottom line. Doing so in no way suggests that you are forcing some conclusion on clients that doesn't fit their circumstances. Doctors don't hand you the results of tests and photocopies of pages from a pharmacopoeia. They combine the test results with the case history and their observations into a specific evaluation (diagnosis)—a process involving the same logic as the synthesis step in evaluation—and then they provide recommendations tailored to your condition and needs, commonly involving what is known as a prescription. That's the nature of professional consulting, and it is that way for good reasons which will now be considered. To those who favor stopping before the last step, one must say: If you don't like the heat, stay out of the kitchen—don't try to talk the customers into eating raw vegetables. That's not the chef's job and the people who come to restaurants don't find it helpful.

In fact, F5 advocates the abrogation of the professional responsibility of the evaluator at what is often the most critical moment—the moment when the client most needs professional help. There are three reasons why this is the moment of the professional's maximum value rather than the moment to withdraw. First, the fragments (the "bare facts" or subevaluations) may be extremely numerous and of totally different types, with the result that the client is simply confused by the complexity of the integrative task. This is typical when the person lacking area-specific experience encounters the need to evaluate complex products like houses, computer software, and public service programs. A good evaluator who is, or is cooperating with, a specialist in the area, should know how to deal with this complexity in a systematic way that assists the clients to see what will be best from their point of view.

Second, the last step in a complex evaluation, the synthesis or combinatorial step, is made much more difficult than its predecessors by the intrusion of confounding influences. For this is the moment when clients begin to see the looming shape of some of the possible evaluative conclusions, which means that their other agendas, ego-involvements, and general anxiety about criticism (or the reactions of others to it) come to bear with greatest force. Furthermore, memories of what other people have done at this point—with good or bad results—begin to flood in, along with the media messages of vendors. This is exactly the time when the independent professional can be most useful in preserving the objectivity of the process. In recommending amputation of a leg, the doctor is taking the extra step to the bottom line, and is there to defend it, knowing that you won't like it. That's what being a professional involves, not sitting back on one's facts.

Third, the last step is methodologically the most difficult step, and it seems clear that in many cases the coy posture of the Fifth Fallacy conceals or is driven by simple ignorance of how to justify "the final inference." The difficulties are threefold. First, there is the question of whether you have covered all aspects or components of whatever it is that you have evaluated. There is no simple algorithm for this, although reading every evaluation of comparable evaluands is a good start, and in every specific area there are relevant checklists (albeit of highly variable quality). Second, there is the question whether the criteria or components you have identified are independent. If they are not, the synthesis will normally double-weight the overlap. Substantial logical skills help here, but it also helps to have a local expert with well-tried checklists. However, the checklists, even if well-tried, are much more likely to involve this error than the error of incompleteness. Third, and most seriously, there is the mighty problem of exactly how to combine the bits and pieces—your subconclusions—into the overall conclusion. This is the problem of identifying and justifying "the combinatorial algorithm."

An algorithm that we frequently and almost intuitively use is the "weight and sum" approach (for example, in product evaluation and in marking student papers), but it involves many extremely dubious assumptions about the distribution of utility.[18] There are some acceptable pragmatic solutions to this problem, none of them as simple as the original.[19] While this is no place for the details, it's possible to indicate the general reason why a solution is in principle possible without imposing one's own values or someone else's values on the client. It's possible because one can tie the weights to the *client's* needs (and other values), to the needs of impacted groups, and to legality, accuracy, etc. (the contextual values), something which the evaluator should long since have determined in working through the evaluation task.

Thus, F5 involves a common misconception of evaluation services that might be described as the "two-legged stool" view. From one point of view, evaluation (like most professional consulting) necessarily involves three components: data about the thing being evaluated; data about the client, environment, and background; and the analysis of that total set of data. Much scientific research not aimed at evaluative conclusions quite properly omits the second component. But evaluation research, like most professional consulting, can very rarely omit it. Hence there is no question of us lacking the knowledge required to take the third step in an analytic evaluation. Not only should the evaluators already have this knowledge (and have used it several times), but it's reasonable to expect that the version of it which they have is more complete and accurate in crucial respects than the version which the client intuits. Even when clients are the sole source of specific values—as distinct from the general values of ethics and the law—the evaluator (who here functions as the knowledge engineer in expert systems research) will normally have clarified the client's values profile with some probing questions, and perhaps filtered out some inconsistencies and fantasies, thus refining the relative weightings of the values on the way to identifying the winner. How else would the candidates for consideration, the options for the decision maker, be identified? How else could one decide on the dimensions along which performance is to be measured?

Pushing onwards to judgment is not always appropriate, although it is normally appropriate. There are three relatively rare cases in which a single winner should not be declared by the evaluator. But in all of them, the evaluator has gone far beyond "determining the facts" and handing these over to the client. In all of them, the evaluator has completed what we might call the vertical integration of facts and values for each candidate, and only holds back on the horizontal comparison. First, even with the best photofinish equipment, there are sometimes dead heats in horse races. The result can then be determined by the toss of a coin, but just in case the client sees something in one of the alternatives which had not previously seemed important, it's appropriate to give the client the chance to make the final selection. That's why the doctor will sometimes leave it up to the patient to make a choice between two therapies after they have been described in some detail. Sometimes, too, the horse race is just a qualification race against the clock; winning isn't the point. In competency testing or certification, a number of candidates qualify, and the tests are not designed to find a winner. Second, generalizing this point, it's often sensible to expect that the clients can do some fine-tuning of their values in the light of the specific alternatives that are leading as they come down the straight, even if they would not dead heat on their own. So, at that point, turning the choice back to the client, while maintaining close touch, is often a good procedure, if the problem of undue influence from seeing the outcome appears not to be serious. Third, with some clients, it's best to let them feel that they drew the conclusion even though it's clear enough for the evaluator to announce. Some decision makers, for example, are seriously threatened by the idea that if evaluators draw conclusions, the administrator's power has been undermined. This is confused thinking, but it's often less important to educate clients about this point than to get the right decision made immediately.

The Need for an Overall Conclusion

So the fifth fallacy consists of the idea that it's *always* proper to avoid the inference to an overall conclusion, that *all* the runners can be given the chance of legitimate last minute redemption by the client. Short of traumatic emotional conversion, this is absurd; fragmentary evaluation is simply balking at the last hurdle because it's the last one. The whole process of evaluation *began* with a set of candidates that were picked on the basis of the client's needs and preferences (as well as their performance); and it proceeds to identify the best-performing candidates in the light of those values. There's nothing special about the last, comparative, step except that the implications of those values are now becoming clear. Remember that in most of these cases, the client's request was: "Which alternative should I buy/support/do?" And that question is not answered until one alternative is shown to be the winner, or one of the winners.

If this argument is correct, then analytic summative evaluation should normally proceed to an overall conclusion, typically a comparative rating, and will be incomplete if it does not. Nor is this conclusion restricted to summative evaluation. The following proposition about formative evaluation is also in error:

The Sixth Fallacy (F6) maintains that in *formative evaluation*, it is only necessary to point out various respects in which improvement is needed. It is not necessary to draw any overall conclusion.

This is often advanced as tenable even if F5 cannot be maintained for summative evaluation. Does it really do any harm? The answer is that it is one of the most dangerous of our agenda of mistakes.

Applied to teacher development, for example, this proposition often leads to citing a number of "directions of needed improvement," without struggling for an overall rating. This seems not only reasonable but possibly more humane. Unfortunately, one cannot conclude from the fact that a performance is deficient in a number of respects that the effort of changing is worthwhile, and certainly not that the way to improve it is to try to improve these respects directly.

There are no doubt respects in which one can fault Frank Lloyd Wright's designs, including the clarity of his lettering, for example. It does not follow that he would have been well-advised to spend substantial time on rectifying this or other deficiencies. The cost might be far larger than the benefits. Fragmentary evaluation can cause much more trouble than it's worth; it should be put in the context of an overall rating which tells you, for example, that you are already very good and only very small benefits could possibly accrue from addressing the alleged imperfections.

Particularly, but not only, when more than one problem is identified, a further difficulty comes in. It may be that attempts to improve one aspect of one's performance or program will simply produce other effects with results that represent a net loss. Most of these fragmentary evaluations rest on the assumption of causal independence of the dimensions of deficit, an assumption which is very often false. In fact, it involves exactly the fault referred to in the medical and psychotherapeutic areas as "treating the symptoms." There may well be some underlying condition which *must* be addressed in order to mitigate the observed symptoms; worse, it may be the case that tackling the symptoms directly will produce more unfortunate side effects than it will produce immediate or long-term benefits. In the teaching case, for example, it is often the case that the observed deficits are not important compared to the underlying failure of enthusiasm for teaching, or failure to commit to continual self-development. If the deeper cause is addressed, the observable weaknesses will vanish; if it is not, addressing them directly may lead to losses in other areas that will add up to produce a worse situation overall.

Of course, the "friendly formative" image is facilitated by a piecemeal approach; there are no threatening overall conclusions, no deep diagnoses. It's just that improvement is poorly served, and that's what formative evaluation is supposed to be all about.

In the engineering and instructional technology areas, one sometimes encounters the view that formative evaluation is the same as troubleshooting.[20] If this just means dealing with observable defects on an ad hoc basis, it is a version of the sixth fallacy. It's true that troubleshooting, in this sense, is better than making no attempt at improvement at all, but is also very likely to yield an unbalanced impression, which is a poor basis for *planned* improvement. The stronger sense of troubleshooting involves finding the root cause of the surface problems and that's what we need for full remediation. Formative evaluations with an overall conclusion are the first step toward finding the root cause, but remediation takes us far beyond that into diagnosis and prescription, discussed below.

In an emergency, the diagnosis and prescription phases may have to be bypassed, at least temporarily. If the ambulance brings in an accident victim who is hemorrhaging, we don't run a full work-up before stemming the flow of blood. But we must do what we can toward a complete rather than a fragmentary formative evaluation. That is, we must try to identify the relative importance of the major problems and the overall level of severity. Hemorrhaging has a good prima facie claim to being the leading problem, but *still* one has to check the skin color for signs of cyanosis; no good stemming the bleeding of a patient who will be dead of asphyxiation by the time we succeed. Then, as soon as possible, one tries for the deeper analysis that goes beyond evaluation to causation and prescription. The same applies to less traumatic cases like a computer crash, where one must take a breath and review where the back-up is, if any, and how important the lost files are, and so on, before starting the remediation.

Notice the difference between what is being recommended here and the typical formative teacher evaluation by a teacher supervisor/principal, which consists of shooting from the hip based on observations of small samples of classroom behavior. Doing so is indeed providing formative evaluation, but it is not providing *a* formative evaluation—that is, a serious and systematic evaluation, including an overall conclusion, which is the essential basis for remediation. Of course, for that one would need information on how much the students are learning, and of what quality, and whether this quality is being identified by good testing and recognized by appropriate grades. But, of course, that takes a little more effort than commenting on the style we can see immediately.

Aren't we being unrealistic in this demand for serious formative evaluation with an overall conclusion? Paul Diederich, a pioneer in upgrading the quality of evaluation in marking student essay papers, used to say that it was a great mistake to keep issuing grades all the time to students who were not doing well, because it simply discouraged them. This may appear inconsistent with the argument here, and that concern gives us a chance to clarify the flaw in the fifth fallacy. F5 says that it's not necessary to *draw* an overall conclusion. That's incorrect, for the reasons given, but drawing a conclusion doesn't mean that one should constantly *broadcast* the conclusion. If doing so will adversely affect motivation, as with students, it can be withheld most of the time and replaced with specific helpful advice. From time to time, however, in line with the evaluator's obligations to any client (including student clients) that include avoiding the possibility of misunderstanding or self-deception about the quality of performance and of progress, some overview of both must be provided.

Of course, the teacher/child relationship is not the same as the relationship of an evaluator to an adult client (including an adult student). In the latter case the importance of not discouraging the learner is normally much less than the importance of reasonably complete disclosure. Principals are all too often inclined to think of themselves as dealing with students when evaluating beginning teachers, instead of as dealing with professionals at the workplace. While there is some truth in the view that most teachers still have much to learn, just like principals and professors, it is professionally improper to treat them as students because it treats a professional as less than a professional. Doctors are now moving away from a period when they treated patients, especially female and aged patients, in a correspondingly inappropriate manner.

A second reason for disclosure is the high error rate in teacher evaluations and medical evaluations; clients should be given the information which makes it possible for them to decide whether a second opinion is desirable. Of course, parents tend to think that this is equivalent to getting a higher grade, when in fact it is usually the reverse, since students tend to get much better grades than their work deserves, partly because of the one-sided pressure placed on teachers when they give low grades.[21]

Hence the general conclusion is that overall evaluations, not just fragmentary ones, must be inferred in the formative as well as in the summative situation, and only in special cases should they be withheld from those to whom—or to whose work—they refer.

Psychological, Social, and Political Considerations

Most of the objections to evaluation focus on summative evaluation, probably because it is more commonly criterion-referenced and is circulated to a wider audience than formative. It is thus much more threatening to one's ego, and even the prospect of it is anxiety-provoking. Reference to the possibly inhibiting effect on students of too many grades during a term, even formative grades, is not the first reference we have made to psychological considerations. There was, for example, the suggestion that some evaluators prefer a "kinder, gentler" approach. It seems clear that there are massive differences between evaluators on the dimension of willingness to say what the client—or the evaluee—doesn't want to hear. At one end of the spectrum, the school principal, like a parent of spoiled children, is often simply unwilling to say critical things to a teacher—someone with whom he or she has to live from day to day. Outside the protected climate of government-funded schools, any manager would say that this is clear evidence of incompetent management.

In education, however, there is no shortage of those who argue that there shouldn't be any teacher evaluation, or that there should only be peer evaluation of teachers, or that teacher evaluations should always be fragmentary, or that principals should only be teacher-helpers, etc.[22] In fact, this approach is not restricted to teacher evaluation; analogous unwillingness to come to negative conclusions, or to get to the bottom line at all, or to use evaluative language, has surfaced in attempts to reform the evaluation of students. And it has characterized many program evaluators and evaluation theorists. Apart from Cronbach and his associates, examples include much of the British work in program evaluation, the position which came to be known as the North Dakota school, and many aspects of Robert Stake's later work.

The problem with the "kinder, gentler" approach is that it throws away half the benefits of evaluation when used as part of the process of improvement. While there is some role for evaluation in pure research, much of its value comes from the way in which it improves things that can be improved, increases efficiency in the use of resources, and provides accountability where appropriate. Evaluators are well aware of the drawbacks of doing evaluation in a *context* where its results will have no effect on practice. They should realize that if it is done in a *way* which cuts half of the possible conclusions off from practice, one loses half the benefits. Conceptually speaking, half the benefits come from each half of the spectrum of ratings: half come from identifying the best candidates (e.g., when you buy, promote, or hire), the other half from identifying the weaker ones (when you withdraw support, distribute scarce remedial resources, or prevent continued abuse of consumers). So the truth is simple: if there's no "downside risk," that is, if evaluation is only done to distribute rewards, half the payoff from evaluation is thrown away. One frequently encounters a failure to realize this, e.g., when districts try to "sell" teachers on a new system of evaluation—"We promise that it will not be used punitively, only constructively." This is precisely comparable to offering high-yield investments without risk.

Such promises result in discarding half of the benefits of the evaluation. What benefits are left may be worth less than the cost of the evaluation process itself. (On the other hand, when the full payoff from evaluation is used, the benefits are likely to more than pay for the evaluation.) So it is hard not to react to promises like "only constructive evaluations will be used" with despair: "There goes the ball game!" But it isn't a ball game; it's the education of millions and the future of the country. For many of those millions education is thwarted the moment you abandon the possibility of dismissing for incompetence.

The real situation is even worse, because the two halves of the evaluation scale are coupled. When you restrict evaluation to the upper half of the scale ("half-scale" evaluation), you almost guarantee that those performing on the lower half will deteriorate further. Their level of performance is not just going to stay the same, that is, remain unsatisfactory. It's going to get worse, move nearer to disastrous, because you have just removed a major reason for a continuing effort on their part. This can, of course, be done in other ways, for example, by making the rules for dismissing incompetent personnel so complex and time-intensive that administrators are not willing to start the process, as in much of the federal bureaucracy and in many school districts.

But the worst treachery to the student or consumer comes about when you announce in advance that you won't produce or circulate negative summative evaluations. One sees in consumer magazines or government units which argue that "there's no point" in publishing negative product evaluations; and again, throughout the world, in the unwillingness of centers set up to evaluate computer courseware (i.e., educational software) to publish critical comments.[23] It's quite clear there is a point in not publishing negative reviews—you avoid alienating potential advertisers or creating political adversaries—just as there's a point in not alienating the teachers' union or individual teachers, or private sector producers. The problem is that if you rate that kind of point higher than service to the customer or student who will benefit in terms of money and quality of life from your publication of negative results, you reveal the shoddiness of your true values. The same problem comes up in countries where the libel laws are excessively protective (Australia, for example), and people quote the possibility of a lawsuit as an excuse for pulling punches. Evaluators often have to say what has to be said and realize that the legal problems, like the problem of creating distress, are part of the job and are to be avoided only where doing so does not entail abandoning your clients or professional standards.

The psychological problems with the evaluator's role are serious. One or two erstwhile program evaluators of some distinction have pulled out of the game entirely because of the psychological stresses involved. It's quite common for younger evaluators to "go native," that is, psychologically join the staff of the program they are supposed to be evaluating and become advocates instead of evaluators. (The two roles are not incompatible, but we are talking of cases where they are not reconciled, only switched.) The usual symptom is simple overrating—giving unjustifiably favorable evaluations, switching to "half-scale" evaluation. Those with a theoretical turn of mind try to show that evaluation really *means* never having to say anything negative. The true conclusion is the commonsensical one: professional evaluation is just as incompatible with "half-scale" evaluation as it is with fragmentary evaluation, or with evaluation which fails to look at comparisons, or at costs, or at ethical issues such as discrimination in personnel practice when evaluating a program or an institution. There's no real excuse for overfavorable evaluation—*Consumer Reports*, the Federal Drug Administration, the Better Business Bureau, and fifty specialist magazines do it right most of the time—although there are indeed many difficulties in the way, political and psychological as well as methodological.

Of course, any claim about psychological motivation is a double-edged weapon. If one argues that the main reason evaluators avoid negative conclusions is that they haven't the courage for it, they may well reply that the only reason one defends the propriety of negative conclusions is that one wants to be able to wield a whip—an unhealthy lust for power. The decision must be made on the relative social utility of the two approaches, not on the motives of their advocates. To extend the previous argument, social utility appears to have been amply demonstrated in the fields of product and service and medical nostrum evaluation, where billions of dollars and thousands of lives a year are saved by willingness to buy or ban products on the basis of "full-scale," integrated, comparative, cost-related, summative evaluation. It has also been demonstrated in the field of personnel evaluation—outside a few government bureaucracies including much of education. It has been demonstrated in the evaluation of educational materials in those organizations where the savings from good choices are credited to the organization, such as the U.S. Air Force Training Command. It is difficult not to regard it as profoundly significant that none of the advocates of the restricted kinds of evaluation we have been discussing (formative only, fragmentary only, and half-scale only) appears to have had experience in any of these fields. What possible argument could there be to show that, even though summative evaluation of personnel and products and services is not only useful but best done on a full scale, the corresponding evaluation of teachers or programs should be run under severe censorship? This does have the appearance of special pleading. Despite the psychological and political risks of serious evaluation, the costs of not doing it are greater.

Dimensional vs. Component Evaluation

The previous discussion suggests that analytic evaluation must not stop at subevaluations (let alone at the descriptive stage) but rather proceed to an overall conclusion. We must now look more at the *kind* of detail that analytic evaluation provides, the deeper kind of analysis that often makes it more attractive than global or black box evaluation. We can illustrate the two different ways in which it does this by going back to the example of essay grading. One approach would provide subevaluations of performance on several *aspects* or *dimensions* of the essay; this might include the originality, the organization, and the grammar. The other approach breaks the evaluand into *parts* or *components* and evaluates those; teachers quite often provide subevaluations of the opening, the development, and the closing sections of an essay. The key difference between "component evaluation" and "dimensional evaluation" is that *dimensions are pervasive throughout an evaluand*, and *components are spatio-temporally separate regions of it*. Since it is often easier to replace or upgrade components than dimensions, component evaluation is often more helpful in the formative role than is dimensional evaluation. Should we focus on it exclusively? One sometimes hears this demand in teacher evaluation: "Tell me exactly what I'm doing wrong, and I'll do it right; just telling me that certain aspects of what I'm doing are unsatisfactory is simply not helpful. I need to know what to improve."

The Seventh Fallacy (F7) maintains that formative evaluation, at least in most contexts, should be done in terms of component evaluation rather than dimensional evaluation.

One practical reason against F7 is that component evaluation is often much more expensive than dimensional evaluation. Another is that it is often more difficult, and in many cases impossible. Consumer product evaluation is usually done in terms of dimensions: television sets, for example, are typically evaluated in terms of color purity, convergence, resolution, distortion, reliability, cost, sound quality, fringe area reception, etc. These are all dimensions, and incidentally they provide quite useful information to the manufacturer for improvement purposes. However, it would be considerably more useful to a television manufacturer who wishes to improve the product if the evaluation were expanded in terms of the quality of the components of the television set, for then the defective ones could be replaced or upgraded. But to do this would require perhaps ten times the budget for the evaluation, and it would require expertise that may not be available anywhere, since the fault may lie in subtle aspects of the design not yet codified as weaknesses in the body of scientific/ technological knowledge. In any case, that kind of effort would be entirely inappropriate since the membership of Consumers Union is not interested in making television sets, only in buying them, and dimensional evaluation is all and exactly what they need in order to tailor the research results to their own needs.

Dimensional evaluation has another advantage over component evaluation. We earlier identified several reasons why would-be evaluators in the analytic mode balk at the integration step, one of which was its methodological difficulty. That difficulty was said to have three causes: the three problems of identifying completeness, independence, and a valid integrative algorithm. If our analytic evaluation is in terms of components, we must add another pair of problems to that list, the problems of evaluating architecture and assembly. For the merit of a whole is not the sum of the merits of its parts; it also involves the merit of the way in which they have been put together (a) by design (architecture) and (b) in practice (assembly).

Thus dimensional evaluation is often cheaper, it is often possible instead of impossible, it is often very useful in the formative context, it is often incomparably superior for summative purposes, and it is often simpler to combine its elements than the elements of component evaluation. Hence the idea that formative evaluation should always be not only analytic but, specifically, the component type of analytic evaluation, as suggested in the first paragraph of this section, is extremely unrealistic. The mistaken view probably originated in an intuition along the lines of "If I don't know what parts to improve, how can I possibly improve?" We need to sort out a good answer to this perfectly sensible question, if we are going to reject the apparently plausible answer of F7. To do so, we must first face some more fundamental difficulties with the whole line of argument which suggests that analytic evaluation is the way to generate suggestions for improvement.

Evaluation vs. Diagnosis

The logic of evaluation and improvement is more complicated than appears at first sight. While analytic evaluation does result in subevaluations, and while these are often helpful in generating suggestions for improvement, they are not themselves—nor do they entail—recommendations for improvement. The doctor's report on someone in for an annual check-up is a paradigm example of analytic evaluation, but it doesn't include or entail any prescriptions, though the doctor is expected to provide these after consideration of the results. Prescription calls for further skills, in, for example, pharmacology and dietetics.

Even diagnosis, the usual intermediate step between the discovery of disorder (resulting from a formal or informal evaluation) and making recommendations, generally calls on further skills beyond the results of testing, examining, and case-history analysis. Those results—the usual subevaluations generated in the course of a check-up—make up the components in a component-type analytic evaluation. The tests reveal that the blood uric acid level is too high. Inspection shows obesity. The case history reveals family conditions likely to produce extreme stress. These are certainly evaluations of components of the totality that is a patient's health. But, typically, they are not, nor do they entail, a diagnosis (let alone a prescription). They have to be put together, interpreted, matched to patterns of disease and disorder.

Sometimes, one can almost read the bare evaluative conclusions off tables that provide acceptable ranges for each variable—not quite, because of interaction or configural effects, but nearly. And you can often integrate or synthesize those simple subevaluative conclusions into one kind of overall evaluation ("You're in reasonably good shape for your age, although it wouldn't hurt to bring the cholesterol down a little") without any great expertise in diagnostics. But serious diagnosis requires you to be able to recognize the syndromes for all likely illnesses in the data before you. In these days of fast and frequent travel, that doesn't leave much out. Then you have to know how to do differential diagnosis, which often means knowing which further tests are called for. Sometimes all this cannot be done at one session, because the diagnosis may depend on how a patient reacts to medication or other thereapeutic regimens, or it may require extended periods of interactive observation, for example, in diagnosing exotica like pseudoneurotic schizophrenia. The idea that an analytic formative evaluation automatically spins off a diagnosis is, sadly enough, simply a myth. Of course, there is no sharp line between diagnosis and global evaluations, or between diagnosis and other types of analytic evaluations.

Is a diagnosis evaluative? One doesn't diagnose conditions of good health. It is part of the meaning of the word that it consists of the classification of disorder/malfunction/disease. Hence the conclusion of a diagnosis is always (negatively) evaluative; to say that you have cancer implies that you are not well. Nevertheless, we are inclined to say that the evaluation comes first, and the diagnosis is a taxonomical or explanatory exercise that comes after the evaluation; it *presupposes* rather than performs the (negative) evaluation. The content *of the diagnosis*, by contrast with the material it works on, is a classification.

This temporal sequence—evaluation, then diagnosis—is some-times collapsed. Sometimes the diagnosis is instantaneous, unmediated: the mechanic at the garage where you are getting fuel says, "Sounds to me as if a bearing is going in that engine." For the mechanic, that characteristic rattle of a deteriorating bearing tells its story instantly: malaise is identified and diagnosed in one perception. (In this particular case, the diagnosis is in fact a component [analytic] evaluation.)

Still, a difference remains between most diagnoses and most evaluations. Evaluations usually begin with data and end up with an evaluative conclusion. In most evaluations, we feel it would be begging the question to begin with the assumption that the result is unfavorable; but in diagnosis, that is by definition the nature of the task. The real point is that diagnosis is an exercise in *the classification of a condition already known to be bad*; it is not an exercise in *determining whether and to what extent or in what respects something is good or bad*, i.e., evaluating it. But one must remember that the conclusion of a diagnosis is nevertheless an evaluative conclusion, even if the evaluative element is, so to speak, inherited by the diagnostician (who may simply be the physician of first recourse, who has put on this hat as soon as the evaluation shows the patient is in trouble).

To keep this in perspective, one must remember that some analytic evaluations begin after a global evaluation has identified malaise or at least probable malaise. So, even if diagnosis typically comes after a negative evaluation has taken place, that does not categorically exclude it from the class of evaluation types. Program evaluators are familiar with something like diagnosis. It occurs in the situation where a client says: "I'm not hiring you to tell me that I've got serious problems with this program; I already know that, and what I want you to do is to find out what the trouble is." That's very like a request for a diagnosis, and one would be likely to respond to it with a component evaluation. We do not have an elaborate taxonomy of program disorders, so component evaluation is much nearer to being diagnosis in the program evaluation area than it is in the medical area.

In the personnel area, since humans are involved, we can and do apply much of our taxonomy of human conditions in a process that is obviously diagnostic. "He's simply unable to delegate authority" is a diagnostic remark. (The associated overall evaluative remark would be something like "He's not working out as a manager.") This particular diagnostic remark is quite like a fragment of a dimensional evaluation, but, unlike such a fragment, it often carries the heavier burden of being presented as *the* diagnosis.

Diagnoses are not, in themselves, the same as either component evaluations or dimensional evaluations. A doctor may conclude that you are suffering from some rare tropical disease, without even knowing which parts of your system are under attack and by what agency. It's clear, first, that you aren't well—the symptoms of high fever, giddiness, fatigue, etc. are parts of an analytic evaluation which justifies that conclusion (an adult will already have made the global evaluation). In a second process, diagnosis, the expert identifies the syndrome—the configuration of symptoms and context—as a case of disease X. Diagnoses are exercises in this kind of "identification," where the term means classification or labeling, and they are, in a weak sense, explanatory. They are perhaps most closely related to what has elsewhere been called perspectival evaluation—the attempt to present the evaluand in a certain way, thought to be illuminating.[24]

Thus, in the medical case, and perhaps in some other cases such as personnel review, the diagnosis goes beyond the primary evaluation. A diagnosis may be offered as part of a formative evaluation (the mechanic) or of a summative evaluation (as in a post mortem). But it is not a necessary part of—or consequence of—every analytic evaluation.

There is one other interesting feature of the medical case. A patient's presenting symptomatology is often enough to establish serious illness, even though no comprehensive work-up has been done. So evaluation and diagnosis are often correctly and appropriately done without waiting for a *complete* evaluation. Again, however, this is an emergency override of ideal principles and does not justify most "trouble-shooting" approaches as a substitute for serious formative evaluation.

This analysis has substantial bearing on our main line of argument. Diagnosis, where it is something distinct from dimensional or component evaluation (e.g., in the medical context), is done because it is usually the best route to recommendations. But it may and often does represent *a step beyond the evaluation itself, and it may still be some distance from the recommendations.*

Evaluation vs. Causation

Very often, the next step after diagnosis is determining causation; and typically we have to go through that step before moving to recommendations, including pharmaceutical or regimen prescriptions.

(Sometimes the diagnosis itself includes causation,[25] but such cases are atypical.) Usually, the process of determining the causation of a condition—in medical parlance, etiology—is not a spin-off from the basic check-up (the evaluation) and is only facilitated by the diagnosis. For example: the (component) evaluation is serious illness involving weight loss, hair loss, lassitude, and vomiting; the diagnosis is lead poisoning; the etiology is flaking paint getting into the food preparation process in ghetto housing. It is sometimes essential to determine causation in order to decide how to treat a condition; but it is sometimes not essential (as in the case of cancer). One can even treat symptoms directly, without a diagnosis (as in the case of nasal congestion).

Even where etiology is essential to determine treatment (as in the case of identifying the cause of infant trauma as child abuse), the treatment is typically not entailed by the etiology (major decisions have to be made about the legal situation with removing the child from the home before one can decide between hospitalization, foster home care, injunctions, etc., and they are not just medical alternatives). Thus, there are typically two entirely different disciplines, diagnosis and etiology—both of them often parts of medical expertise, to be sure, but separate parts of it—between the evaluation and the recommendations. Graphically, one should think in terms of a sequence of overlapping circles representing the domains of description, evaluation, diagnosis, etiology, and recommendations. It's often a long way from the first to the last.

The world is a complicated place, and evaluation's essential place in it is not as a source of causal explanations or recommendations but merely as a determiner of merit, worth, or well-being. Hence the idea that we should always use formative rather than summative evaluation "since it generates helpful suggestions," is wrong for one more reason. Formative evaluation does not, of its nature, generate recommendations at all. When it appears to do so, the recommendations are often "symptom-treatment" and may do more harm than good. Those who are good at evaluation are not necessarily good at generating recommendations; in fact, they are in some ways much less likely to be able to do that. For their evaluations tend to improve if they are not too closely tied to the field (as long as they have consultants to ensure accuracy about the field), while the expertise of the field is typically essential to provide diagnosis, etiology, and recommendations.

So the ideal solution, if you want recommendations, is not simply to get an evaluator who knows something about the field. The paradigm example of that, the school principal serving as both evaluator and remediator, is a major disaster. That approach is a disaster because the evaluation quality is often bad (e.g., omits subject matter competence, focuses on style, uses tiny samples) and the advice is often biased (implicit assumption that "what worked for me is best for you" plus coauthorship and other role conflicts[26]). The medical model shows the way: very stiff training for the general practitioner combined with very heavy use of the specialist/second opinion, with a system of secondary controls via the hospital review committees. There can be economy versions of this when we are not in life-threatening realms, but at the least one needs to *ensure the separation of the evaluation role from the helper role.*

Evaluation vs. Prescription

The idea that good evaluation produces etiology or recommendations can be seen in one way as mere confusion, or as an optimistic view of a good evaluator's skill repertoire. But there are times when it appears to be part of the straw man approach to destroying the opponent by caricature. A limiting case of this is illustrated by the following remark, sometimes put forward as if it were an insight:

The Eighth Fallacy (F8) is that the real test of, for example, a teacher evaluation system is whether it causes teachers to improve.

Is one to take this literally or just as an indication that one would hope to get this payoff, and many systems can't deliver it? Taken literally—as it is often meant—as a statement of a necessary condition for a good system, it is absurd. Evaluation systems are systems for identifying merit and worth, health and illness, function and dysfunction. Whether their use produces benefits or not in the teacher evaluation case obviously depends on many factors other than the merit of the evaluation system: the efficiency of the manager using the system, the extent to which benefits and penalties can be connected to the results, the cooperation of those to whom they apply, and, of course, the teachers' ability to improve. If a teachers' union refuses to cooperate with a system, it is often because many of their members are very anxious not to be evaluated, and they judge their power is great enough to get away with opposition. It rarely has much to do with the quality of the system itself. It is an interesting thought that the usual supporter of F8 has never thought how absurd it would be if applied to the kind of evaluation they do all the time, the evaluation of students. Do we really think that the real test of the Law School Admission Test is whether those who take it improve their thinking? The real test is whether or not it identifies the best candidates for law school, and anything else it does is a side effect. Nice if you can get it, but not to be confused with merit.

The Eighth Fallacy is a special case of an error which at one time afflicted almost everyone in the professional evaluation community[27] and is still popular. This was the error of supposing that it is a criterion of merit for an evaluation that its recommendations are implemented. Now, it is a criterion of merit for an evaluation to be done in such a way as to *facilitate* implementation, where doing so does not compromise the validity of the evaluation. For example, it is important that evaluations be written in a way which is comprehensible to the client, that they address the issues of importance to the client, etc. While it is naturally and properly a matter of *interest* to evaluators to look at implementation, and properly a matter of concern if it turns out that implementation is low, the job of the evaluator stops at the point where that of the decision-maker client begins. People may read superb road tests and buy the worst of the cars evaluated; the psychosociology of that phenomenon is interesting but not part of the discipline of evaluation. (Or at best it is part of a fringe discipline from which one might hope to uncover hints for the improvement of the basic process of evaluation.) To think otherwise is self-indulgent; it is to suppose that the doctor owns the patient, that the adviser is king. Territorial aggrandizement is unprofessional.

It's time to look at a special case which forces us to a more sensible view of the scope and limitations of evaluation. This is the case of how simple global evaluations can help with improvement, despite their apparent lack of resources for this purpose. It constitutes the final refutation of F4, the claim that formative evaluation cannot be global.

Global Formative Evaluation

Global evaluation is sometimes all that is available, and it alone can be very useful for formative purposes. One sometimes hears it said that it's improper to do—and act on—summative teacher evaluation if the evaluator can't make remedial suggestions. But it is normally thought to be part of the professional repertoire to work out how to improve oneself in the light of adverse, but well-supported, global

evaluations. It isn't the job of *Consumer Reports* or of school superintendents to work out the prescription for improvement; it's only up to
them to determine objectively whether the work is satisfactory. We
normally expect them to supplement this with one kind of specification
of deficiency, namely subscores on the respects (dimensions) in which
work or output is evaluated. Going beyond this into component
analysis will still fall short of recommendations, and is far beyond the
obligations and often the capacity of the employer.

When sales managers fire an employee for "failing to deliver" after
repeated warnings, they will often have no clear idea whether the
salesperson is congenitally incapable of doing a good job, alcoholic, or
simply lazy (the diagnosis). It's the results that count, and should
count, and in the case of teacher evaluation, it's the results with the
students that count and should count. It is primarily the obligation of
professional or skillwork employees, not of the employer, to go from
the evaluation to the remediation. It is thus not in the least unethical to
use an objective summative evaluation process which provides no
component-type analysis, even if it were the case that such an analysis
would generate recommendations. It may be all that one can afford, or
more important, all that one has the expertise for (think of consumer
product evaluation and civilian review boards of police conduct). In
the case of teachers, of course, the relevant approach is "evaluation by
results," that is, looking at how well students from comparable classes
perform on a standardized test. This has been used as a basis for
personnel action, and has survived court test.

Responding to a global evaluation—or to a sketchy dimensional
evaluation—given in a formative context may require getting some
help from peers, experts, consumers, or a library. The kind of
feedback you would be working with can range from an annual
review discussion with one's superior, or bad sales of your new
textbook. Or it may be a matter of self-evaluation, of running over the
relevant checklist and reflecting on how you are performing the
duties. Doing that may suggest some variations in approach, coupled
with careful evaluation of the results. It may even be sensible, or it
may not, to ask the superior for suggestions. There are problems with
doing so; it's not just that superiors may not be able to produce any
suggestions, but that it may not be appropriate for them to do so. This
is the strong objection to the usual argument that it's improper for
them *not* to do so. (The weaker objection is that it's often not part of
what they can do or are in a position to do.)

The more serious problem is that for a superior to make specific suggestions—the analogy is with medical prescriptions—concurrently with an evaluation, or in response to a request, involves some risk of conflict of interest. There are two possible outcomes if recommendations are provided. In the first case, the superior's suggestions are judged unhelpful and ignored by the recipient; in that case, the evaluator faces a problem of avoiding irritation or resentment when next evaluating this individual. Alternatively, the suggestions are accepted, in which case the two individuals then become coauthors of a work of which they are going to be the evaluator. This dilemma is best handled by separating the roles of evaluator and helper. There should be little or no increase in cost from doing this, since the time spent by the principal on discussion of the evaluation with the person being evaluated can be halved if it is not expected to cover remediation. Separating the roles makes clear that what is at stake here is protecting the rights of the teacher, and increasing the utility of the help available. The teacher should not be in a position of being afraid that confessions of inadequacy to the only available helper will count against him or her for summative evaluation purposes. To ensure that helpers are coaching their clients toward the actual standards being used in the summative situation, the helpers should sit in on personnel decision-making committees from time to time, although only being allowed to discuss matters of general standards.

It follows from this dilemma for the principal that the teacher should be careful about requesting or expecting remedial suggestions from the same person who is to do the later evaluation. They may find themselves unable to benefit from the suggestions and must then risk disfavor in ignoring them; or, if they adopt the suggestions, they may find that the principal is gone next year, and the replacement has different ideas about style. We here see a second type of reason why treating the evaluator as having remediation duties is risky business.

Field Expertise vs. Evaluation Expertise

In the case of teaching (similar examples are found in many other areas) principals usually confuse the evaluation and helper roles by reasoning in the following way. They rightly believe that they "know how to teach" because they know what worked for them, with their personality and their subject matter and their students, in their day. They tend to convert this into believing that they "know how to teach" in the sense of knowing how to set other teachers straight. Alas, what they do know, important though it is, is a totally inadequate foundation for supposing that they know how a quite different person should teach a quite different subject, to quite different students, in a quite different decade. Principals all too often provide an extreme example of treating field expertise as if it were evaluation expertise. The skills involved in doing something well look as if they are important for helping others do it better, which is seen as a key part of formative evaluation; formative evaluation is seen as the key kind of evaluation, e.g., because it's seen as more humane than summative; and we finish up with the school principal being the key summative evaluator as a kind of afterthought.

This argument is wrong at every step. Some of the best athletic coaches are totally incompetent in the sport they coach, not merely below world class. We've seen this lately in gymnastics, but we've also had at least one great swimming coach who couldn't swim— Frank Kiphuth. Some of the best athletes are hopeless coaches, like good teachers who make bad teacher-helpers. Similarly, some of the best evaluators are, and some are not, experts in whatever it is they evaluate. The evaluation of evaluators has to be done on the merit of their evaluations, not of their coaching skill, let alone of their equivalent of athletic ability (teaching ability, in our example).

The fact is that principals have to be, at least, competent site managers. That means they are not worth anything at all unless they can do sound *summative* evaluation, and implement the results. Anything else is icing on the cake. In the first place, the formative evaluation is worth nothing at all unless it at least includes a preview of good summative evaluation. In the second place, a summative evaluation is quite a good starting point for improvement, even if it is global. It tells you how well you are doing, which is the essential starting point.

It will be clear that we have undermined the ninth fallacy, which follows:

The Ninth Fallacy (F9) is the belief that competent evaluation of those performing a certain job requires demonstrated skill in performing that job.

This requirement has actually been built into some teacher contracts, which stipulate that teacher evaluation can only be performed by those who have demonstrated competence at that level of teaching. That's putting the formative cart before the summative horse. It would mean that *Consumer Reports* has no right to evaluate things they can't design, that juries can't pass judgment on doctors, that readers can't see the flaw in a detective novel unless they are authors, etc. Good suggestions for improvement are nice if you can get them; good evaluation even without suggestions for improvement is the first essential for improvement as well as for accountability. It must be remembered that summative evaluation alone can lead to improving the performance of the teaching faculty at a school, even if none of them uses it as a basis for professional self-development because one can always replace poor performers with better ones. Accountability requires that to be done if guided self-improvement does not remedy the deficiencies.

The best evaluators are often those who come at the task from the consumer's viewpoint, not from the vendor's—and formative is vendor's evaluation. The best software reviewers aren't programmers; they are expert users. The demand that they be programmers would simply be a sign that the consumer's interests have been overridden by the vendors' interests. The best evaluators of in-service medical education, if you have to pick one group, are the recipients of the education; and so on. The best teacher evaluation officer for a large city school district may come in with a background in industry or in the health field, topped off by some years in the district office. They might *never* have taught, or never at the precollege level; but they may be very good at determining whether the evidence available justifies the conclusion that someone is teaching well or badly. Their relevant experience is of the right kind: they most certainly have *been* taught.

They may also be able to make very useful suggestions about areas for improvement, on the basis of the evidence in front of them. For the nature of teacher evaluation, disasters apart, is quite complex since the duties are quite complex. That means analytic evaluation is virtually essential, apart from cases of outlandish behavior which might allow a global negative judgment. Hence a review of this kind of data will quickly reveal strengths and weaknesses in subject matter knowledge, classroom control, test construction, communication, lesson preparation, etc.; this spins off from analytic evaluation, whether done for formative or for summative purposes. Once such weaknesses have been mentioned, the teacher is in a good position to generate useful remedial suggestions for trial runs, without getting into problems of coauthorship or rejection of suggestions from the evaluator. There are some thousands of well-supported suggestions for handling such difficulties in the literature of teaching techniques, with many of which the teachers should be familiar—and know how to access the others.[28]

You see a corresponding fallacy turning up in program evaluation, the great fallacy of supposing that, for example, medical or law school accreditation is best done by representatives of medical schools or law schools. Of course, you must have field experts *on* the evaluation/accreditation team, but they are far more contaminated than an experienced program evaluator, and the results show it. They are prone to the belief that the ways things have always been done, which is of course the way they do it, is the right way; they are somewhat loath to criticize people who are colleagues in an extended sense (it reflects on the discipline); they are greatly affected by "how it would look" if Harvard Medical was disaccredited; they look ahead nervously to the time when these people they are now evaluating will be on the team that evaluates them; they don't like the idea of "outsiders" having any say in evaluating their turf; they think outsiders will make blunders because of their ignorance of the field; and they know very little about the tricks of the trade and the traps for young players in program evaluation. It's a poor profile for an evaluator. In reading the results in a number of cases I have found it impossible not to be struck by their variable quality, including an extreme variation in the list of topics considered, and the rarity of serious needs assessment or follow-up.

Accreditation does at least represent lip service to the notion of external evaluation. But it's often not enough to go outside your own campus: you may have to go outside your own discipline. Off-site evaluators are not external enough to warrant validity, let alone credibility with professional evaluators and savvy academic administrations. Of course, there are trade-offs—advantages from using same-field experts as evaluators—which include realistic standards; likelihood of including workable recommendations; tricks of the trade which will lead to getting better data and avoiding being taken in by well-known deceptions; and increased chances of implementation because of continued peer pressure and the acknowledged status of the evaluator. These are not to be dismissed lightly.

The solution is obvious: always use both professional evaluators and field experts on reviews of technical areas.

Legal Ambivalence about Formative and Summative Evaluation

A number of legal opinions have been handed down on the legitimacy of dismissals based on evaluations in the educational and other areas, which raise serious problems for the evaluator. These opinions may be summarized as follows: dismissal (usually of tenured staff) is only acceptable if prior evaluations have indicated (a) the respects in which improvement is to be made; (b) the amount of improvement which has to be made on these dimensions; and if (c) a reasonable time is provided for improvement to be made.

This is a tough requirement on the employer, the requirement of analytic formative evaluation. Many of them feel that a valid global evaluation demonstrating failure to achieve the (reasonable) goals of the job (e.g., successful learning by the students) should be enough to justify replacement of professionals who are supposed to know how to get the job done. Fairness requires advance warning in terms of an "early warning" global formative evaluation. But very frequently something else is read into the above, which represents a complete mistake.

The Tenth Fallacy (F10) is the view that an evaluator/employer must say how improvements are to be made by an unsatisfactory employee, *in the sense that* the evaluator must provide effective remedial recommendations, i.e., ones which will work in the particular case.

One might as well insist that safety inspectors not close a bridge judged dangerous if they cannot see a way to redesign it. It is arguably reasonable to require valid analytic evaluation prior to dismissal. It is not reasonable to require that these formative evaluations include prescriptions of remediating behavior which are: (a) within the power of the candidate to perform, and (b) if performed, will ensure that the candidate will meet the required standards. Not only is our knowledge of remediation far from complete, it is clear enough that some people will never be able to do some jobs for which they might be mistakenly hired. One can hardly argue that, since the welfare of the public is so much less important than that of the employee who fails to teach children (or do bypass surgery) effectively, one should continue to allow the employee to practice his or her profession until the employer can find a way to remediate him or her. It is to be hoped that the courts will clarify the situation and avoid requiring the impossible.

Notice that these cases do not prescribe that the decisive summative evaluation has to be analytic; they simply exemplify situations where the law requires that negative summative decisions must be preceded by analytic formative evaluation.

Reasonable Expectations

For the most part, the message of this chapter has been strongly cautionary. It is an attempt to prevent unrealistic expectations of the evaluator, and to prevent inappropriate assumptions of expertise by the evaluator. Nevertheless, it is important to avoid leaving a totally negative impression. It is not trivial that global approaches, which are easier, cheaper, and can sometimes more easily achieve validity, can be used intelligently for formative evaluation. And it is most important that summative evaluations, often analytic in order to achieve credibility or insight or validity, will frequently spin off unmistakable implications for improvement. For example, on present evidence, it seems arguable that the only valid approach to summative teacher evaluation consists of determining the extent to which the nine or ten groups of duties of the teacher are performed with competence or excellence.[29] One of these groups refers to knowledge of subject matter, including the disciplines taught as part of the job description and also the across-the-curriculum subject matters like literacy. One can take account of the warnings above about the need to place fragmentary criticisms in the context of an overall rating, and the need to be wary of the possibility of interactions, and still find it easy enough to indicate a need for substantial improvement in subject-matter knowledge, when one finds incorrect answers being given in class or credited in tests. This kind of situation often occurs.

The arguments here are just intended to make one avoid the assumption that evaluation skills somehow confer certain types of subject-matter expertise on the evaluator. Even if you find exactly which component of a program is responsible for its overall poor performance, and can conclude that something needs to be done about it, there's no reason to think that you are in any position to recommend that the component should be dropped rather than replaced, redesigned, or its personnel retrained. Evaluation contracts require expertise, but it is not the expertise of repairers; not even the expertise of causal analysis.

Conclusions

It is suggested in the above that a better understanding of the formative/summative distinction can be achieved by noting the way it relates to some distinctions developed here, particularly the analytic/global and component/dimension distinctions. Some effort is also made to clarify the relation of the formative/summative distinction to the well-known external/internal distinction, and to the less well-understood distinctions among evaluation, diagnosis, causation, and prescription. If one doesn't master these methodological/conceptual foundations, the chance of successful practice is reduced.

A major theme here has been the defense of summative evaluation and global evaluation against various attacks. It is about as intelligent to attack one of these in favor of the alternatives as it would be to attack reading as against writing.

But none of the conceptual clarifications provides a substitute for the skills of *doing* good formative or summative evaluation, skills which are still rare. In the quarter century since evaluation as a discipline emerged, it must be realized that although the subject has come a long way, the territory of good evaluation practice is still extremely small. The society is at risk from this. We've been emphasizing examples from medical practice and teacher evaluation throughout; in this last section, it may be useful, in order to see the extent of the problem, to focus on applied evaluation in the product area.

The best-known story here is that of perhaps the most important development in applied formative evaluation, the Quality Circles approach. It was invented by an American, could not be sold to anyone in the United States, was enthusiastically adopted by the Japanese, and became the basis for the success of the Japanese automobile and other industries. But most people think that's an old story. Even if we had to re-import it, surely the Japanese car plants in the United States show that we have finally learned that lesson. Unfortunately not; it appears to need Japanese managers to swing the balance, and outside the automobile area, the lesson appears to be largely unheard—not just the Quality Circles lesson, but the lesson of the importance of systematic formative evaluation.

Even the most powerful and successful companies in the most modern industries are usually highly incompetent at, or only marginally interested in, serious formative evaluation, despite massive

publicity to the contrary. Examples from the computer area include
IBM, Ashton-Tate, Claris, Borland, and Lotus[30]; on occasions, even
Microsoft. The highly visible and not disputed result is the release of
strings of products that are demonstrably, extensively, avoidably, and
seriously flawed.[31] This simple weakness in applied evaluation, by
itself, has cost a hundred well-funded high-tech companies their lives
in the past few years. It is more depressing still to note that that
academic courseware, admittedly less well funded, very rarely shows
the slightest grasp of minimal standards of formative evaluation. In
fact, the most widely used of all high-tech computer-assisted
instructional systems, the PLATO system, after decades of
development starting at the University of Illinois, shows about
twenty-two errors of design in the interface screens that come up in
the first few minutes of use.[32] And it's very difficult to find one of the
5000 courses in its repertoire that avoids gross errors of design which
would have been identified by even the slightest effort at formative
evaluation.[33] It's not as if it's all that hard to do these things right;
apart from the Honda/Toyota/Nissan paradigm, there are a number
of examples in the computer area.[34]

But formative evaluation is not the only weakness in the high-tech
area. Consumers are not the only big losers; investors and taxpayers
also pay a bill. The quality of summative evaluation illustrated when
companies like IBM, Ashton-Tate, and Lotus buy a new product
(that is, buy the company which created the product) is appalling. In
nearly all areas where our tax funds are spent, the summative evaluation on the basis of which products are bought is still abysmal, and if
it were not for the pressure brought to bear by the General
Accounting Office it would be farcical across the board instead of
abysmal. The farce is still alive and well in the military procurement
area.[35]

There are a few rays of sunshine in the area where evaluators run
their own businesses. Consumers Union still does invaluable summative evaluation, and has been joined by scores of increasingly
sophisticated magazines largely devoted to consumer product evaluation. But Consumers Union still makes mistakes, still refuses to
announce or discuss its evaluation methodology, a fact which must
make its cofounder, the distinguished practical logician Stuart Chase,
turn in his grave.[36] And the magazine reviews are, with very rare
exceptions, seriously biased in half a dozen ways, e.g., by advertiser
pressure, enthusiast bias (new is wonderful), the substitution of

60   FORMATIVE/SUMMATIVE EVALUATION

specification one-upmanship for improvements in consumer-detectable benefits.

Still greater problems arise in the application of good evaluation practices in government and industry. There, special interest groups and power elites still have far too much influence, and cost everyone far too much. The battle for quality, efficiency, equity, and accountability is not the stuff of which headlines are made, but it is a battle against forces of incompetence and corruption, and a battle for the life and leadership role of this society. In the long run, it's as important as many bloodier battles, and ethically more important than most of them.

FOOTNOTES

1. Michael Scriven, "The Methodology of Evaluation," in *Perspectives of Curriculum Evaluation*, ed. Robert E. Stake, AERA Monograph Series on Curriculum Evaluation, no. 1 (Chicago: Rand McNally, 1967).

2. See James D. Russell and Bonnie L. Blake, "Formative and Summative Evaluation of Instructional Products and Learners," *Educational Technology* 28 (September 1988): 22-28.

3. To be exact, summative evaluation relates to a class of purposes rather than to a single purpose as does formative evaluation. Note that formative evaluation, although it is particularly important in the process of creation, is not confined to that process. Good management arranges for recurrent formative evaluation during the life of a program, since its worth or merit can easily deteriorate, absolutely or relative to the changing ensemble of other available options.

4. Evidence of this is to be found in any issue of *Consumer Reports* or in the specialized consumer magazines, e.g., from the microcomputer, audio/video, or automobile areas.

5. Some support for this claim comes from the occasional overviews by the General Accounting Office or the Audit Agencies, but for the most part it is based on twenty years of doing and reviewing program evaluations.

6. Lee J. Cronbach, "Course Improvement through Evaluation," *Teachers College Record* 64 (1963): 672-683.

7. Scriven, "The Methodology of Evaluation."

8. This view appears to imply the sometimes unpopular view that norm-referenced assessment is as useful as criterion-referenced assessment. A case can be made for that, but the point strikes deeper, since in most cases the criteria are *implicitly* comparative, that is, they are norm-referenced at one remove. Since the comparisons need not be explicit, people sometimes think there is more of a role for noncomparative evaluation than is really the case. For example, when the road-holding of the new Ferrari 384 is described as "impressive," this is implicitly comparative since it would not be impressive if every Hyundai model met this standard. Even terms like "excellent" when applied to braking (or essay-writing) performance are implicitly comparative, because the standards steadily shift with advances in the norms, whether

of technology or education. The same is true with "healthy" and "competent" in the medical and educational fields. One can say that they are not *directly* comparative to the immediate reference group, as norm-referenced testing is, and for this reason criterion-referenced testing is sometimes much more appropriate than norm-referenced testing. But the criteria, *to be useful*, are almost always based on norms from a wider context. There are indeed absolute standards; for example, if a car usually catches fire when you start it, one would no doubt describe it as "unsatisfactory" on some cosmic scale. But you cannot do a great deal of useful evaluation using only such standards. Getting every answer right on a test is not automatically a sign of excellence; it depends on the relevance of the test to the student population to which it has been administered.

9. Lee J. Cronbach et al., *Towards Reform of Program Evaluation: Aims, Methods, and Institutional Arrangements* (San Francisco: Jossey-Bass, 1980), p. 82.

10. Jan Lokan and Philip McKenzie, eds., *Teacher Appraisal* (Melbourne: Australian Council for Educational Research, 1989).

11. Cronbach et al., *Towards Reform of Program Evaluation*, p. 62.

12. This case illustrates the fact that summative is not just retrodictive evaluation; it is often predictive in purpose. Evaluations of candidates for Nobel Prizes are retrodictive; evaluations of the same candidates for purposes of employment are predictive of future merit, and the logic is different (e.g., trends in productivity become crucial, rather than mere totality and quality of production). Formative evaluation, although future-oriented, is only conditionally predictive: if so and so were to be done, the product would be better. (There is an assumption that no other circumstances change.)

13. Lee J. Cronbach and Patrick Suppes, *Research for Tomorrow's Schools: Disciplined Inquiry for Education* (New York: Macmillan, 1969).

14. Cronbach later came to think that it was too simple to regard evaluation as decision-oriented (see Cronbach et al., *Towards Reform of Program Evaluation*), but not because he wanted to promote it to conclusion-oriented research. It was part of his continued attempt to salvage his original view that formative is more important than summative.

15. Robert Karplus, director of the SCIS science curriculum project, was one of the first to put this into print in a pamphlet on multiple approaches to formative evaluation.

16. The usual form of "cheating" here is to send the product out to external reviewers, but select the reviewers for the potential of future sales based on flattery rather than on acuity. Many of those used in this way are executives, not users of the project. A recent example is Claris's abuse of beta-testing MacWrite II. See "Review of MacWrite II," *University MicroNews* 16 (May 1989): 92.

17. One might, of course, define "analytic evaluation" so that it includes or refers solely to causal explanation of the global rating. But that would have two undesirable effects. First, we would need to coin another name for the subevaluations, since they are a very useful and distinct feature of many evaluations. Second, it would confuse the distinction between evaluation and explanation, which are usefully distinguished.

There is an interesting sense in which analytic evaluation can sometimes lead to causal explanations, even of grades awarded globally. The original paper in the debate between the use of expert judgment and rules as a basis for decision making—the "clinical vs. statistical" debate—focuses on the question of the factors which influence judges in evaluating the quality of ears of corn entered in the competition at the state fair. This was an empirical effort to reconstruct cognitive processes by varying the stimuli rather than depending on introspection. The result was a hypothetical version of analytic evaluation which can be thought of as providing a causal model of the way the judge's brain worked, regardless of how the judge conceptualized the process. But that is a case of what we might call the reconstructive use of analytic evaluation; its normal use is prescriptive ("Marks will be allocated in the following way: 10 for originality, 5 for literature search, . . .") or constructive ("Since I gave him 3 for originality, 2 for literature search, . . . I have to give him a C+ overall"). In an unbiased evaluator doing analytic evaluation, the subevaluations may in fact provide the causal explanation of the overall grade. But the process may be much more complex than that and arguably should be with a sense of the overall worth of the work interacting with the prima facie subscores. In such cases, it is not that the reported subevaluations are rationalizations of the intuitive rating; it is just that both contribute to the optimal grading process.

18. This might involve weighting each criterion of merit, perhaps on a 1 to 5 scale, then scoring each candidate on each of these criteria by rating their performance on, say, a 1 to 10 scale, then multiplying the scores by the weights, and summing the results for each candidate. Then the one with the most points is, according to this algorithm, the best. In testing, this often boils down to giving a certain number of marks for each question, and scoring out of that number. Most academics and teachers are so used to doing this that we are not even conscious of the underlying assumptions.

19. Details are provided in Michael Scriven, "A Model for Evaluative Reasoning: The Multiple Matrix Method," in *Critical Reasoning in Contemporary Culture: Theoretical Perspectives on the Meaning, Conditions, and Goals of Critical Reasoning*, ed. Richard A. Talaska (Albany, NY: State University of New York Press, forthcoming). Preprints obtainable from the author.

20. For example, see Walter Dick, "Formative Evaluation: Prospects for the Future," *Educational Technology* 27 (October 1987): 55-57.

21. This is often a serious problem with community control of schools, where life can and is made miserable for the teacher and principal by parents complaining about grades which "handicap" their children in the search for acceptance by high-ranking colleges, i.e., anything less than an A. At the tertiary level, the same effect is produced by the policy of body-count approaches to allocation of resources; departments and colleges whose life depends on their enrollments are not open-minded about "tough" grading.

22. Several examples of this are provided in Michael Scriven, "The Dependence of Teacher Development on Teacher Evaluation," in *Promoting Teachers' Professional Development*, ed. Phil Hughes (Melbourne: Australian Council for Educational Research, 1990).

23. Nigel Dolan has just completed a comprehensive survey of and visits to most of these centers, on which this conclusion is based. The research is in progress at the Department of Education, University of Western Australia. Unfortunately, this result does not show that courseware is good; it just shows that its evaluation is bad. The most heavily developed courseware in the most competitive market with the largest possible financial gains is the typing tutor market and the results there are very poor indeed. The one exception is slightly above "Acceptable." See Nigel Dolan, "Inadequate Quality Control of Educational Software: A Case Study of Typing Tutors," *Educational Research and Perspectives* 14, no. 1 (June 1987): 136-149. What is missing in most courseware evaluations, apart from courage, are: the comparative dimension, reasonable definitions of standards, consistency, and overall conclusions that follow from the subevaluations (they are nearly always softened). In the volumes of reviews published one constantly finds nothing rated below "Good," the usual "half-scale" fallacy.

24. Some remarks extracted from the entry on Perspectival Evaluation: "Advocate-adversary is a special case of perspectival evaluation; consumer-based or manager-based evaluations are special perspectives. As in architecture, multiple perspectives are

required in order to see something in full depth." Michael Scriven, *Evaluation Thesaurus*, 3d ed. (Inverness, CA: Edgepress, 1980).

25. For example, the diagnosis of paresis definitionally entails that a prior infection with syphilis is causative, and it can be done directly by the identification of spirochetes in the brain.

26. The other role conflict besides the fact that the evaluator is later reviewing a product which he or she helped to create (the coauthorship bias) is the conflict between wanting to get on well with faculty, to facilitate everyday operations and atmosphere, and wanting to do the best possible evaluation, which may involve comments that will produce very hostile reactions.

27. This means the community of those committed to the development of the modern discipline of evaluation. The Japanese had a profession of sword evaluators centuries ago. They allegedly used felons for criterion-referenced testing, and they certainly signed the tang of the blades from great swordsmiths, thereby adding substantially to their value.

28. A recent project devoted to putting short descriptions of all describable teaching techniques into an electronic database flattened out after around 2500 entries, after abstracting about 80 books and other references (MENTOR/DB). The idea was to facilitate retrieval against keywords or search on any text string. (Currently available in FileMaker II format for the Macintosh; A HyperCard version should be completed early in 1990; hardcopy also available but searching is slow! Details on request from the author.)

29. See, for example, Michael Scriven, "Duty-Based Teacher Evaluation," *Journal of Personnel Evaluation in Education* 1, no 4 (1988): 319-334.

30. Some details are in Michael Scriven, "The Evaluation of Microcomputer Products," *Studies in Educational Evaluation*, in press.

31. Two simple examples: the IBM word processor, one of the most expensive on the market, is not even mentioned in any serious discussions of the state of the art; IBM portable computers have long been a standing joke (the current one [they had to withdraw its two predecessors] has now caught up with the state of the art as it was two years ago, just in time to be out of date again, as the scene shifts to the battery powered ultralites).

32. Some details were provided in Michael Scriven and Kerry Adams, "An Evaluation of the PLATO Installation at the University of Western Australia," unpublished report, 1988.

33. We ran a reward system for student "explorers" to run overlapping searches through the repertoire for promising courses, which were then followed up.

34. Hardware examples: Compaq, Intel, Apple, Dell, Imprimis, Northgate, Canon (printer division). Software examples: Fox, Symantec, Norton/Mace/Central Point, Silicon Beach, T/Maker, CE, Paragon. Note the disproportionate number of small companies in these lists.

35. Evidence for this is provided in most General Accounting Office reports on purchasing practices in various agencies, but is also evident from looking at what agencies purchase (it is widely publicized by the lucky vendors) and comparing it to the available product evaluations, making all possible allowances for discounts and special contexts. The same is true, but to a lesser extent, in the spending of the shareholder's funds in public companies, as one can see from the same type of evidence.

36. Possibly the most pervasive methodological error in their current practice is the intermittent use of a numerical weight and sum approach, which can be identified by their use of a Total Score. This leads to substantial errors because of its oversimplified

assumptions about distributions of utility; the problems are evident in their recent evaluation of lap-top computers (*Consumer Reports*, September, 1989). Details of the fallacies in this approach are provided in Scriven, "A Model for Evaluative Reasoning." They occasionally still fall into the trap of accepting vendor definitions of function, a version of the fallacy of defining evaluation as determining goal-achievement, which is monitoring, not evaluation (important from the point of view of managers, not consumers).

Evaluation's Countenance

In the mid-1960s, when evaluation had just become the focus of intense scholarly scrutiny, there seemed to be little agreement about the roles that evaluation could play in the broad educational enterprise; and there was also a lack of consensus about what evaluations should *look like*—about their "countenance," as it were. So a number of people made pioneering efforts of description, and these writings set the agenda for much subsequent discussion. The descriptions were not primarily naturalistic, in the sense that they described what evaluations *appeared* to be; they were predominately *normative*, in that they showed what, in the mind of each author, an evaluation *ought* to be. One such influential paper was "The Countenance of Educational Evaluation" (1967) by Robert Stake of the Center for Instructional Research and Curriculum Evaluation (CIRCE) at the University of Illinois at Urbana-Champaign. (CIRCE was a testing center that was converted by Thomas Hastings, Lee Cronbach, and Jack Easley into a technical assistance center for curriculum reform projects nationwide.)

Stake opened by arguing that different segments of the population (what we might now call different stakeholders) expected different things from educational evaluations; and he suggested that many educators leaned toward informal evaluations of their programs and were skeptical about the value of formal evaluations. Turning to what formal evaluations should be like, Stake presented a 3x4 matrix to classify data that could be collected. He was not suggesting that data for all of these cells had to be collected in any one evaluation, but rather he offered the matrix as a way of reminding evaluators of the possibilities that were open. However, in a time when evaluators were hungry for guidance, many grasped his ideas as a prescription—as a "countenance model."

Basically, Stake distinguished a half matrix of "descriptions" from the remaining six blocks of "judgments." When describing a program, one could record antecedent intentions of the program, intended transactions (e.g., the things that were intended to be done in the classroom by the teacher delivering the program to students), and intended outcomes; and one could record observed antecedents,

65

observed transactions, and observed outcomes. Turning to judgments, he distinguished the standards or generic expectations concerning antecedents, transactions, and outcomes of such programs; and separately the judgments specific to this program, again regarding antecedents, transactions, and outcomes.

Stake went on to argue that there should be a logical link between the antecedents, transactions, and outcomes; in other words, the proposed or actual transactions should make sense in the light of the antecedent beliefs or desires, and there should be grounds for believing that the transactions would lead to the achievement of the outcomes. Furthermore, ideally one would hope that there would be congruence between the things that were intended and the things that were observed. Stake suggested that different combinations of data from the matrix would be needed in different evaluation situations and that it would be a mistake to standardize the process of evaluating: many countenances rather than one.

CHAPTER III

Retrospective on
"The Countenance of Educational Evaluation"[1]

ROBERT E. STAKE

The Circumstances in 1965

President Johnson, President Conant, Mrs. Hull (Sara's teacher) and Mr. Tykociner (the man next door) have all passed away. Back in 1966, when I opened "the countenance paper" with reference to the four of them, they all were alive and active in that decade's educational reform. Hearts and minds were rallied. Program evaluation would be a major player in the reform.

I opened the paper informally—using those personally important names—to indicate widespread lack of consensus about what is high-quality education and to advocate aid to both practitioner and public interpretation.

Fellow evaluation specialists had been offering a variety of methodological views. Benjamin Bloom, Thomas Hastings, and George Madaus spoke of evaluation as a special arrangement of student testing.[2] James Popham advocated inquiries structured to behavioral objectives.[3] For Donald Campbell, the orientation was experimentation; for Lee Cronbach, instructional development; for Daniel Stufflebeam, administrative decision making; and for Michael Scriven, consumer service.[4] In 1965, the schools had a new array of curriculum packages and an emerging zeal for extending educational opportunity to the underprivileged[5] and a new technical specialty, educational program evaluation, charged to discover which practices worked best.

The Cronbach-Scriven dialogue. In 1963, Cronbach challenged evaluation strategists who were seeking a universally best instructional treatment and one-size-fits-all reform curriculum.[6] He urged turning even more evaluation effort toward assisting curriculum developers to discern the students or classroom types who work well with each exercise or pedagogical ploy. In 1964, with Cronbach presiding, the executive committee of the American Educational Research Association (AERA) set up a committee to study the need for standards for the conduct of evaluation studies, noting the *Technical Recommendations for Psychological Tests and Diagnostic Techniques*.[7] Committee members were N. L. Gage, Wells Hively, John Major, and myself. Our study persuaded us the time was wrong for settling into standard designs; rather, expansion, experimentation, and borrowing from other disciplines were needed. We proposed that instead of commissioning a book of standards, AERA should sponsor a monograph series on curriculum evaluation to help explore design options.[8] In AERA's next presidency, Benjamin Bloom's, it was done.

The first volume[9] of the series included Scriven's "The Methodology of Evaluation," setting forth criteria for classifying evaluation situations. Early drafts of this monograph had been prepared for the Educational Consortium for Social Science, to which Scriven and I were advisors. At board meetings, Scriven enjoyed taking issue with Cronbach's 1963 paper, particularly disputing the priority on formative evaluation. In confrontational language (especially in early drafts) Scriven advocated instead that consumers receive summative evaluation services, a scholarly endeavor that program evaluators could and should provide.

Thomas Hastings, Jack Easley, and I persuaded Scriven and Cronbach to come to Champaign-Urbana and clarify their differences. Robert Glaser joined the discussions too. That evening Cronbach made a remark that puzzled me for years, yet presaged the direction my work would take in the 1970s. He said something like, "What the evaluation field needs is a good social anthropologist." He was acknowledging the situational or cultural character of instructional programs and their resistance to sweeping generalization. Scriven, in some ways the absolutist insisting that standards of quality not be dominated by parochial interests, did not contend that curricula are situation-indifferent. But he counseled evaluators to inform administrators, teachers, and parents (in whatever situation) which instructional arrangements are needed.

It was during these meetings that I realized even greater arrays of data could be used in evaluation studies: few ingredients were absolutely essential, much was optional, and good design depended on questions needing answers, which changed as time passed. In keeping with the conclusions of the AERA committee, my aim was to explore and legitimate evaluation adaptations to local circumstances and program uniqueness. The first draft of the countenance paper emerged not too long after the Champaign-Urbana discussions.

Reconsidering the priority on outcomes. Like the version appearing in *Teachers College Record* in April, 1967, early drafts featured graphic representations. What later became a 13-cell matrix of data eligible for collection by evaluators started out as a three-ring overlapping Venn diagram, like a Ballantine Beer ad. Descriptions and judgments were stacked in a third dimension. An even more complex version portrayed the passing of time, acknowledging need for repeated measures in planning, implementing, and closing periods of a program. I wanted to encourage a more chronological or historical view of teaching and learning, not the stages of Jean Piaget nor the hierarchies of Robert Gagné, but capturing the month-to-month evolution of teaching a particular course in a world not indifferent to Christmas programs, basketball playoffs, and spring vacation. Later, with disappointment, but in the interests of simplicity, I gave up this stronger representation of *real time*.

The circles I sketched in 1965 represented three main categories: goals, inputs, and outputs. Most social-science-based evaluation designs, then as now, put a premium on effects, particularly student achievement. As one specially trained in testing, I had wanted very much to measure the merits and shortcomings of the new curricula with tests. Re-educated by watching Cronbach and Hastings, I found little in test results of the early 1960s to tell us what evaluators, program developers, and consumers wanted to know. What appeared as important attainment was often attributable to prior student knowledge. On standardized tests we failed to show accomplishment of reform goals and seldom found crucial differences between experimental and control groups. On tests custom-built for the program under study, we often felt that the facts learned had been directly taught and that anticipated understandings, applications, and extrapolations were left untested. My attentions swung from the quality of outcomes to the quality of activities. In 1966, I was calling the activities "transactions."

The circles in my early drawings overlapped and the shared areas were for contingency data, those showing relationships among goals, inputs, and outputs. In another year I had shifted to matrix representation and used a separate graphic to countenance these functional relationships.

Low interest in formal standards. For evaluators using my grid, the columns for Standards and Judgments were not found useful, perhaps not even understood. Standards data were intended to indicate quality levels for judging programs in general, independent of how this program was faring. Judgment data were intended to indicate quality levels (for antecedents, transactions, and outcomes) of the evaluand as seen by on-site observers. People sometimes define the process of evaluating as discerning discrepancies between aim and actuality.[10] Similarly, my standards data were background to help explain what people intended the program to be, and my judgment data were to indicate quality level of outcomes or discrepancies actually found.

It slowly became obvious to me that formal standards (as opposed to implicit intentions) are often used and seldom identified. When the National Science Foundation was in political trouble in 1976, Harvey Averch got them out of trouble by committing the education directorate of the foundation to an evaluation philosophy zeroing in on discrepancy between intent and accomplishment, but did not commit it to explicating standards implicit in the rationale.[11] Data on discrepancies between intents and standards turn out to be of small value. They are important rhetoric but incidental to real decisions of program worth.

I did not mean to invite people to sort data into the cells of my grid. I shivered at the possibility that my matrix might cause practitioners to spend long hours sorting data—much as they, to Bloom's eventual dismay, spent long hours sorting statements of objectives or test items into the six *Taxonomy* categories.[12] I tried to emphasize that in considering what data might be useful, the matrix should stretch one's mind. More of this in the section on models and persuasions.

Conceptual Structures

The main purpose of the countenance paper was to suggest that the array of data for evaluation studies was far more extensive than even the largest studies had encompassed. My purpose was not to spell out how to evaluate a program. I did not see the countenance grid as a model for conducting a study. Further, I knew the methods I personally used were weak. Yet I felt I should give some advice on how to carry out a study, at least to identify some primary moves.

Models and persuasions. The literature of program evaluation methodology soon referenced many models, e.g., the discrepancy model, the adversary model, the goal-free model, the countenance model. These "models" clearly differentiated approaches to evaluation but it was problematic to call them models. The term model over-promises. People start relying on it as a blueprint, with a "parts inventory" and a "directions for assembly," so that, if followed carefully, a satisfactory evaluation could be assembled.

The term "model" suggests a representation of considerable complexity and completeness. Such detail was not then present in any of the methodological advocacies within program evaluation, nor is it today. Our so-called models are merely advocacies alluding to a few of the many responsibilities and identifying a few of the many inquiry opportunities of even the simplest evaluation study.

Evaluation models do exist. The actual conduct and report of a program evaluation can serve as model for subsequent work.[13] No actual study, however, will epitomize an approach such as "the CIPP model"[14] and, even more important, many quite different evaluation studies can represent such approaches accurately.

What we have in the evaluation literature are not models but approaches or persuasions. Ernest House reminded us that evaluation theorists promote their concerns, advocate particular commitments, and emphasize particular purviews.[15] These are persuasions, not prescriptions. They are important as preventive counsel but deal with only a few of our technical and conceptual flaws. So far none of them has been a full methodological statement. We still have to rely on unexplicated ways of data gathering and data processing. The evaluator, not the "model-builder," has the responsibility to put these all together, with or without certain "persuasions."

Stated oversimplistically, several of the important persuasions have been:

an accountability persuasion to assure that new promises, previous goal commitments, and community customs are honored;

a case study persuasion to give focus to the contexts and complexity of a single educational program;

a decision-oriented persuasion for the consideration of options and implications of administrative operations;

a connoisseurship persuasion to engage and honor expert judgment;

a democratic persuasion to resist authoritarian fiat and techno-logical fix;

an ethnographic persuasion to emphasize cultural relationships;

an experimental persuasion to establish data-analysis controls so that an influence or effect can be relatively cleanly assessed;

a goal-free persuasion to reduce bias by sequestering sponsors and program personnel;

an illuminative persuasion to portray events as readers themselves might see them;

a judicial persuasion to optimize presentation of the program's pros and cons; and

a naturalistic persuasion to study ordinary events in natural settings.

When put into practice these different persuasions overlap and coalesce. Each has something important to say, but none is a model.[16]

I had no foresight as to how frequently people would refer to *the countenance model*. My words and graphics did model something, but were far too vague to guide the conduct of an evaluation study. I came to be distressed by people referring to my persuasion as *the countenance model*. The countenance paper was an overview of data available for an evaluative study. I advocated broader selection, especially more use of "process data." I was not offering a model for conducting a study. I found people brandishing the term *countenance model* and, while using some of the language (e.g., antecedents and contingencies), ignoring the countenance article's persuasions (e.g., lengthy observation, relying little on formal statements and instruments, and working toward full description).

Comparison and judgment. In 1965, I believed in comparisons. I considered myself a social scientist and social science featured comparisons as primary steps to understanding. We compared carefully designated groups with reference to one or more criterion variables, often over time. For theory building, it *is* important to cultivate constructs (e.g., reading comprehension, admissibility, leadership), to obtain measurements as indicators of those constructs, and to make comparisons that show relationships among constructs. For program evaluation, it now seems important to me to keep language natural, paralleling perhaps the thinking of practitioners and clients. Of course, these people use constructs (e.g., model program, effective teaching, leadership) but they see the constructs more as emerging from experience, less as structuring it. Thus in most ordinary thinking comparisons are indirect, muted, present but not dominating and discrete as they are in our correlational or experimental studies.

In the countenance paper, I proposed we approximate evaluative thinking by examining the congruence between intended and observed antecedents, between intended and observed transactions, and between intended and observed outcomes. If people were not consciously making these comparisons, they were doing so covertly. They would probably do it better consciously, and better still, deliberatively—or so went my thinking. As Ernest House noted,[17] I started to speak more as an intuitivist, claiming superiority of intuitive over rational processes for many complex tasks. I rationalize this conclusion by observing many of our best thinkers to be largely intuitive in their thinking and by noting how unrewarded are our efforts to convert decision makers into rational thinkers. It may make us feel good but it seldom does much real good to try to nudge our readers away from intuitive thinking. People recognize the value of something inferentially and simultaneously as they come to know it, not apparently comparing it to real or abstract standards.

Implicit standards. In their separate ways, Michael Polanyi and Robert Pirsig have discussed such tacit understandings.[18] The two of them helped us acknowledge that people *have* standards, that people may make some standards explicit and may refer to the standards to explain or justify their valuings. It is not apparent, however, that people arrive at a sense of value by comparing the case to initial intentions or to other standards. By 1975, I realized I had erred in stating in the countenance paper that assessing congruence was an essential step in processing descriptive data, or even that evaluators could improve their judgments of quality by identifying congruence between intent and outcome. It may be useful in describing a program to point out congruence or lack of it, but that is for the purpose of making the case understandable, not for indicating program merit.

Similarly, I erred in representing the act of judging as making relative comparisons between this program and others. People cannot judge the quality of one case without knowledge of other cases, but often they will not explicitly compare this case with other cases in reaching judgments of quality. And I know of no grounds for claiming they should. Even in 1963, Cronbach was urging fewer formal comparisons.[19] Here too it took me several years to follow his lead.

Good conceptual structure is characteristic of all good thinking. In designing evaluation studies each of us has sought good structures. As did Popham, many chose *objectives* for conceptual structure. Others chose *cause-and-effect relationships*, *indicators*, or *issues*. Structures help us compose interpretable collections of diverse data. Structures force our attention onto high-priority matters and away from low priorities. But our intended priorities are vulnerable. Inquiries can suffer from being too focused. That probably occurs as frequently as inquiries being intellectually flimsy. Comparisons give sharp focus but on matters often of little relevance to clients and practitioners. The countenance paper, I believe, did a good job of structuring eligible data but a poor job of structuring the process of evaluation. As indicated below, it took me another ten years to contrive a process structure.

Need for a Social Anthropological View

In the countenance paper I said, "Today, educators fail to perceive what formal evaluation could do for them. They should be imploring measurement specialists to develop a methodology that reflects the fullness, the complexity, and the importance of their programs. They are not." I was presuming that it would be useful to understand their programs better than they do. When I wrote it, there was neighborhood and national confidence in the schools. Sputnik had warned national policymakers that United States education might be lagging and academics agreed, but the common perception was that the schools were okay, they just needed maybe to upgrade career counseling and instructional materials. Professional educators anticipated curricular restructuring and racial desegregation. It seemed a bit premature to study a system that seemed to work well but would soon make big changes.

Taking stock or taking cover. Educators did not implore evaluators to help them understand. Shortly thereafter, in the late 1960s, a social upheaval bared the need for sweeping changes in education. Many people young and old wanted to liberate the educational system. Many more wanted it returned to an earlier authoritarian pedagogy and to circumscribed "basics" curricula. Soon, few were happy with the middle-of-the-road national system.

To most people the neighborhood school still seemed pretty good. But the media repeatedly portrayed lack of restraint and ignorance among youth. Apparently the schools were failing to do their jobs. Stung by criticism, school people withdrew from the challenges of Sputnik and curriculum reform and defined a narrow set of objectives for which teachers might be held accountable.

Under the pressure of accountability, much of the appetite for understanding was overwhelmed by a craving for protection.

Educators implored measurement specialists to develop a methodology that pointed to the shortcomings of students. By 1980, student assessment rather than program evaluation was the major player in the school improvement movement.

Accountability and assessment became the grand sweep of educational change. When shortcomings were found, efforts were redoubled. If change seemed needed, educator experience would point the way. Restoration was a political and intuitive endeavor, and little support could be expected from research and evaluative study. That has been the larger picture of school reform from 1975 to the present.

The local picture often was different. Within some schools, classrooms, and networks of educators, curiosity endured. What additional knowledge might improve things? Pretty clearly there was a confidence in local knowledge, situational knowledge, and teacher-based knowledge, rather than the knowledge produced by large research and development centers. Many saw need for full description.

Descriptive studies. In the countenance paper, I endorsed full description but set my sights too low. Agreeing with Bloom and his *Taxonomy* co-authors, I urged amplification of outcome variables into the higher-order processes. I extended full description to include the generalizations about educational practice that Cronbach elucidated in 1963. It took me some time to realize how much well-studied contextual (antecedent) and process (transaction) data were needed. Outcome data can ascertain there is a problem and mobilize reformers to seek remedy—but outcome data seldom guide crucial change. That is so partly because the linkages between educational practice and student cognition are complex and obscure. I know of no reason to doubt that good teaching results in good learning. So I see good description telling about the conditions likely to foster or inhibit good teaching.

Educational reform does not occur because a legislature or other policy-setting group gets explicit or pushy about what teachers should do differently. For reform to occur in this society, teachers need to understand the implications of their actions and need opportunity and protection for holding fast or for changing—as they see fit. The countenance paper was propelled in part by the common belief that central policy could profitably redirect educational practice. I held too much to the view that the important readers were people with research, administrative, and political authority. That was a mistake. I now see the important readers to be the immediate stakeholders of the immediate evaluand: teachers, local administrators, community leaders.

To an extent, all of us, practitioners or whatever, need to be told what to do. That does not mean that we will do it, particularly not if we see it undermining our standing. That does not mean the more telling the better. An evaluator needs to tell us some things, to convey some summary of findings plus guidance to change our practices, whether didactically or informally through vignette and quotation. The countenance paper was right that far. Not many authorities and practitioners may be persuaded, or even take heed, but the responsibility to give counsel exists.

What will practitioners heed? They heed stories of people in a plight like their own.[20] They attend to experiential accounts. A good account invites them to recognize the circumstances, never identical to the reader's own, but described in sufficient detail so the reader can decide their similarity and pertinence. Often what needs to be described are people, their activities over time, their physical and social surroundings. What was needed in 1965 and still today is social anthropological viewing—not anthropological interpretation as much as anthropological sensitivity to culture, kinship, and ritual.

Attention to contexts becomes increasingly persuasive. People see their own lives, their destinies, shaped by immediate contexts: poverty, grace, competition, aspiration, handicap. They know contexts shape other lives as well. They know the quality of a program can be affected by noise level or arrangement of chairs. To understand a program requires knowledge of its contexts, contexts experienced by those who participate. Evaluation is served by experiential accounts.

Case Study. I remember Cronbach once pointing out that all program evaluations are case studies. Regardless of the complexity of the program, regardless of the number of schools and children involved, the program itself is a case and the methods of case study should be pertinent.

Case study is inquiry about a particular object rather than about a population of objects or about relationships among variables that describe objects. A case study may contribute to generalization but is an exercise in particularization. Evaluators and evaluation audiences are interested in generalization but an evaluation contract usually holds understanding the quality of the particular program as a first order of business. Generalizations about other cases and recommendations for subsequent treatment may or may not be expected.

Cronbach has persisted in drawing attention to the *population* of programs, schools, and teachers of which those being evaluated might be considered a sample.[21] I think neither evaluators nor readers are well served by talk about populations. The utility of the evaluation study is not determined by whether the studied case and the cases to which the findings will be extrapolated are from a common population. To gain understanding, readers fit the present case in among the cases they have experienced; to take action, readers associate the present case with those to be treated. Each reader brings his or her own reference populations but seeks application to cases more than generalization to populations. The task of the evaluator is to tell enough about the antecedents, transactions, and outcomes so that readers can relate the evaluator's report to what they already know.

The evaluator can give deliberate attention to readers' conceptual and experiential backgrounds so as to enrich *their* interpreting, their "naturalistic generalization," as Deborah Trumbull and I called it.[22] The evaluator is obligated then to describe the new case in ways likely to facilitate the reader's own comparing and contrasting. In 1965, I had no expectation of turning my evaluation work into what Jerome Bruner called "discovery learning."[23] But as I worked on the countenance paper and in the years to follow, my notion of evaluators as surrogate decision makers faded, and I came to see us more as facilitators of decision makers who were, at least for the business at hand, the principal investigators.

I want us, as evaluation specialists, to think of ourselves as facilitators of inquiry but not part of the remediation team. Many, including Michael Patton, Thomas Cook, William Shadish, and Laura Leviton,[24] link evaluation too closely, I believe, to remediation. My experience has been that the evaluation can miss important problems, can too quickly move away from study of the problem, if remediation is the product. And too often, evaluators imply an enduring usefulness by emphasizing issues along their own lines of expertise. For ethical as well as epistemological reasons, the evaluator should seldom be a part of the remediation team. Case study should be oriented to understanding the case more or less as a whole, not for patching its pieces and fixing its problems.

Responsive Evaluation

A major weakness of the countenance paper was a shortage of procedural guidelines to match the epistemological and political sweep of its data matrices. While on sabbatical leave in Sweden in 1973, I came to believe that even the rational Swedes jumped great gaps between data and interpretation, that the intuitive and experiential side of program development and operation remained a domain to which program evaluators needed to accommodate. Even in a relatively homogeneous social system, the situationality of education was apparent. I decided that the procedures of evaluation research needed to be carefully responsive to the activity and contexts of teaching and learning. Drawing heavily from Ulf Lundgren, Barry MacDonald, and David Hamilton, I presented a paper at the University of Gothenburg extending the countenance ideas into a procedural statement which I labeled "responsive evaluation."[25]

Responsive evaluation is a persuasion to concentrate early attention on the activity, uniqueness, and social plurality of the program in order to see what data gathering and interpretive schemes might be useful for indicating program quality. In a way it corresponds to Wholey's "evaluability,"[26] for it postpones designing the study until the evaluand is well understood. The conceptual structure is an *issue list*, an identification of high priority puzzlements and problems to enhance understanding of this particular program, given the evaluation resources at hand. Beyond early hesitance, responsive evaluation calls for continuing adaptation of evaluation goal-setting to emerging and evolutionary features of the program, i.e., progressive focusing.

I chose *issues* as my conceptual organizers because they draw thinking toward the complexity, particularity, and subjective valuing already felt by persons associated with the program. Issue questions such as "Are the published admission criteria observed?" and "Do the simulation exercises confuse students about authoritative sources of information?" are raised, some from acquaintance with similar programs, but most from on-site contacts. The evaluator inquires, negotiates, and selects a few issues around which to organize the study.

To become acquainted with a program's issues, the evaluator observes ways program people work, interviews stakeholders, and examines documents. These are not necessarily the data-gathering methods for informing and interpreting the issues, but for initial planning. Management of the study remains flexible whether quantitative or qualitative data subsequently dominate. The complexity of substantive issues goes far beyond the complexities anticipated in the countenance paper. When it came time to amplify the Gothenburg paper, I found it preferable to concentrate on particular subject matters, as in "To Evaluate an Arts Program"[27] or *Case Studies in Science Education*,[28] the latter co-directed with Jack Easley.

Qualitative methods. A common misunderstanding has been that responsive evaluation requires naturalistic study. Although most who have chosen to call their evaluating responsive have had leanings toward naturalistic case study,[29] the essence of responsiveness is adaptation to prevailing conditions. Relativism before naturalism. Evaluators, staff, and sponsors discuss alternative approaches; they negotiate. Knowing more about what different methods accomplish and what this evaluation team can do well, and because work never mirrors intent, the evaluator ultimately determines what the methods will be.

But with strong intent to know personal histories and social interaction, it is not a surprise when the dominant method of responsive evaluation turns out to be ethnographic, naturalistic, and phenomenological. Still, it is not uncommon for major attention to be given to goal-oriented instrumentation. It depends on the situation. Usually people are treated more as informants than as subjects, questioned not so much to see how they have changed but to indicate the changes they see. If done well, the methods fit the "here and now," serving immediate need for understanding of the various parties concerned, as voiced in the countenance paper.

Those who object to the responsive approach often do so on the grounds that too much attention is given to subjective data such as testimony of participants. Responsive evaluators try through triangulated description to show the reliability of observations.[30] Part of the description, especially that about the worth of the program, is revealed in how people subjectively perceive what is going on. Placing value on the program is not seen as separate from perceiving the program.

The researchers' own perceptions are also recognized as subjective—in choosing what to observe, in observing, and in reporting the observations. One tries in responsive evaluation to make those value commitments more recognizable. Issues are not avoided just because they are inextricably subjective. When reporting, care is taken to illuminate the subjectivity of data and interpretations, thus facilitating the reader's own interpretation. The evaluator makes his or her assertions[31] but the reader is encouraged to reach beyond the evaluator's understanding.

Political dimensions. Objection to responsive evaluation is also expressed in the belief that the program staff, the funding agency, or the research community should specify the research questions. Such questions are often worthy of study but in program evaluation for public use, they should not dominate. The public believes that when a program is evaluated a wide array of important concerns are examined. Embezzlement, racial discrimination, inconsistency in philosophy, and thwarting of creativity may be unmentioned in the contract, and barely in the evaluation specialist's range of view, but such shortcomings belong to the public image of evaluation, and the responsible evaluator at least tries not to be blind to them.

Evaluation is invoked for many purposes, many of them with little concern about the production of information. Evaluation studies are prescribed to legitimatize authority and to protect program operations from criticism. Evaluation requirements are sometimes laid down for the purpose of promulgating standards. These efforts at extending control over education are part of the ordinary politics of education. Some evaluators despair at seeing their informational products disregarded, not realizing the information was only a secondary purpose. Disappointment rightly turns to indignation and protest when sponsors are deceptive in their disposition of the evaluation or use it to undermine legitimate interests. Responsive evaluation was not intended as an instrument of reform, though reformists might find it useful. It was intended to serve the diverse people most affected by the program at hand. Still, it is likely to produce some findings and cause political maneuverings they will not like.

Over the years MacDonald, House, and Cronbach led the way in pointing out the political character of program evaluation studies.[32] In the countenance paper I announced that for the moment I was ducking "the politics of evaluation" but I appealed for a more pluralistic consideration of values. Views then seem pretty naive now. Even if we evaluators could do all we propose to do, which we cannot, too many people have too much invested in change or in the status quo to allow our findings to determine the direction of educational reform.

Twenty years after our AERA committee deliberations, meta-evaluation standards were developed.[33] The *Joint Standards* give us basis for empirically understanding the strength and weakness of tactics and persuasions. Yet formal meta-evaluation studies seldom occur. The professional associations, notably the American Evaluation Association and Division H of the American Educational Research Association, have been weak catalysts for critical analysis of the work of their members. Funding agencies seldom find meta-evaluation studies worthy of funding.[34] The advice of the countenance paper has not been adequately tested. But even if the various persuasions had been better evaluated, we still would follow our intuitions more than our research in proposing new studies and teaching others our craft.

Epistemological Grounds

The epistemological foundation of the countenance paper was a hypothetical set of functional relationships between teaching and learning. I implied that under specified antecedent conditions, outcomes would co-vary with variation in observed transactions. And ultimately, school improvement would be based on these co-variations, identified by program evaluators who would express them as limited generalizations for the use of policymakers and practitioners. In 1965, I felt simplistic input-output relationships were being overly relied on; that generalizations needed to be much more conditional; but that if extensive records of contexts, activities, accomplishments, and side effects were kept, contingencies could be isolated by evaluators and put to good use by educators. I believed that, in a real sense, specific teaching resulted in specific learning.

Constructed Reality. Recent discussions among evaluation theorists draw attention to implicit and explicit definitions of reality.[35] Our evaluation studies reflect our epistemological views. I think it important to amplify my own views here, particularly to indicate why, even as an evaluator believing it our responsibility to judge program quality, I am reticent to promise or pursue authoritative summary judgments. In a chapter in this volume, Michael Scriven implies, as he has over the years, that teaching has measurable effects, that a competent evaluator can know a program well enough and can and must combine perceptions of merit and shortcoming to arrive at an epistemologically sound summary judgment of quality. In the following paragraphs I reject that view—once my own.

It has become increasingly apparent to me that educators, as most people, work from experiential understandings, that their knowledge and all knowledge is a human construction. Since writing the countenance paper, I have increasingly replaced realist presumption with constructivist hesitation. I have worked less and less to capture that which can be specified and objectively measured and more to understand what is being commonly intuited. I reasoned: Knowledge begins in the sensory experience of external stimuli. It originates in outside action but, as constructivists emphasize, only the inside interpretation is known. As far as we can tell, nothing about the stimulus is registered in awareness and memory other than our interpretations of it. This registration is not necessarily either conscious or rational.

In our minds, new perceptions of stimuli mix with old. They become complexes of perception, some of which we recognize as generalizations. Some aspects of knowledge seem generated entirely from internal deliberation, i.e., pondering, without immediate external stimulation. But no aspects of knowledge are purely of the external world, devoid of human construction.

I came to think of three realities. One is the outside world, that external reality capable of stimulating us in simple ways but of which we know nothing besides its stimulation. Another is a reality formed of interpretations of simple stimulation, an experiential reality we know so well that we seldom doubt its correspondence to that first reality. The third is a world devised of our most complex interpretations, our rational reality. The second and third, of course, blend into each other. A common human view is that the outside world, reality number one, exists, corresponding nicely to our notion of it, reality number two. This correspondence cannot be tested. Nothing of that outside world can register independent of our constructed interpretation. But the view is esteemed. The extreme counterclaim, that the world is entirely illusory, has little popularity.

Each human being has his or her own version of worlds two and three. The versions evolve. Still, a person's world remains largely the same from day to day and two people sharing experience devise similar realities. They are stimulated at the same time and they speak to each other, sharing responses, each influencing the other's interpretation: "Isn't she the teacher?" "Is that textbook any good?" Many stimulations from other humans are perceived to be indications of generalization. Views which appear to be held by large numbers of people or by people respected are held credible, even factual.

We are comfortable with the view that books and people exist. Denial of an independent reality (beyond human construction) is unsupportable by evidence and is socially disconcerting. In our daily affairs, the price of believing in reality number one, even if it did not exist, is small. For self-guidance, we might turn Unamuno's phrase thus: "Even if there is no independent reality, let us live as if there were." Letting children play in the street or tripling the amount of achievement testing—the consequences would be distressing if we stopped supposing reality number one exists.

The appetizing belief, mine too, is the nonparsimonious view that all three realities exist and have important effects on experience. Which reality to believe the more important, like the question of nature and nurture, is academic. It is important to remember we can jeopardize our lot by neglecting any of the three.

The aim of empirical research is not to discover reality number one, for that is impossible, but to construct a clearer reality number two and a more sophisticated reality number three, particularly ones which will ring true even in the face of disciplined skepticism. Science strives to build universal understandings. The understanding reached by each individual will, of course, be somewhat unique but much is held in common. Although the reality we seek is of our own making, it is a collective making. We seek the well-tuned reality, one bearing up under scrutiny and challenge.

As the evaluation study draws to a close, how well-tuned and how challenge-resisting are the comprehensions of the competent evaluator? To make valid summary judgments, evaluators must comprehend the thrusts and sweep of the program. They must comprehend processes and products and relationships among them. They must comprehend needs, resources, and valuings of stakeholders. They must comprehend standards of quality. Having no nonsubjective access to reality number one and having only impressions, many weakly triangulated, their comprehensions are laced with presumption. Even the nature of the program is epistemologically indefinite; so too are its effects and usefulness. I believe that it is not just the weakness of the evaluator's methods but that in reality number one, the program and its working exist not as a definite object but as evolving nebulae. But whether actually indefinite and ephemeral or just complex and out of reach, evaluators have good reason to be modest in their claims. Evaluators can provide useful descriptions and must summarize merit as they see it, but acknowledging amorphous and obscured realities, educational evaluators should not expect to make strong summary judgments of program quality.

Relativism, not egalitarianism. Reality is relative, but every person's personal reality is not of equal social importance. Some interpretations are better than others. People have ways of agreeing on which are the best explanations. Of course, majority and consensus views are not always right. Personal civility or political ideology may call for respecting every view but scientific study does not.

Egon Guba and Yvonna Lincoln especially are pushing evaluators to pay attention to concepts of reality. In *Fourth Generation Evaluation*[36] they have identified several levels of belief in independent and constructed realities. Such belief is often linked to belief of how we come to know what we know, but ontology and epistemology are not interdeterminate. Belief in independent reality does not commit one to viewing the world as homogeneous and generalizable. Nor does belief in construction commit one to viewing the world as heterogeneous and particularistic. Realists as well as constructivists believe that generalizations are regularly limited by local conditions. "Do teachers always prefer authoritarian milieus or only under certain conditions?" Although idealists, relativists, situationalists, and other champions of local knowledge often resist broad generalization and are found to support constructivist ontology, their support for a contextualist epistemology is a correlate, not a derivative, of that ontology.

Contextualists find value in case studies because the design allows or demands extra attention to physical, temporal, historical, social, political, economic, and aesthetic contexts. Contextualist epistemology requires in-depth description, leaving less time for the refinement of theme and construct.

Many realists are fond of case studies. Physicians, realtors, social workers, many of whom are realists, are professionally committed to case study. In educational research, naturalistic, phenomenological, and hermeneutic case studies are most often done by researchers with constructivist persuasions. Why this occurs is not clear to me.[37] It is not uncommon to find case study researchers espousing a constructivist view of reality but the two persuasions are not one and the same.

Research does not discover truth, for truth is beyond reach. When researchers' impressions attain a certain redundancy, meanings take the form of generalization. A researcher's descriptions and assertions portray a part of his or her experienced reality. A reader modifies his or her generalizations, often in the direction of the researcher's assertions. Cronbach said, "Generalizations decay."[38] Though less parsimonious, it is better to say that generalizations wax and wane. They change in complexity and relevance; the conviction with which they are held changes too. The researcher's role in this reconstruction of personal knowledge can be significant.

Multiple Realities. In the countenance paper, I spoke of multiple purposes, observations, and value judgments. People do not see things the same. Even then, I objected to the idea that the evaluator's job is to identify the correct view or consensus. Deviant and contradictory views may help us understand a program. Credit the evaluator who coherently portrays a variety of expectations, interpretations, and judgments.

Subscription to a constructivist view eases the dismay of finding incompatible testimonials, although the burden of ascertaining a proper record increases. People do not just disagree, they live in different realities. People live quietly and often proudly with their peculiar ways of seeing things. The evaluator errs in too noisily depicting the peculiarities as much as too quietly. With matrixed rows and columns in the countenance paper, I implied irreducible perceptions, multiple perceptions. Today multiple views help legitimate resistance to bureaucratic overstandardization.

But, anything goes? Not at all. Every measurement and vignette needs verification. The evaluator triangulates, not to indicate the multiplicity of views but to ascertain that each separate view has been properly perceived. Among those views that can be verified, only some will be deemed sufficiently relevant to the issues, sufficiently a contribution to understanding, to be reported. In the countenance paper, the goal was choosing among eligible data types. That choice was not the greatest problem then nor is it now. The greatest problem is helping others understand the complexity of quality. To do so we structure reports not with a data matrix but with issues, descriptions, and assertions, choosing each for its capacity to diminish misunderstandings and to enhance interpretation among people expected not to see eye to eye.

How evaluators perceive knowledge influences their designs and reporting. As I have taken up constructionist views, I have increasingly seen the role of research as delivering portrayals and assertions to readers so that they may modify their already elaborately constructed generalizations.

The Circumstances in 1990

Twenty-five years after publication of the countenance paper, there appears little audience for advice on program evaluation. Schools and specific programs continue to be evaluated but not with the strong social science expectation of the 1960s. Few programs are funded with special dollars, and little expectation is raised that formal evaluation will occur. The rhetoric of accountability has increased but formal attention is almost entirely deflected away from looking at quality of instruction to looking at level of student performance.

Research methods for investigating teaching and learning have changed substantially in the same period. Among the changes are substantial increases in naturalistic, contextual, and phenomenological studies. Although many studies attend to issues of quality, few are billed as program evaluations. Evaluation continues to be a main concern among researchers, practitioners, policymakers, and the public—but the response from program evaluators in the late 1960s and early 1970s did not encourage further investment of funds and careers. It is not just that federal funding is no longer available. There is little continuing expectation[39] that accounting and performance measurement based in educational research will pay off—even if we could afford it.

Education is not being adequately portrayed by the spokespersons for education, its critics, or its evaluators. I note again my words in the countenance paper, "Educators . . . should be imploring measurements specialists to develop a methodology that reflects the fullness, the complexity, and the importance of their programs." Goal statements, course descriptions, student achievement, teacher customs, and the words of the philosophers are not nicely interchangeable. The reality of education is much more complex and often much more robust than the representation.

Education turned out to be not as comprehensible, and the profession and public not as susceptible to rational persuasion, as we educational researchers thought in 1965. Today, as student assessment rivets attention and energy, the authority of those who have studied education deeply is not held in greater respect than the authority of those who merely have been greatly disappointed by the schools. Disregard is not reserved just for the educational evaluator but for the curriculum scholar, the educational philosopher, the policy analyst, the instructional researcher. It soothes us to think that the indifference to human need of the Reagan years was our nemesis, but the truth is that the society gave applied educational research more than a decade to show the way to upgrade the schools—and we failed. The schools are in poorer shape today than they were in 1965. If the bottom line is school reform, the countenance persuasion was no better than the rest. In that regard, it too failed to address the realities of education.

President Johnson, President Conant, Mrs. Hull (Sara's teacher) and Mr. Tykociner (the man next door) had a 1960s confidence in our understanding of education that two decades later is found suspect.

FOOTNOTES

1. The original "countenance" paper, "The Countenance of Educational Evaluation," appeared in *Teachers College Record* 68 (April 1967): 523-540.

2. Benjamin S. Bloom, J. Thomas Hastings, and George F. Madaus, *Handbook on Formative and Summative Evaluation* (New York: McGraw-Hill, 1970).

3. W. James Popham, ed., *Evaluation in Education* (Berkeley, CA: McCutchan

Publishing Corp., 1971).

4. Donald T. Campbell, "Reforms as Experiments," *American Psychologist* 24 (1969): 409-429; Lee J. Cronbach, "Course Improvement through Evaluation," *Teachers College Record* 64, no. 8 (1963): 672-683; Daniel L. Stufflebeam, William J. Foley, William J. Gephart, Egon G. Guba, Robert L. Hammond, Howard O. Merriman, and Malcolm M. Provus, *Educational Evaluation and Decision Making* (Itasca, IL.: Peacock Publishers, 1971): Michael Scriven, "The Methodology of Evaluation," in *Perspectives of Curriculum Evaluation*, ed. Robert E. Stake, AERA Monograph Series on Curriculum Evaluation, No. 1 (Chicago: Rand McNally, 1967), pp. 39-83.

5. James B. Conant, *Slums and Suburbs: A Commentary on Schools in Metropolitan Areas* (New York: McGraw-Hill, 1961).

6. Cronbach, "Course Improvement through Evaluation."

7. American Psychological Association, *Technical Recommendations for Psychological Tests and Diagnostic Techniques* (Washington, DC: American Psychological Association, 1954).

8. As described in my introduction to *Perspectives of Curriculum Evaluation*, ed. Stake.

9. Robert E. Stake, ed., *Perspectives of Curriculum Evaluation*.

10. As did Malcolm Provus in *Discrepancy Evaluation* (Berkeley, CA: McCutchan Publishing Corp., 1971).

11. Robert E. Stake, John A. Easley, Jr., and others, *Case Studies in Science Education* (Washington, DC: U.S. Government Printing Office, 1978).

12. Benjamin S. Bloom, ed., *Taxonomy of Educational Objectives: The Classification of Educational Goals, Handbook 1: Cognitive Domain* (New York: Longman, 1956).

13. The model serves merely for reference. Adaptations to unique contexts are desired and inevitable.

14. CIPP is the acronym used by Daniel Stufflebeam identifying the need for study of Context, Input, Process, and Product. See Stufflebeam et al., *Educational Evaluation and Decision Making*.

15. Ernest R. House, *Evaluating with Validity* (Beverly Hills, CA: Sage, 1980).

16. Michael Scriven provides a synopsis of each of these persuasions in his *Evaluation Thesaurus* (Inverness, CA: Edgepress, 1980).

17. House, *Evaluating with Validity*, p. 63.

18. Michael Polanyi, *Personal Knowledge: Toward a Post-Critical Philosophy* (Chicago: University of Chicago Press, 1962); Robert Pirsig, *Zen and the Art of Motorcycle Maintenance* (New York: William Morrow, 1974).

19. Cronbach, "Course Improvement through Evaluation."

20. Terry Denny, "In Defense of Story Telling as a First Step in Educational Research," Paper No. 12 (Kalamazoo, MI: Evaluation Center, Western Michigan University, 1978).

21. Cronbach's *UTOS is a population large or small which the decision maker has in mind. Lee J. Cronbach, *Designing Evaluations of Educational and Social Programs* (San Francisco: Jossey-Bass, 1982).

22. Robert E. Stake and Deborah Trumbull, "Naturalistic Generalization," *Review Journal of Philosophy and Social Science* 7, nos. 1-2 (1982): 1-12.

23. See Jerome Bruner, *The Process of Education* (Cambridge, MA: Harvard University Press, 1960).

24. See Michael Q. Patton, *Creative Evaluation* (Beverly Hills, CA: Sage, 1981); Thomas D. Cook, Laura C. Leviton, and William R. Shadish, Jr., "Program Evaluation," in *Handbook of Social Psychology*, vol. 1, 3d ed., ed. Gardner Lindzey and Elliott Aronson (New York: Random House, 1985), pp. 699-777.

25. Robert E. Stake, "Program Evaluation, Particularly Responsive Evaluation," in *New Trends in Evaluation*, Report No. 35 (Gothenburg, Sweden: Institute of Education, University of Gothenburg, 1974), pp. 1-20. For updated traces of those influences, see Ulf Lundgren, *Curriculum Theory: Between Hope and Happening: Text and Context in Curriculum* (Geelong, Australia: Deakin University, 1983); Barry MacDonald, "A Political Classification of Evaluation Studies," in *Beyond the Numbers Game*, ed. David Hamilton et al. (London: Macmillan, 1977); and David Hamilton, "Making Sense of Curriculum Evaluation: Continuities and Discontinuities in an Educational Idea," in *Review of Research in Education*, vol. 5, ed. Lee Shulman (Itasca, IL: Peacock, 1977).

26. J. S. Wholey, *Evaluation: Promise and Performance* (Washington, DC: Urban Institute, 1979).

27. Robert E. Stake, *Evaluating the Arts in Education: A Responsive Approach* (Columbus, OH: Charles Merrill, 1975).

28. Stake, Easley, et al., *Case Studies in Science Education.*

29. Egon Guba and Yvonna Lincoln thoughtfully opted for the composite name "naturalistic responsive evaluation." See their *Effective Evaluation* (San Francisco: Jossey-Bass, 1981).

30. This problem was neglected in the "countenance" paper. See Norman Denzin, *The Research Act* (Chicago: Aldine, 1970).

31. Frederick Erickson has characterized qualitative studies more as interpretative than naturalistic studies with the key production being *assertions*. See his "Qualitative Methods in Research on Teaching," in *Handbook of Research on Teaching*, 3d ed., ed. Merlin C. Wittrock (New York: Basic Books, 1986), pp. 119-161.

32. See MacDonald, "A Political Classification of Evaluation Studies"; Ernest House, ed., *School Evaluation: Politics and Process* (Berkeley, CA: McCutchan Publishing Corp., 1973); and Lee J. Cronbach, "Remarks to the New Society," *Evaluation Research Society News Letter* 1, no. 1 (1977).

33. Joint Committee on Standards for Educational Evaluation, *Standards for Evaluations of Educational Programs, Projects, and Materials* (New York: McGraw-Hill, 1981).

34. An exception occurred when NIE official Norman Gold managed to have stakeholder evaluation studied, as detailed in Robert E. Stake, *Quieting Reform: Social Science and Social Action in an Urban Youth Program* (Urbana-Champaign: University of Illinois Press, 1986).

35. See Guba and Lincoln, *Effective Evaluation*, and William R. Shadish, Jr., Thomas Cook, and Laura C. Leviton, *Foundations of Program Evaluation* (Newbury Park: Sage Publications, 1990).

36. Egon Guba and Yvonna Lincoln, *Fourth Generation Evaluation* (San Francisco: Jossey-Bass, 1989).

37. See ibid. for development of the rationale.

38. Lee J. Cronbach, "Beyond the Two Disciplines of Scientific Psychology," *American Psychologist* 30 (February 1975): 122.

39. The misanthropy of technology in social affairs was nicely portrayed for scholars by Jürgen Habermas in *Knowledge and Human Interests* (New York: Basic Books, 1970); for popular audiences by David Halberstam in *The Best and the Brightest* (New York: Random House, 1972); and for educational evaluators by Charles E. Lindbloom and David K. Cohen in *Usable Knowledge: Social Science and Social Problem Solving* (New Haven: Yale University Press, 1979).

Evaluation Theory Development

In the first half of the decade of the 1960s, evaluation was most commonly conceived in terms of a precise statement of program objectives, followed by accurate measurement of the degree of their attainment; but by the middle of the decade alternative emphases were beginning to be discussed. A watershed was the publication in 1963 of Lee Cronbach's influential paper "Course Improvement through Evaluation," in which he advocated a different role for evaluation— the role Michael Scriven shortly afterwards labeled as "formative." Daniel Stufflebeam soon followed with his decision-oriented CIPP (Context, Input, Process, Product) model, and the floodgates started to open.

The result of this activity was that near the end of the decade the field was quite unsettled, with various evaluators and evaluation theorists holding different conceptions of the nature of the evaluation enterprise. The ferment was reflected in the statement that started to appear in the literature to the effect that evaluators urgently needed to reach agreement on the *definition* of evaluation; another symptom was the call for an overarching *theory* of evaluation. (The widely held assumption seems to have been that a coherent or unified view of evaluation was awaiting discovery—it was a sign of the immaturity of the field that there were rival accounts of the nature of evaluation. On the other hand, as early as 1967, Scriven had been comfortable with the view that evaluation could undertake—or could be assigned—a variety of different roles.)

In 1969, Marvin Alkin, of the Center for the Study of Evaluation at UCLA, published his paper on "Evaluation Theory Development" in *Evaluation Comment*. The paper accurately reflected the intellectual climate, and the intellectual uncertainties, of the period. According to Alkin, a theory of evaluation should present a conceptual scheme that would classify areas of evaluation, it should clarify the kinds of data and analyses appropriate to each of these areas, and it should provide systems of generalizations about the use of various evaluation techniques. Alkin spelled out four key assumptions that he then held about evaluation, and on the basis of these he went on to offer a definition: Evaluation is the process of ascertaining the decision areas

89

of concern, selecting appropriate information, and collecting and analyzing information in order to report summary data useful to decision makers in selecting among alternatives.

In the following chapter Alkin revisits the topic of his 1969 paper, and he shows how he—and the field—continued to progress over the next two decades.

CHAPTER IV

Evaluation Theory Development: II

MARVIN C. ALKIN

"Carol (Weiss), you and Michael (Patton) disagree on the issue of the evaluator's possibility of affecting use. This has been demonstrated in your interchange in *Evaluation Practice*.[1] But, let me ask you: How do you think your views would differ with respect to the role of a substantive field's theory as a guide for the evaluator?" And so Gretchen, posing as Carol, and Karin, role-playing Michael, debate the question during a "Meeting of the Minds" format in my Education 202 class, intuiting the views of Weiss and Patton and basing their arguments on the written formulations of the theorists. Despite the enormous expertise that Gretchen, Karin, and other students gain during their course of study, their interpretations of the views of evaluation theorists are sometimes wrong. To these students and to other readers of the evaluation literature, theorists are portrayed solely by their writings. And that is the main deficiency.

Evaluators' written statements of theory do not provide a full insight into their views on evaluation. There are several reasons. First, since such theorizing is viewed by the reader as fixed in the written word, it often goes unchanged over time. Secondly, the reader is limited to what appears on the printed page and is often not aware of the nuances that were part of the author's reasoning at the time the paper was written. For example, it is often difficult for the reader to discern the extent to which statements are tentative conjectures or resolved issues. It is often difficult to determine the extent to which the theorist considered an apparent thesis "essential" or "peripheral." Further, it is difficult for an author/theorist to portray the nature of the interrelationships (and interdependencies) between ideas, and even more difficult for the reader to discern them. Finally, even at a particular time, theorists are restricted by page limitations (as I am in this chapter) and thus, cannot put down in writing *all* of their thoughts.

An example of the problems in interpreting "theories" is provided
in an exercise reported in *Studies in Educational Evaluation*.[2] In this
exercise my students portrayed evaluation theorists based upon their
prior writings and indicated how they might have changed "their"
prior views based on the conceptual stimulus of having read a certain
book. One interchange in particular exemplified the extent to which a
theorist's writings can fail to portray him adequately at a later time.
The frustration of a theorist in recognizing his prior *public* self was
exemplified by Guba who noted "I am not the 'real' Guba . . . That
Egon Guba was the one working and writing seven to ten years ago
. . . The real Egon Guba of 1978 . . . is really quite different from
what Elaine has suggested."[3] And, I would venture to say that the
Egon Guba of 1990 is again quite different.

All of this directs us to the questions: Who was the Marvin C.
Alkin of 1969? Who is the Marvin C. Alkin of today? How and why
did he change? In considering these questions this chapter becomes an
exploration of the nature of evaluation theorizing as well as a
statement about my personal views on evaluation.[4] To a large extent
I use my views on evaluation and how they have changed over time
as a case study of the evaluation theory development/formation
process.

1969: Evaluation Theory Development

The original "Evaluation Theory Development" article[5]
(hereafter referred to as ETD), which I have been asked to address,
had four major sections. These sections will be used as a basis for
structuring this discussion. (In actuality, a fifth section of the article,
which will not be further discussed, presented views on how the
Center for the Study of Evaluation could best foster its evaluation
improvement and theory development goals by various planned
projects, including the development of an evaluation kit and the
initiation of the Instructional Objectives Exchange.) The four major
sections of ETD to be discussed here are: emphasis on theory
building, assumptions about evaluation, evaluation definition, and
evaluation need areas.

EMPHASIS ON THEORY BUILDING

On reflection, almost two decades later, the most impressive aspect
of the original ETD was its emphasis on the importance of
systematically considering (and developing) evaluation theory. ETD

was not intended to be a fully developed theory of evaluation. Instead, it was intended as a "rationale for conducting evaluations in a certain way, that is, based on a *specified set of assumptions* which in turn underlie a *precise definition* of what an evaluation is supposed to do or be." The goal was expressed of ultimately developing propositions, as part of a theory of evaluation, which would "enable one to predict, fully, the appropriateness of utilizing various evaluation strategies. . . ."[6] The goals of systematically engaging in the process of developing evaluation theory, and of conducting research that would add to our understandings of evaluations, have pervaded my work since the writing of ETD. Over time I have further clarified my assumptions about the particular "brand" of evaluation that I espouse (user-oriented/utilization-focused). Given these certain assumptions about the purposes of evaluation, I have learned a good deal more about the conditions under which the purposes are most likely to be met.[7]

Another area associated with evaluation theory building is the concern for ways in which evaluation theorists change their views over time and the kinds of influences that modify those views.[8] The issue of comparative evaluation theory—that is, the way in which theorists agree and differ—is explored in my own studies already noted, and by my students as well.

However, I, and we as a discipline, still have not made very much progress toward developing an evaluation theory. A list of propositions on which all evaluators agree has not yet been defined. Clearly, an analysis of all (or a representative set of) theoretic points of view on evaluation would yield a list of common beliefs and assumptions about evaluation. For example, do all evaluation theorists agree that evaluation involves the collection of data (broadly defined)? Would all evaluation theorists adhere to the Evaluation Standards[9] as *requisite* elements in an evaluation? Perhaps more importantly, are there generalizations that can be made about those who would, and those who would not, agree to the necessity of particular standards?

Clearly, the theory development goal asserted in ETD established a worthy direction for further writings in the evaluation field. Unfortunately, most of the writings in the field have been confined largely to providing prescriptions as to how one might conduct an evaluation. These prescriptions have been based on assumptions about the priorities and purposes of evaluation that are usually only implicit.

ASSUMPTIONS ABOUT EVALUATION

The original ETD made explicit four assumptions about evaluation upon which a subsequent definition and strategies were to be dependent. Those assumptions were:

1. Evaluation is a process of gathering information.
2. The information collected in an evaluation will be used mainly to make decisions about alternative courses of action.
3. Evaluation information should be presented to the decision maker in a form that he can use effectively and which is designed to help rather than confuse or mislead him.[10]
4. Different kinds of decisions require different kinds of evaluation procedures.

Generally, I agree with all of the assumptions. *Specifically*, I can today find fault in each. Evaluation certainly involves gathering information, but we must be careful that the word "information" is not too narrowly defined. There are a variety of ways in which the evaluator becomes informed about the entity being evaluated. A significant clarification of that assumption also requires that the information gathering be "systematic." Although I never intended that the evaluator's activities be less than systematic, that important clarification might be necessary to establish firmly that evaluation is a form of disciplined inquiry; for were it not, the development of evaluation theory would hardly be worth discussing.

Now we turn to the second assumption: ". . . used *mainly* to make decisions about alternative courses of action." Certainly, in a great many instances there will be decisions made, and decisions by their very nature focus on a choice between alternatives. The statement was never meant to imply that all evaluations lead specifically to a decision. However, the manner in which this statement was made (and statements like it that were made by others) has led to interpretations that clearly overstate the case. Those who have been critical of "decision-oriented" evaluation have painted a picture of the major theorists of this type in the late 1960s and early 1970s (e.g., Stufflebeam, Provus, and myself) as being concerned exclusively with "decisions" and naively assuming that eager "decision makers" sit in wait for evaluations so that they might make "decisions." This view, of course, is a preposterous overstatement. I do allow that we provided the basis for these slings and arrows in ill-drafted statements like Assumption 2, however well intentioned they were at that time.

The statement about "information presented to the decision

maker" in Assumption 3 is a continuation of the same theme and offers many of the same problems. I still maintain that information has to be presented to someone or to a number of someones. (I now prefer to think of these someones as "users" or "potential users.") The essence of Assumption 3 is that one of the things that differentiates "evaluation" from "research" is the presence of an intended user who has specific concerns that we hope can be acted on as a result of the evaluation. Clearly the 1969 term "the decision maker" was far too limited, and I would not say that now.

The remainder of the statement in Assumption 3 has been critical in my developing views on evaluation in the last several decades: "in a form that he can use effectively and which is designed to help rather than to confuse or mislead him." An important thrust within this assumption is the notion of *evaluation use* and the obligation of the evaluator to be responsive to performing and presenting an evaluation in a manner that might enhance that use. My research on evaluation utilization over the years has been designed with this purpose in mind.

The last assumption in ETD dealt with the recognition that evaluations serve multiple purposes, particularly with respect to the kinds of decisions that might be made. The notion of evaluation procedures that are tailored to the kind of decision to be made was prevalent in the 1960s and 1970s as a number of us sought to understand and describe the nature of the evaluation enterprise. For example, Stufflebeam focused on Planning, Structuring, Implementing, and Recycling Decisions, which required Context, Input, Process, and Product evaluations respectively.[11] Typically, "kinds of decisions" referred to stages or phases of an evaluation, each of which had a different purpose.

My current criticism of the fourth assumption is that while the idea was sound, it tended to treat evaluation as too mechanistic: a step-by-step, cookbook kind of activity. Hence, many of the personal and human aspects of conducting an evaluation were masked by the strong emphasis on evaluation stages or types of decisions. Thus, while I still agree with Assumption 4 as a way to think about evaluation, I feel that its effect on the conduct of evaluation has not been entirely positive. I will have further comments about this matter in a subsequent section of this chapter.

DEFINITION OF EVALUATION

The definition proffered in ETD was derived quite naturally from the set of assumptions and is subject to the same caveats:

Evaluation is the process of ascertaining the decision areas of concern, selecting appropriate information, and collecting and analyzing information in order to report summary data useful to decision makers in selecting among alternatives.[12]

One key phrase of this definition is: "ascertaining the decision areas of concern." Unlike a research study, an evaluation has specific potential users who are likely to benefit from the results of the evaluation. Typically, there is a sense of immediacy connected to the evaluation. Thus, a program that is being judged in its field setting will have areas of concern related to it. As noted in ETD, "the decision maker, and not the evaluator, determines the nature of the domain to be examined." Evaluators have input into this process, and by doing so may affect it. Evaluators do this when they "point out inconsistencies, potential difficulties, or additional data that might modify the decision makers' views on the relevance of certain concerns."

Even the original ETD, despite some of its faulty verbiage, recognized that there would not always be a specific preidentified decision maker. In such instances, the evaluator played a more imminent role in ascertaining the decision areas of concern. The 1969 article acknowledged that the evaluator might conduct an evaluative study of an educational institution "without having been commissioned by a specific decision maker." In such instances, I noted, "there is a preconception on the part of the evaluator as to which decision maker or potential decision groups he is directing his work towards."[13] This was referred to as the notion of "preconception of decision maker." This notion substantially broadened the role of defined decision maker, but did it in a way that still maintained a meaningful distinction between evaluation and research.

My current views on evaluation are not satisfied simply with this notion of preconception; today I would require the evaluator to make an effort to engage these "preconceived decision makers" in order to better understand and refine their concerns. Moreover, this interaction with the potential user(s) currently is viewed as a critical element in eliciting the commitment usually associated with high levels of evaluation use. Thus, the overriding concern is for the evaluator to engage in efforts likely to lead to higher levels of use; this concern has modified my views on the sufficiency of "preconceived" or presumed decision makers.

Current views of evaluator responsiveness to multiple stakeholders were portended in the 1969 ETD:

The summary data is provided to be of use to the decision maker. It has already been alluded to in this paper that we are using the term "decision maker" to apply both to an explicit contractor of evaluation services as well as a potential but only implicit decision maker or group. Moreover, we are using the term "decision maker" to apply both to an individual with organizational "line" authority (e.g. a school principal) as well as to other publics that participate in the decision process or in the development of educational policy decisions. Throughout this paper, whenever we refer to "decision maker" it is in the generic sense discussed above.[14]

I now believe that this view (as well as current derivatives) is weak. Again, this judgment stems from the concern for evaluation use which has, for me, become the dominant evaluation assumption. While not usually prone to quoting the Bible, I am nonetheless now reminded of the saying from the book of Matthew: "No man can serve two masters, for either he will hate the one and love the other, or he will be devoted to the one and despise the other" (Matthew 6:24). The proliferation of decision makers or stakeholders, in my view, decreases the likelihood that an evaluator can be sufficiently attentive to the information needs of each (and I would maintain that there would usually be differences in these information needs). Note also the previously discussed assumption (Assumption 3) related to providing information in a form that can be effectively used. Thus, when one conceives of multiple decision makers/stakeholders, the effectiveness of the evaluation is reduced (using "potential use" as the primary effectiveness criterion).

EVALUATION NEED AREAS

An understanding of the evaluation need areas presented in ETD is best viewed within the historical context that produced them. I think it is fair to say that in the early 1960s, evaluation was generally viewed as related to performance and outcome measures. Within that context, Cronbach's paper on "Course Improvement through Evaluation" was extremely important.[15] The idea that someone as prestigious as Cronbach sanctioned alternative purposes for evaluation provided impetus for a series of writings on "evaluation theory." Scriven's important monograph formalized and expanded on the notions put forth by Cronbach by making the formative-summative distinction that we know all too well.[16] Both of these works called attention to different kinds of evaluation or different purposes of evaluation. Consequently, in the middle and late 1960s a number of theorists attempted to define the various dimensions or kinds of evaluation. In particular, Stufflebeam presented his Context, Input, Process, Product (CIPP) model; Provus's notion of Discrepancy Evaluation also depicted specific evaluation stages.[17]

The evaluation need areas presented in ETD were part of that intellectual stream of thought. "Systems assessment" (subsequently renamed "needs assessment") was in many ways similar to Stufflebeam's context evaluation. "Program planning evaluation" was a more unique entity that recognized the important evaluative function of determining the extent to which the program plan, as a statement written prior to implementation, was conceptually sound and had a reasonable face-valid relationship to the desired outcomes. Thus, the examination of a program plan in terms of its assumptions, intents, and stipulated procedures was recognized as a valid evaluation role. The validity of these stipulated procedures was examined in terms of their logical relationships to desired outcomes as well as through an examination of relevant literature.

The next two need areas (program implementation evaluation and program improvement) focused on the formative stage, but recognized the distinction between implementation (process) and improvement (outcomes).

"Program certification" was similar to summative evaluation. The term for this need area stemmed from a long-held belief that there really was no such thing as a "summative evaluation" in which a program is no longer undergoing change. The implications of the term "summative evaluation" appeared to be so heavily allied with performing a research-like evaluation that I distanced myself from it. (Indeed, I have long thought that the term "summary formative" or simply "summary" would be more appropriate for describing this evaluation area.)

Do I still agree with these evaluation need areas? Generally, yes! They are reasonable areas about which an evaluation can provide information. One could make changes, however. Indeed, I subsequently suggested the need for distinguishing the process and product summative evaluation areas. I did this by creating a category called "documentation evaluation" in which the program process is fully documented before it is considered for broader implementation.[18] A number of additional need areas were suggested by a National Academy of Science committee of which I was a member.[19] And, I would certainly consider evaluability assessment[20] as another candidate for inclusion. However, were I rewriting ETD at this time

I probably would not bother to focus on these changes. Simply put, I am not that excited about need areas as the primary focus in defining evaluation. Although the evaluation need areas provide a context for thinking about the evaluation, for better understanding the nature of possible user concerns, and for considering the adequacy of prior evaluation stages (and thus making appropriate stipulations in the evaluation), a need area focus is "overblown." I react quite negatively to thinking that defines each need area as a unique set of step-by-step evaluative procedures. The personal aspects of evaluation behavior are much more important.

Change Influences

There are many ways in which theorists come to modify their views on evaluation—and even ultimately their written "theories," although this comes to pass much more slowly. Many of these change influences were outlined in a paper by Alkin and Ellett.[21] In this section, I will consider the change influences and discuss some of the ways in which they may have caused me to reflect on my views of evaluation and ultimately to modify them.

CONFRONTATION WITH ONE'S OWN THEORIES AND OTHERS' INTERPRETATION OF THEM

The simplest kind of confrontation with one's own views (and potentially the most discouraging) is a letter from a practitioner who claims to be an advocate, a devotee, or an adherent to your theoretic position. Sometimes, these "groupie" letters can be alarming: you struggle to distance yourself from overly simplistic statements that aren't quite what you thought was "you." You feel the strong urge to go to the window and yell "I don't know Harry Holmes from Hilo, Hawaii, and his views of evaluation *do not* correspond to mine." And you further think, "Please, please let him not write an article citing me." While such confrontational stimuli provide an uncomfortable few moments, or hours, they very rarely are powerful enough to overcome inertia and disrupt an already busy schedule to review old publications and rewrite them. However, seeds for potential change are planted.

A more powerful stimulus to action are the views and interpretations of colleagues, particularly those whom you know and respect. (The opinions of others can be more easily rationalized and discounted.) As Ellett and I have noted: "Portrayal of one's evaluation theory by others often leads to stark interpretations—perhaps different from what theorists thought they had said or from views currently held."[22] I have noticed these interpretations in various evaluation textbooks that present overviews of theories.[23] A better example of the influence of others' interpretations of one's theories presented itself during my guest lectures in a colleague's introductory course in evaluation at UCLA. Popham's views on evaluation are different from mine and his questions forced me to struggle to understand his interpretations of decision-and-user oriented evaluations and to clarify my own thinking. In particular, I now better understand the bounds of the evaluator in framing the evaluation issues.

CONFRONTATION WITH OTHER THEORIES

We might read the views of another evaluation theorist, perhaps in a journal article, and find a basis for comparison with our own thoughts about evaluation. Alternatively, other evaluation theorists might suggest avenues or strategies that we had not previously considered. These kinds of confrontations may lead us to modify our own views of evaluation. A theorist also might read (or "be confronted with," as I am now describing it) the views of a theorist who is not in evaluation. The potential applicability of such ideas to evaluation might alter one's own views—and in some cases the results may be quite dramatic. Probably the classic example is found in the work of House, who has shown in a number of his papers the influence of John Rawls.[24] More dramatic is the way in which the book by Perelman and Olbrechts-Tyteca formed the primary intellectual basis for House's monograph *The Logic of Evaluative Argument*.[25]

In most instances, it is difficult to identify specific "confrontations" that have had dramatic influence. One can more easily point to shadings of disagreement with the works of some authors and other interesting thoughts that were ultimately incorporated into one's own views. And so what follows for me is a potpourri of ideas proposed by other theorists upon which I have reflected—accepting some, rejecting others—but in most instances these ideas have had some impact upon my own views of evaluation. Clearly, they represent only a very limited listing of such instances.

Stake's work has always been a source of intellectual stimulation for me. His work on stakeholders[26] has led me to reflect upon the role that interested constituencies ought to play within an evaluation.

Stake's discussion of stakeholders has led me to distinguish between various stakeholder roles: (a) stakeholder as primary user; (b) stakeholder as a source of information for framing the evaluation; (c) stakeholder as a source of data during the evaluation; and (d) stakeholder as audience for the evaluation report.

With respect to the first of these roles, an important stakeholder might be identified as a primary user in many instances, but this is not always the case, and certainly this role does not apply to all stakeholders. I am guided in my views on evaluation by the evidence that where there is an interested potential user (or limited number of users) who wants the evaluation information and is in a position to do something about it, use will occur. Thus, since *all* stakeholders are not necessarily the primary potential users of the evaluation, their role in my view is diminished.

Even if some stakeholders are not identified as primary users, they still may be an important source for framing the evaluation. However, this is not, in my view, the evaluator's prerogative. Information about the stakeholder's expectations for the evaluation could conceivably be utilized as input to the primary user or to primary user groups as they frame the evaluation; but, this is not a foregone conclusion. I have real problems about the extent to which the evaluator independently acquires information from stakeholders on their desired evaluation without the interest and the concurrence of primary users.

Stakeholders as a source of data? There are many sources of data that might be examined within the course of an evaluation. Various stakeholders can provide valuable information about the program, that is, they can be an important part of the database. Does that mean that they should always be a part of the database? Not always, and certainly inclusion of information from this source would be dependent upon the issues identified by primary users before and during the evaluation.

Finally, there may be many audiences for an evaluation report. Various stakeholders very likely would be potential recipients of the report. Again, this is determined by the nature of the evaluation issues, etc.

Another confrontation with evaluation theories is found in my consideration of the work of Michael Patton. In this case the confrontation is really more of a reaffirmation and redefinition of positions I have long held. Patton read much of my early work on evaluation and decision making and undoubtedly was influenced, to some extent, by this work. I, on the other hand, have greatly respected

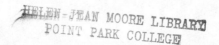

his ability to articulate and extend these views. Thus, these evaluation positions, placed into writing and expanded, have presented the opportunity for further reflection. His identification of the "active-reactive-adaptive" role[27] prompted reflection on my own views and reinforced some of them. I had long recognized a necessity for the evaluator to play an active role in the conduct of the evaluation. My own research on evaluation utilization (to be discussed subsequently) reaffirmed the necessity of an active, involved evaluator, one whose presence increased the likelihood of utilization. The notion of "reactive" had undoubtedly been present in my writings from the time of the 1969 ETD. That is, the evaluator needed to work with decision makers to help them identify decision areas of concerns; thus, the evaluator was responding to information needs. Unfortunately, this notion was a kind of static reaction that failed to identify changing needs and changing user concerns. So, the notion of an adapting, reacting evaluator interacting with and sensitive to the *changing* nature of evaluation concerns—rather than being statically fixed on identified decisions—was one that had begun to emerge in my thinking and whose development had been greatly enhanced by Patton's work.

Confrontation with other theories takes place in a number of different ways. Sometimes the confrontation leads to agreement and clarification of one's own views. Other times one finds that he is in disagreement with the viewpoint and through this disagreement clarifies his own views. Several minor examples will perhaps suffice. Patton comments that there is no need for an evaluation report: one of the areas of decision that he focuses on with potential users is determining whether an evaluation report is necessary. In my own writings I have routinely discussed the evaluation report presented by evaluators without giving very much active thought to whether I thought such reports were necessary. While I do not find difficulty agreeing intellectually with Patton on the notion that there may be situations where written reports are not required, I find that in the fifty or sixty evaluations I have done, each has included a written report. I maintain that evaluators can (and should) be inventive in the way in which they report their findings and ought to be attentive to presenting information in as user-friendly a manner as possible; however, I am unable at this point to accept the notion of no written documentation of the findings whatsoever.

As another example, I find Wholey's notion of "evaluability assessment" quite appealing.[28] These ideas go beyond those I have stated over the years that relate to the necessity of the evaluator "framing the decision context."[29] I feel that it is important to identify the likelihood that reasonable information can be collected within the available budget and that the evaluation will have sufficient value to be usable. Although the notion of conducting an evaluability assessment is quite appealing, I am struck by the formality of the procedure and personally would advocate that the evaluator engage in a more informal assessment of the likely impact of any evaluation in relation to its costs at its outset.

CONFRONTATION WITH CONSOLIDATION AND CATEGORIZATION SCHEMES

It is said we are known by the company we keep. In categorization schemes our company is cast upon us. Struggles with thoughts about what we have in common with our newfound "bedfellows" may lead to further changes in our theoretic positions on evaluation. Put simply, if we believe that we don't fit in the same category as a particular theorist, we struggle to determine the attribute of our written theoretic position that might have led to the unwanted classification, and we subsequently reflect on its continued pertinence to our views.

A number of evaluation category systems have been produced over the years. In most such listings, I have been categorically linked with Daniel Stufflebeam.[30] In the years that I refer to as "early Alkin" (the 1960s and 1970s) I found this to be appropriate. More recently I have not found this to be a comfortable classification fit. One reaction to these category systems is the development of a system of my own,[31] in which I place myself squarely in a user-oriented evaluation "camp" along with Michael Patton; this category is associated with a subcategory of decision-oriented evaluators (such as Stufflebeam and Malcolm Provus).

More recently, a student of mine conducted a data-based study using multidimensional scaling to classify theorists based upon the pattern of their responses to theory and practice issues.[32] In this category system I note that in terms of the pattern of responses I am most closely allied with Robert Stake and next most closely allied with Ernest House and Michael Patton, and then with Elliot Eisner and Michael Scriven. This recent study has prompted me to consider what aspects of my stated views on evaluation caused me to be categorically placed closer to Stake than to Patton and placed closer to Eisner than I previously would have predicted. Have my views on the role of the evaluator—that is, as a skilled professional who has personal impact upon an evaluation—placed my thinking closer to an evaluation connoisseurship than I had realized? This is an area of current introspection.

ONE'S OWN RESEARCH

When theorists conduct research about evaluation and the evaluation process, insights are often gained which enrich their theoretical perspectives. A study that I conducted with several of my students in the early 1970s provided such an instance. We examined the relationships among characteristics of Title VII evaluation reports (primarily methodology and size) and the impact on federal decision making (subsequent budget, perceived quality) and local decision making (stated impact).[33] There was little evidence of a relationship between the evaluation report and budget changes, which reinforced views that I had on the importance of evaluation report timing. More importantly, the success of the evaluation in the view of local decision makers (often unrelated to evaluation report characteristics) led me to question my prior emphasis on the evaluation report as the output of the evaluator's activities. The impact of an evaluation is not based simply on a final report, but on the more informal interim reporting activities as well as by the evaluation process itself. This study had impact on my theoretic views of evaluation and also provided the impetus for my thinking about users rather than decision makers and led to my subsequent studies of evaluation utilization.

The various evaluation utilization studies provided understanding into the conditions under which evaluation was most likely to have impact.[34] Convinced of the importance of the evaluator working in ways that "make a difference," my own views about evaluation have thus been shaped further. Some of these views on the appropriate characteristics and actions of evaluators were summarized in a paper at the 1985 meeting of the American Educational Research Association: "While the factors cited by evaluators tended to confirm the utilization framework already developed, users' comments suggested some additional factors that . . . merit further discussion for the insight they give into utilization: level of evaluator effort, leadership behavior, user involvement, evaluation reporting, evaluator involvement in implementing recommendations."[35]

A study of the costs of evaluation[36] provided further evidence of evaluation as a costly endeavor, particularly as it related to professional personnel costs. As a consequence I became more conscious of the need to devise effective means of conducting evaluations. Evaluators can do far more than is typically done within restrictive budgets by being creative in the way in which they organize their time to accomplish specified activities. Thus, notions about evaluation as a management task have become more prominent in my thinking.

An evaluation always provides an opportunity to field test the currency of one's theoretic views. Performing an evaluation is not likely to modify one's perspective drastically; instead, each situation presents new challenges and new ways of thinking about specific procedural issues. (A general prescription that I might offer is that those who write about evaluation should spend more time *doing* evaluations.)

Years of evaluating integration programs in the Los Angeles Unified School District have taught me that the process of obtaining agreement and approvals can be painstakingly slow, and that each step of the evaluation process must sometimes be approached with caution. Is this unique to the Los Angeles school district? Certainly not! Rather, it is a lesson to be learned and incorporated into one's evaluation model as it pertains to a certain class of evaluation situations.

About eight years ago, I was contracted to do an evaluation of a Title VII program of a very small local school district. The "program" to be evaluated was virtually nonexistent, and the desired outcomes were not well specified. One possible approach to the situation might have been to say, "When you get a program and you know what you want evaluated, let me know." The situation forced me to face the issue of the role of the evaluator in helping to frame program objectives and, through feedback on implementation (or lack thereof), provide guidance for the creation of a program. As a consequence of that experience, I was more willing to accept a proactive role for evaluators—but within limits.

Conducting evaluations in field settings (as opposed to stating positions in theoretical writings) imposes cost constraints upon the evaluator. Conflict between wanting to conduct a quality evaluation and having to work within the available budget made me more attentive to devising efficient evaluation methods for a study in the Grossmont (CA) High School District. This was an implementation evaluation in which a district administrator, as the primary user, wanted a monthly report on the program's implementation. The report was obtained by developing an efficient program monitoring system for all program elements and using a form that was up-dated each month. The efficiency of the program monitoring procedure[37] assured that resources would be available for a monthly interview and document review associated with a qualitative evaluation on a specific topic.

A project at the University of California, Santa Barbara, provides another example of the use of efficient procedures—and more. This three-year project, which influences mathematics teaching in two counties, had reasonably well-defined objectives specified in its National Science Foundation proposal. The evaluation design statement that I prepared started with the NSF objectives, then presented interpretations, understandings, and operationalizations, and concluded with a three-year timeline of associated evaluator activities and products. The evaluation design statement/timeline (entered into the computer) provided the opportunity to record the completion of individual tasks, modifications, and deletions, and allowed us to add evaluation activities to meet new needs as they emerged. The original document plus the six dated "up-date versions" provide a historical perspective on the operationalization of a user-oriented adaptive/reactive approach. I know it is possible. I have done it.

About fifteen years ago I had opportunity to conduct an evaluation of the educational program of the juvenile detention facilities of another western state. This experience helped me to understand how far an evaluator's credibility can lead him when he finds that a program is "an educational disaster area." More importantly, it convinced me of the importance of user involvement and participation at important stages of the evaluation. It seems that an influential member of the state legislature was an observer at a portion of the evaluation review. He concurred with my "educational disaster area" assessment and was able to mute objections to my opinion, which was quoted in the state's newspapers.

My work with the California Community College Chancellor's office in developing a procedure for the evaluation of the Extended Opportunities Programs and Services (EOPS) program provided me with an opportunity to test the extent to which informed and interested users could extend the evaluator's capabilities and further enhance utilization. My work with Ron Dyste and subsequently Rod Tarrer and Peter White led to the requirement of reports from colleges responding to evaluation findings and recommendations; it also triggered subsequent interaction between the Chancellor's office and colleges based on the evaluation recommendations. Moreover, the yearly program application forms on which colleges indicate their activities and functions for the upcoming year have been modified to allow for the inclusion of subsequent evaluation feedback directly on the forms, thereby making the process more meaningful to the colleges.

Finally, I would cite my experience with the Caribbean Agricultural Extension Program. As the head of an evaluation team (with Michael Patton as client and primary user), I have had the opportunity to observe (and partially to frame) the optimal role of an informed utilization-oriented client. I believe that in these roles Patton and I have both learned more about the capabilities of the user-oriented evaluator, the extent of impact of use-oriented clients, and the interaction between the two.[38]

INFLUENCES OF PERSONAL INTERACTIONS

Since the time of my earliest writings on evaluation, I have recognized that my own evaluation stance is quite different from those whose orientation leans more to "evaluation as research." Although I have understood in general terms the implications of the distinction between these points of view, the interchanges that I have had over the years with Carol Weiss have greatly illuminated significant differences between a research orientation to evaluation and a utilization orientation. For instance, Weiss had the following to say during a discussion about the differences between these two views: "We're talking about decision making as if information leads to decisions. Decisions are the product of enormous numbers of interacting variables . . . so many things besides information. Even the best and the greatest evaluations only minimally affect how decisions get made."[39] Weiss's position is that evaluation is to be problem-oriented, rather than person-oriented, and that the impact of evaluation will be the solution of a problem, rather than an impact on a particular person.

Further Thoughts on Current Views

As I reflect on the original ETD, my reactions to it, and the various change influences, some additional personal thoughts emerge. Over the years I have been struck by the way in which most of the writing in evaluation (including my own) tends to be mechanistic and prescriptive in nature, seeming to imply that there are certain specific procedures to be followed, or certain protocols which, if done properly, will lead to a professional and expert evaluation. What bothers me about all this is that I have become convinced over the years that even though the human aspects of evaluation are very critical, they are often not discussed; indeed, they are largely ignored in the evaluation literature. We know that since evaluations are conducted by human beings, the personal element is of necessity present. These human beings (evaluators) have personal qualities that affect the way in which an evaluation is conducted. We know certain things from our research on evaluation utilization about the conditions under which evaluators can be most effective (and I suspect other things from my own observations and conduct of evaluations).

Successful evaluators must be intelligent so that they are able to understand situations and make reasonable choices and decisions. They must act in a professional manner so that their status and the legitimacy of their results are not questioned. Evaluators must be sensitive to situations and must understand organizational dynamics. It is easy to picture an evaluator going through the motions of collecting data that are meaningless because the evaluator did not understand the organizational context in which those data were collected. Moreover, evaluators must be skilled in personal dynamics; they must be able to recognize that the kinds of interrelationships that they develop will influence the way in which they are able to collect data and the respect and accord that are ultimately provided to their evaluation.

Another aspect about the nature of the evaluator that I have learned from my research on utilization is that evaluators must *want* to do an evaluation that will make a difference. Such an orientation increases the likelihood that evaluators will pursue evaluative studies that are meaningful and likely to be used. And, I am convinced that the desire to make a difference is more likely to orient evaluators toward "likely users."

The evaluator has bounds on the extent to which the evaluation conducted can be oriented *solely* toward issues of concern to preidentified potential users. The alternatives in this regard are very tricky and constitute an issue that I have struggled with for a number of years. To the extent to which the potential users identify issues of concern that appear to be unethical, illegal, immoral, or just downright wrong, what is the evaluator to do? My own view is that the appropriate stance for an evaluator is to point out initially potential dilemmas and concerns that relate to these identified areas. In short, the evaluator may try to use the persuasion of logical argument to modify the potential issues. But what if they can't be modified? If the issues of concern are unethical, illegal, or immoral, then clearly the evaluator could and should decline from participating in the evaluation. If, on the other hand they are, in the judgment of the evaluator, simply wrong or slightly off target, the question remains can the evaluator, within those constraints, still provide information that is likely to have a positive impact upon the program? These are issues with which evaluators must deal in determining whether they can in good conscience participate in an evaluation.

Now with respect to methodology, I believe that in performing an evaluation, evaluators may call upon whatever methodologies are appropriate, consistent with the desire to engage in systematic data collection. I am not bound to particular methodological techniques. Indeed, depending upon the nature of the issues on which data are being collected, the evaluator should be open to using whatever methods are appropriate, and indeed, "inventing" methodologies that fit the situation. The evaluator must be consistently and continuously aware of the need for data collection activities to be conducted in as systematic a manner as possible; yet, the evaluation must not be so severely limited by this constraint that user concerns are not addressed.

Analysis procedures that are employed should be appropriate to the data collected, and analyses should always be done in a way that recognizes the evaluator's obligation to communicate to potential users. This communication should be in forms that are meaningful and likely to enhance the possibility of use. The evaluator's job is not to "dazzle" or to impress with sophisticated expertise, but rather to *communicate* in ways that demonstrate that systematic work has taken place and that stress the presence of the issues to be resolved.

Postnote. And so Gretchen and Karin, I ask you, "Who is the Marvin C. Alkin today? What are his evaluation views? Would you know from this paper?" I think, hopefully, that you will have a somewhat better understanding of my work. But, given the limitations of theoretical writings, our "off paper" interactions would provide you with insights well beyond this chapter.

FOOTNOTES

1. Carol H. Weiss, "Evaluation for Decisions: Is Anybody There? Does Anybody Care?" *Evaluation Practice* 9, no. 1 (1988): 5-19; idem, "If Program Decisions Hinged Only on Information: A Response to Patton," *Evaluation Practice* 9, no. 3 (1988): 15-28; Michael Q. Patton, "The Evaluator's Responsibility for Utilization," *Evaluation Practice* 9, no. 2 (1988): 5-24; idem, "How Primary Is Your Identity as an Evaluator?" *Evaluation Practice* 9, no. 2 (1988): 87-92.

2. Marvin C. Alkin, "An Approach to Evaluation Theory Development," *Studies in Educational Evaluation* 5, no. 2 (1979): 125-127.

3. Egon G. Guba, " 'The New Rhetoric' of Egon Guba Compared to That of 10 Years Ago," *Studies in Educational Evaluation* 5, no. 2 (1979): 139.

4. A friend and colleague, Frederick Ellett, upon reacting to a draft of this chapter, felt that I should say the following: "I think you need to rephrase or reword 'your *personal views* on evaluation.' For what 'your personal views' really amount to in this context is 'your *theoretical views*,' which happened to have focused primarily on evaluation use, views that have been problem (theory)-driven and responsive to various change influences. . . . You should not portray your views as merely personal; your paper nicely demonstrates how your theoretical stance, claims, and conceptions have been responsive to theoretically relevant material."

5. Marvin C. Alkin, "Evaluation Theory Development," *Evaluation Comment* 2, no. 1 (1969): 2-7.

6. Ibid., p. 2.

7. Alkin, "An Approach to Evaluation Theory Development"; ibid., *A Guide for Evaluation Decision Makers* (Beverly Hills, CA: Sage Publications, 1985).

8. Alkin, "An Approach to Evaluation Theory Development."

9. Joint Committee on Standards for Educational Evaluation, *Standards for Evaluations of Educational Programs, Projects, and Materials* (New York: McGraw-Hill, 1981).

10. In the 1960s we were much less sensitive to sexually biased language. My belated apologies.

11. Daniel Stufflebeam, William J. Foley, William J. Gephart, Egon G. Guba, Robert L. Hammond, Howard O. Merriman, and Malcolm M. Provus, *Educational Evaluation and Decision Making* (Itasca, IL.: F. E. Peacock Publishers, 1971).

12. Alkin, "Evaluation Theory Development," p. 2.

13. Ibid.

14. Ibid., p. 3.

15. Lee J. Cronbach, "Course Improvement through Evaluation," *Teachers College Record* 64 (1963): 672-683.

16. Michael Scriven, "The Methodology of Evaluation," in *Perspectives of Curriculum Evaluation*, ed. Robert E. Stake, AERA Monograph Series on Curriculum Evaluation, no. 1 (Chicago: Rand McNally, 1967), pp. 39-83.

17. Malcolm M. Provus, *Discrepancy Evaluation* (Berkeley, CA: McCutchan Publishing Corp., 1971).

18. Marvin C. Alkin and Carol T. Fitz-Gibbon, "Methods and Theories of Evaluating Programs," *Journal of Research and Development in Education* 8, no. 3 (1975): 2-15.

19. Senta A. Raizen and Peter H. Rossi, eds., *Program Evaluation in Education: When? How? To What Ends?* (Washington, DC: National Academy Press, 1981).

20. Joseph S. Wholey, *Evaluation: Promise and Performance* (Washington, DC: Urban Institute, 1979).

21. Marvin C. Alkin and Frederick Ellett, "The Human Activity of Evaluation Theorizing," Center for the Study of Evaluation Working Paper, no. 28 (Los Angeles: Center for the Study of Evaluation, University of California at Los Angeles, 1979).

22. Ibid., p. 9.

23. For example, see Blaine R. Worthen and James R. Sanders, *Educational Evaluation: Theory and Practice* (Worthington, OH: Charles A. Jones, 1973).

24. See Ernest R. House, *Evaluating with Validity* (Beverly Hills, CA: Sage Publications, 1980).

25. Chaim Perelman and L. Olbrechts-Tyteca, *The New Rhetoric: A Treatise on Argumentation* (Notre Dame, IN: University of Notre Dame Press, 1969); Ernest R. House, *The Logic of Evaluative Argument*, Monograph Series on Evaluation, no. 7 (Los Angeles: Center for the Study of Evaluation, University of California at Los Angeles, 1977).

26. Robert E. Stake, "A Theoretical Statement of Responsive Evaluation," *Studies in Educational Evaluation* 2, no. 1 (1976): 19-22.

27. Michael Q. Patton, *Utilization-focused Evaluation*, 2d ed. (Beverly Hills, CA: Sage Publications, 1986), pp. 307-309.

28. Wholey, *Evaluation: Promise and Performance*.

29. Marvin C. Alkin, *Framing the Decision Context*, AERA Cassette Series in Evaluation (Washington, DC: American Educational Research Association, 1976).

30. See Ernest R. House, "Assumptions Underlying Evaluation Models," *Educational Researcher* 7, no. 3 (1978): 4-12; W. James Popham, *Educational Evaluation* (Englewood Cliffs, NJ: Prentice-Hall, 1975); Gene V Glass and Frederick S. Ellett, Jr., "Evaluation Research," in *Annual Review of Psychology* 31 (1980): 211-228.

31. Marvin C. Alkin and Frederick Ellett, "Evaluation Models and Their Development," in *International Encyclopedia of Education: Research and Studies*, ed. Torsten Húsen and T. Neville Postlethwaite (Oxford, England: Pergamon Press, 1985).

32. Janice E. Williams, "A Numerically Developed Taxonomy of Evaluation Theory and Practice," *Evaluation Review* 13, no. 1 (1989): 18-31.

33. Marvin C. Alkin, Jacqueline Kosecoff, Carol Fitz-Gibbon, and Richard Seligman, *Evaluation and Decision Making: The Title VII Experience*, Monograph Series in Evaluation, No. 4 (Los Angeles: Center for the Study of Evaluation, University of California at Los Angeles, 1974).

34. Marvin C. Alkin, Richard Daillak, and Peter White, *Using Evaluations: Does Evaluation Make a Difference?* (Beverly Hills, CA: Sage Publications, 1979); Marvin C. Alkin, Brian M. Stecher, and Frederica L. Geiger, *Title I Evaluation: Utility and Factors Influencing Use* (Northridge, CA: Educational Evaluation Associates, 1982); Brian M. Stecher, Marvin C. Alkin, and Gretchen Flesher, *Patterns of Information Use in School Level Decision Making*, Report no. 160 (Los Angeles: Center for the Study of Evaluation, University of California at Los Angeles, 1981).

35. Joan Ruskus and Marvin C. Alkin, "Factors Common to High-Utilization Evaluations" (Paper presented at the Annual Meeting of the American Educational Research Association, Chicago, 1985), p. 6.

36. Marvin C. Alkin and Brian M. Stecher, "A Study of Evaluation Costs," in *The Costs of Evaluation*, ed. Marvin C. Alkin and Lewis C. Solmon (Beverly Hills, CA: Sage Publications, 1983), pp. 119-132.

37. See Jean King, Lynn L. Morris, and Carol T. Fitz-Gibbon, "How to Assess Program Implementation," in *Program Evaluation Kit*, ed. J. Herman (Beverly Hills, CA: Sage Publications, 1987), p. 124.

38. See Marvin C. Alkin and Michael Q. Patton, "Working Both Sides of the Street," in *The Client Perspective on Evaluation*, ed. Jeri Nowakowski, New Directions for Program Evaluation, no. 36 (San Francisco: Jossey-Bass, 1988), pp. 19-32.

39. Marvin C. Alkin, *Debates on Evaluation* (Beverly Hills, CA: Sage Publications, 1990), p. 43.

Quasi-Experimentation

In the early days of modern program evaluation in education, the favored design was the true experiment. Subjects in a properly selected sample would be randomly assigned to either a treatment or a control group; there would be a pretest and a posttest; and the nineteenth-century British philosopher John Stuart Mill's logical "method of difference" would be applied—the only systematic difference between the experimental and control groups would lie in the treatment that the experimental group would receive. Mill argued persuasively that if analysis of the posttest showed that there was a real (these days we would say significant) difference between the two groups, then that difference had to have been caused by the only factor with respect to which the groups differed; in other words, the treatment was the *cause* of the difference in results. In modern terminology—due chiefly to Donald Campbell—it is said that if properly carried out, an experimental study has a high degree of internal validity.

Fairly quickly, several lines of debate opened up. In the first place, it was argued that true experiments were highly impractical—they were very difficult to conduct in real-life educational settings. For in nonlaboratory settings it was next to impossible to ensure that the experimental and control groups only differed in one respect (the treatment). Chance events like strikes, sickness, and of course attrition (which might or might not be random) were all common threats to the validity of the design and could easily lower internal validity.

Second, it was argued by some (and especially by Lee J. Cronbach and his associates) that evaluators should be more concerned about generalizability of results to other settings than with narrow internal validity. Cronbach argued that to foster generalizability, a design must have high external validity, and unfortunately there was a trade-off required because most often features that maximized external validity lowered internal validity. Campbell responded in defense of internal validity, which he regarded as the *sine qua non* of a design.

Third, it became clear that randomization was often impossible in real-life settings. Schools and other organizations often assign individuals to groups in some systematic way, nullifying the logic of

113

the true experiment. Donald Campbell, and later Cook and Campbell, led the discussion of the logic of quasi-experimental designs—designs that resemble true experiments in all but this one crucial feature. By careful and ingenious planning, it seemed possible (at least to a degree) to guard against the threats to the validity of these quasi designs, and they became very popular among evaluators.

In the following discussion, Thomas Cook traces the history of the recent debates over these interrelated issues.

CHAPTER V

Clarifying the Warrant for Generalized Causal Inferences in Quasi-Experimentation

THOMAS D. COOK

As its etymology suggests, quasi-experimentation is "almost-like" experimentation. But it is not much like experimentation as it is practiced in the natural sciences where materials are often inert, considerable control over testing conditions is possible, and numerically precise predictions are commonplace. Quasi-experimentation evolved from a tradition of experimentation developed by R. A. Fisher for applied agriculture where the treatments are long-lasting, the organisms are growing, and testing has to occur outside the laboratory. Fisher seems to have had little interest in explaining why a particular fertilizer or plant type influenced plant growth, and so his theory of design did not deal in detail with decomposing the cause and effect variables or specifying mediating influences that might have occurred after a treatment varied and before an effect was observed. Fisher's work assumes a "black box" theory of descriptive causation that operates at the molar level of observed manipulanda and outcomes. Its strength lies in identifying what made a difference, not in explaining why a cause-effect relationship came about.

To justify inferences about such descriptive causal connections, Fisher developed a structural theory of research design. It emphasizes when observations are made (with the distinction between pre- and posttreatment measurement being paramount); whether comparison groups are used (with a no-treatment control group being especially salient); and how units are assigned to treatments (with random assignment being preferred but with other modes of controlled assignment not being excluded—e.g., Latin-square designs). In both its purpose and structural attributes, modern quasi-experimentation is like the experimentation Fisher pioneered, except that random assignment is not achieved—by definition! Quasi-experimentation does not have much in common with experiments in the natural sciences, though we later note one way in which the similarity has been increasing.

The last thirty years of systematic program evaluation have witnessed two sets of changes worth discussing in the theory of quasi-experimentation as Donald Campbell and his collaborators have developed it.[1] The first set of changes is internal to the theory. They are not radical, but neither are they trivial. They concern changes in the intellectual warrant justifying the molar descriptive causal conclusions to which all experimentation is addressed: changes in the statistical techniques and rationales now being offered for analyzing quasi-experimental data, and changes in the way "internal" and "external" validity are now understood and in the way debates about their priority are framed.

The second set of changes concerns the role quasi-experimental methods should play within program evaluation. Suchman argued that they should be dominant.[2] He reasoned that the most important evaluation questions deal with *causal* effectiveness; that designs without pretests and comparison groups are "unscientific" and cannot support causal conclusions; that the preferred scientific option is the randomized experiment, but this option can rarely be implemented in field settings; and that quasi-experiments constitute the best fallback option since they were developed for testing causal hypotheses in real-world settings where random assignment is not possible but pretests and comparison groups often are. Suchman's assumptions have come under fire from different quarters for different reasons. The net effect of these attacks has been to dethrone quasi-experimentation from the pinnacle it occupied within evaluation during the 1960s and 1970s. Today it is just one of the many cause-probing techniques available to evaluators who can justify the primacy of descriptive causal questions.

Changes Internal to the Theory of Quasi-Experimentation

THE INTELLECTUAL WARRANT SHARPENED

The intellectual warrant for the randomized experiment is quite clear and comes from sampling theory. If a correct randomization procedure is correctly implemented, the expected pretreatment difference between experimental comparison groups is fully known and will be zero. Sampling theory also indicates the forces on which this warrant depends. Sample sizes have to be large relative to variances; and there must be no treatment-correlated attrition. This is because random assignment creates group comparability *at the pretest*, while Mill's canons require posttest comparability in all things other than treatment exposure. When the assumptions of sampling theory are met, random assignment distributes all known and unknown causes of the dependent variable equally over all the treatment conditions, thereby unconfounding the treatment contrast of substantive interest and all theoretically irrelevant causal forces.

Wanting to develop methods for cause-probing research with long-lasting treatments in open-system contexts, Campbell sought to identify the particular alternative causes that random assignment rules out.[3] He used his own and others' experience to generate a list of these, concentrating on theoretically mundane, nuisance factors that had repeatedly bedevilled causal inference in the past, calling these "threats to internal validity." They are by now well-known and include: selection, history, statistical regression, maturation, instrumentation, and testing, as well as interactions between these forces (e.g., selection-maturation and selection-history). All these threats are assumed to be empirical products and hence subject to modification as experience accumulates. Thus, if a particular alternative interpretation is shown to operate rarely or weakly it would not be retained in the Pantheon of threats. On the other hand, experience might indicate the need to add a new internal validity threat to the list of the day.

For Campbell, who has been heavily influenced by Popper's attack on induction and his advocacy of falsification, the key to confident causal conclusions is the ability to construct a persuasive argument that every plausible and identified threat to internal validity has been ruled out in a particular study. This requires assuming that his list of internal validity threats is comprehensive and that the structural design features he emphasized, such as pretests and comparison groups, can support the burden of falsification placed on them. The warrant for descriptive causal inferences from quasi-experiments is thus triadic: (1) only falsification can be logically justified as a means of certain knowledge; (2) the internal validity threats needing falsification are all known; and (3) Fisher's structural design features constitute the best way of ruling out these threats.

This warrant is more complex than the warrant sampling theory provides for the randomized experiment. It is also weaker. First, there is no guarantee that all relevant threats to internal validity have been identified. Campbell's list of threats is not divinely ordained, as can be observed from the growth in the number of threats from Campbell (1957) to Campbell and Stanley (1966) and then Cook and Campbell

(1979).[4] Also, Campbell himself has insisted that threats are better identified from insider knowledge of the particulars of each study than from any abstract and nonlocal list of threats anyone could generate. Second, while it is necessary to assume that only "plausible" threats need to be ruled out, the concept of plausibility is slippery. Later generations often come to treat as mundane the very phenomena that earlier generations had considered "implausible," while many epistemologists and practicing scientists value theories more if they make predictions that are so "implausible" no other theory could generate them. "Plausibility" judgments are fallible, reflecting the social constructions of a particular time and place. The third weakness in Campbell's warrant follows from Kuhn's attack on science for its incommensurability of theories and the inevitability of theory-laden observations.[5] Popper's falsificationist theory can be expressed as a syllogism: The major premise is the research hypothesis; empirical data provide the minor premise; and the conclusion is whether the data prove the hypothesis false. But if one accepts with Kuhn that causal propositions can never be explicit enough in their conditional structure to function as the major premise of a syllogism, and if one also accepts with him that data can never be pure enough to function as the minor premise, then these two points undermine Popper's theory of certain knowledge of what is false.

By about the mid-1970s, Campbell's original warrant for quasi-experiments was in some disarray. Modifications were needed, and Cook and Campbell sought to make them without totally abandoning the need for falsification linked to an empirical theory of internal validity threats.[6] As regards the comprehensiveness of the list of validity threats, Cook and Campbell sought to enlarge the number of threats in general and of internal validity threats in particular. For this they relied both on theory and the reflections of practicing social scientists who had independently identified new threats while on the job. As regards the slippery conceptual understanding of "plausibility," they did not do as much, merely admitting the ambiguities associated with the term and counselling that all interpretations be checked with persons representing a wide spectrum of competing points of view on the topic under analysis. As regards the dependence on falsification, they sought to complement the falsificationist components of Campbell's warrant with a more verificationist component related to his theory of pattern matching.[7] Concretely, they came to emphasize quasi-experimental designs probing causal hypotheses which were quantitatively specific, multivariate-complex, or both. Specificity and complexity of causal prediction gained a new currency. Simplicity was regrettably abandoned.

Quantitatively specific causal expectations were promoted in two ways. One was the interrupted time series. The inferential key here is that with swift-acting cause-effect links (or when a causal delay period is independently known), a clear expectancy exists about the exact time when a change should occur in the level, slope, or variance of a time series. Thus, the research question is: Do the obtained data match the point-specific time pattern predicted? The second mechanism was the regression-discontinuity design. Here, the prediction is that a discontinuity in regression lines should occur at the exact cutoff point that defines treatment exposure, such as the income eligibility criterion for Medicaid or the grade point criterion for going onto the Dean's List. The research question here is: Does an inflection in the response occur at the cutoff point? In each case, a point-specific hypothesis is under test and matching the data to this expectation provides much of the warrant for causal inference.

However, it is not a flawless warrant. With the regression-discontinuity design, for instance, alternatives based on functional form still have to be dealt with. And with the simplest interrupted time series, problems remain with history, instrumentation, and the modeling of error structures. Nonetheless, the point specificity of prediction limits the kinds of history and instrumentation threats that are viable, making them more contingent, i.e., limited to those events that happen exactly when the treatment takes place. When time intervals are short, the likelihood of such threats is reduced and checking on them is more practical. Similar reasoning holds with the regression-discontinuity design. The smaller the category widths on, say, a quantitative income scale used for treatment assignment, the fewer and more complex are the alternative hypotheses remaining.

Cook and Campbell devoted more space to illustrating the benefits of multivariate-complex causal predictions than point-specific ones.[8] "Nonequivalent dependent variable" designs were discussed that depend upon some of the indicators being theoretically responsive to a treatment but all of them being responsive to the known plausible alternative explanations. Categorizing outcome variables in this way leads to a prediction equivalent to a three-way statistical interaction (between time, treatment group, and dependent variable) instead of the simpler two-way interaction that pertains when a treatment is not expected to influence outcomes differently. Complexity of causal expectation is the inferential key in other designs that Cook and

Campbell discussed,[9] including: (1) designs where a treatment is introduced and later reintroduced, leading to the prediction that the pattern of repeated introductions should be mirrored in the pattern of results; (2) designs with nonequivalent groups but with two pretest measurement waves instead of one, so that the two pretest waves could function as a dry run for the later treatment-control contrasts; (3) designs with multiple nonequivalent comparison groups, particularly those where one comparison group initially outperformed the treatment group and the other underperformed it; and (4) designs where respondents or settings were partitioned so as to create subgroups that differed in the level of treatment exposure and hence expected effect size.

These inference-facilitating design features were discussed separately, but were especially emphasized in designs combining many of them so as to increase the number and specificity of the testable implications of a given causal hypothesis. To give just two examples of the particularly complex quasi-experimental designs Cook and Campbell extolled, one was of an interrupted time-series design (1) to which a no-treatment control series was added; (2) where the original intervention was later introduced to the controls; and (3) where the original treatment series was eventually partitioned into two nonequivalent series, only one of which the treatment should theoretically have influenced. We see here an interrupted time-series design being linked to such other cause-facilitating design features as a no-treatment control series, a replicated treatment, and nonequivalent dependent variables. A second example was of a regression-discontinuity study of how Medicaid affected visits to a physician. Eligibility for Medicaid depends on household income and family size. The typical regression-discontinuity design relates income (the eligibility criterion) to the number of physician visits after Medicaid was passed. The design advocated supplemented this with data on income and physician visits prior to Medicaid becoming law. A discontinuity in the number of physician visits was observed at the exact cutoff point in the year after Medicaid was introduced but not before. Realizing they were denied the simple warrant for causal inference that random assignment provides, theorists of quasi-experimentation moved toward advocating more quantitative specificity and multivariate complexity in the causal hypotheses they sought to see tested. Matching specific or complex causal predictions with obtained data became the order of the day,[10] though neither specificity nor complexity was prized for its own sake.

Specificity and complexity were prized only in the implications of a causal hypothesis.

Meehl has lamented the social sciences' dependence on null hypothesis testing, arguing that for any hypothesis there will almost always be some conditions under which, with large enough samples, the null hypothesis will be rejected.[11] To solve this dilemma he counsels testing hypotheses in the form of exact numerical predictions, as often occurs in the natural sciences. Among social scientists, this advice has largely fallen on deaf ears, presumably because outside economics so few theories are capable of point prediction. The quasi-experimental emphasis on point-specific and multivariate-complex causal predictions comes close to the spirit of Meehl's thinking, however. Though no specific numeric predictions are made, point-specific hypotheses are nonetheless made because change is supposed to occur at a specific point in time or at a specific point on a program-eligibility criterion. With multivariate-complex predictions, the similarity to a single numerical point prediction is less apparent. However, the prediction is about a specific and complex pattern of relationships, and even in Meehl's epistemology no uncertainty is reduced if a theory makes a highly specific numerical prediction *that other theories also make.* Specificity (or multivariate complexity) only facilitates causal inference when no other theory makes the same prediction. The more specific or complex the causal implications are, the less likely it is presumed to be that alternative theories can be found that make the same prediction.

We must be careful here not to claim too much, especially for single studies in which chance could generate differences that the causal hypothesis does not predict and could also obscure true hypothesized differences. In addition, the substantive social science theories generating causal predictions are usually so underspecified that disconfirmed hypotheses can still be reformulated, even if this is more difficult the more specific or complex are the data patterns expected. We can never completely escape from the hot seat on which Kuhn has skewered us if deterministic (rather than probabilistic) knowledge is our goal. Nonetheless, the more quantitatively specific or complex *verified* causal predictions are, the more difficult it will usually be to generate alternative interpretations matching the same data pattern. Explicit here is a narrowing of the conceptual distinction between verification and falsification—suggesting that they complement each other as far as molar causal inferences are concerned.

122   QUASI-EXPERIMENTATION

PROGRESS IN STATISTICAL ANALYSIS

Except for general work by Cochran and specific work by Box on time-series analysis, little work on quasi-experiments took place in statistics until the late 1970s.[12] Then Rubin, Holland, and Rosenbaum entered the fray.[13] Their work added to the criticisms of the randomized experiment, offered an explication of the conceptual difficulties with observational studies (statisticians' name for "quasi-experiments"), and provided four prescriptions for improving causal inferences from quasi-experimental work. The net result of this new interest on the part of formal statisticians has been a narrowing (but not elimination!) of the preference gap between randomized experiments *as they are practiced* and the better quasi-experiments.

Statistical theorizing about quasi-experiments did not come from formal statisticians alone. Other relevant (and even overlapping) traditions of data analysis should be noted. One is in microeconomics, particularly in the context of evaluating job training programs. Goldberger began the effort;[14] Ashenfelter formalized it for the case where the selection process into treatment groups is fully known and depends only on observed quantitative criteria, as in the regression-discontinuity design;[15] and Heckman has constructed a list of models for cases where selection into treatment groups depends on unobserved variables.[16] A closely related tradition uses causal modeling techniques like those incorporated into LISREL[17] or EQS[18] in order to adjust for selection differences using "latent" variables rather than fallible indicators. Illustrations of this tradition in evaluation can be seen in Magidson[19] and in Bentler and Woodward,[20] though most work in this tradition is concerned with causal explanatory processes rather than molar causal relations. The third tradition, emerging from within the theory of quasi-experimentation, emphasizes the inevitable assumption-ladenness of causal inferences from quasi-experimental analyses and suggests the need, not only for probing causal hypotheses that have multiple implications, but also for conducting multiple data analyses to probe the robustness of results across different sets of apparently plausible assumptions about selection processes.[21] We shall thread discussion of these three traditions in with our exposition of the analysis changes that statisticians have recently suggested for observational studies.

In all these data-analytic traditions, scholars have explicated limitations to the randomized field experiment over and above those arising from small sample sizes, treatment-correlated attrition, and inadequately implemented randomization procedures. Rubin has particularly called attention to the assumption that there be no or few crossovers from one treatment group to another, calling this his SUTVA assumption (stable-unit-treatment-values). Quasi-experimentalists had earlier sought to describe some of these social processes, labeling one as "resentful demoralization," another as "compensatory equalization," and another as "compensatory rivalry."[22] In their turn, labor economists have drawn attention to many of the circumstances where it is physically, politically, or ethically infeasible to assign at random, and have also noted the restricted generalizability that results when, as is often the case, the ability to assign at random depends on a confluence of fortuitous local circumstances. And causal modelers have stressed how little information experiments provide about the processes mediating molar cause-effect relationships and about the plethora of molar-level variables with which the treatment might interact. Knowing about such matters would, they contend, increase both predictability and the ability to transfer cause-effect knowledge to settings and persons other than those studied to date.

Advocates of the randomized experiment acknowledge most of these objections. But they also note that some of them can be avoided by careful design, others can be measured, while others are not very important. They also note that these criticisms indicate how experiments can be improved, e.g., through adding measures of attrition, implementation, and causal mediation. They therefore persist in believing that randomized experiments, while not perfect, are still superior to their alternatives when it comes to describing molar causal connections. Even so, random assignment is not always feasible, and some studies that begin as randomized experiments will end up as quasi-experiments because of the differential attrition that results when treatments differ in desirability and have to do so in order to have conceptual integrity. Quasi-experimental data analyses are here to stay. They are a necessity, not a refuge for those too sloppy to do randomized experiments. Realizing this, the statisticians we are discussing believe it is myopic to restrict discussion of experiments to those where random assignment has been initially achieved and subsequently maintained.

The statisticians' explication of the difficulties encountered in analyzing observational data begins with two propositions about causation. First, it only applies to entities that can be manipulated; and second, it can only be understood relative to other potential causes. Thus the question: "Is X a cause of Y?" is meaningless to them; but the question: "Is X a stronger cause of Y than Z?" is more meaningful.

In explicating causation this way, the statisticians make Fisher's type of experimentation central, for in his theory treatment contrasts and the manipulation of independent variables are paradigmatic of experimentation.

Statisticians propose three assumptions that have to be "strongly ignorable" if causal conclusions are to be warranted from quasi-experimental data. The first is the SUTVA ("treatment crossover") assumption mentioned earlier. The second is that all units have to have some probability of entering any treatment group, for otherwise perfect colinearities occur. The third and most important assumption is that the data analysis includes all variables correlated with the outcome that are also correlated with the treatment assignment, i.e., the selection process is perfectly modeled with respect to the constructs in the model, how they functionally relate to each other, and how reliably they are measured. While complete knowledge of the selection process is easily achieved with randomized experiments and regression-discontinuity designs, it is extremely difficult to achieve where administrators select individuals into treatment groups on the basis of unobserved attributes or where individuals self-select themselves into groups. Quasi-experiments obviously lack a counterfactual group that is composed of units whose differences from the treatment group are fully known. Were such information available, most analytic problems would fade away.

To handle the missing counterfactual, statisticians suggest designing research with intact groups that have been deliberately chosen so as to reduce initial differences. This we might call the "matching" prescription. Their second suggestion is to collect data on the selection process directly, measuring the most important constructs so as to arrive at a "propensity score."[23] The third prescription is to collect data from additional comparison groups to enable analyses that make different plausible assumptions about selection bias. The final prescription is in the same vein. It is to conduct "sensitivity analyses," to probe how robust the results are when different plausible assumptions are made about the distribution of likely selection biases. Thus, design is preferred over statistical adjustment; complex predictions are preferred over simple ones; multiple analyses making different assumptions about the selection process are preferred over single analyses that presume to build in the single true or best selection model; and direct, though fallible, measurement of selection processes is preferred over no such measurement and an even larger dependence on assumptions.

In these preferences, the statistical tradition coincides with the quasi-experimental tradition. This does not make the traditions identical, however. Quasi-experimentalists emphasize that theoretical predictions can be complicated by means other than adding extra comparison groups, that sensitivity analyses require clear arguments about the likely direction of bias in any one analysis, and that direct measures of the selection process will probably be incomplete or never independently known to be complete. Thus, their writings display even more tentativeness about final inferences than is the case with statisticians, at least for the most discussed case where a single treatment group is contrasted with one or more nonequivalent comparison groups at a single pretest and a single posttest time point.

Labor economists would presumably endorse the four preferences with which the statisticians and quasi-experimentalists agree. However, there are subtle differences in emphasis between the econometric approach and more design-centered approaches. For many years, labor economists have largely relied on statistical adjustment techniques for testing substantive theory in their field. Yet in a reanalysis of annual earnings data from a randomized experiment on job training, LaLonde[24] and Fraker and Maynard[25] have shown that (1) econometric adjustments taken from Heckman's work provide many different estimates of the training program's effects when quasi-experimental control groups are used, and (2) none of these estimates closely coincides with the estimate when randomized controls are used. These reanalyses have led several well-known labor economists to counsel that molar causal inferences can be justified only from randomized experiments, thereby undermining the decade-long work of Heckman and his colleagues on adjustments for selection bias.

In Heckman and Hotz's[26] rejoinder to LaLonde, they used the same job training data to argue that a particular selection model—based on two separate pretreatment measures of annual income—met certain specification tests and generated an average causal effect no different from the estimate provided by the randomized experiment. The claim was therefore made that a perfect selection adjustment had been achieved. Unfortunately, the demonstration is not very convincing. At the data level, there is the problem of model generality,[27] since the two-wave selection process that fit for youths who were just entering the labor market did not fit for AFDC mothers who were returning to it. Heckman and Hotz invoked a simpler cross-sectional model to describe the selection process for AFDC mothers, but this model could not be subject to restriction tests and was assumed to be correct by fiat. In the randomized experiment, the youth sample for which the two-wave model fit produced no statistically reliable effect. In fact, estimates of the posttreatment income gain were close to zero ($48 in 1978 and $9 in 1979). But when the 1973 and 1974 pretest data were used in the selection modeling, the estimates did not differ from zero, supporting the "no effect" conclusion of Heckman and Hotz. But the effect was a loss of $624 for 1978 earnings and of $806 for 1979 earnings, and the corresponding standard errors were $497 and $586. Since the standard errors were much smaller in the randomized experiment— $144 and $173, respectively—we suspect that the two-wave selection model failed to produce a good estimate of anything with the youth sample. That is, the null hypothesis was accepted in the selection modeling exercise because the theory and measurement were so bad that statistical power was minimal.

To these data-based objections we have to add the philosophical objections of Holland.[28] He pointed out that Heckman's procedures do not logically entail that a selection model is true just because it fits the data. Other models might fit at least as well and might generate quite different results. More importantly, Holland noted that Heckman has now produced many selection models based on quite different assumptions about distributions and functional forms. These models result in different substantive conclusions—as indeed they should since they posit quite different selection processes. The conceptual difficulty, Holland notes, is to know which model to choose for a particular research project, especially if the study design provides little information about group differences in pretreatment performance on the same variable that is measured at the posttest. When several measurement waves exist, Heckman's procedures may generally work better, as with the double-pretest model he used with the youth sample that Cook and Campbell called a "double-pretest design."[29] However, selection modeling is likely to be most problematic when (1) there is no pretest information on the same measure that is used at the posttest, and (2) the comparison groups are poorly matched, as happens if a comparison group has to be constructed from some national data set. Holland characterizes the difference between statisticians and econometricians in terms of the econometricians' greater willingness to accept untested or imperfectly tested assumptions about the distribution of factors correlated with the instrumental variables they choose to represent the selection process.[30]

In all the data-analytic traditions there is a remarkable level of agreement about the kinds of designs likely to give the most complete information about selection. Cases of perfectly known selection come first, e.g., the randomized experiment and regression-discontinuity. Next come designs with extensive pretreatment information on the outcome measures (i.e., time-series designs, whose rich information about "priors" allows maturational trends to be directly estimated, including selection-maturation trends when a control time series is available). Next come designs with two pretreatment measurement waves (the "double pretest" design) so that selection-maturation differences can be directly assessed, even if only over a shorter period. Next come designs with a single pretreatment wave but with multiple comparison groups, hopefully some that initially outperform the presumed controls and others that underperform them. The different data-analytic traditions disagree more when designs have a single pretest measurement wave, nonequivalent groups, and none of the cause-facilitating design features mentioned earlier, especially if the treatment groups are not closely matched initially, the pretest measure is not very reliable, and no direct assessment of group maturation differences is possible. In situations like these, or where no pretest information is available at all on the posttreatment outcome, only non-Bayesian econometricians exhibit much optimism about controlling for selection differences.

We would be remiss if we closed this section on statistical analysis without noting that most of the statistical discussion has been oriented toward ruling out selection bias and simple forms of selection-maturation. Campbell and Boruch identified other internal validity threats that can operate with the most frequently used quasi-experiment that has two or more nonequivalent groups and a single wave of pretest and posttest measurement on the same scale.[31] In discussing adjustments for this situation, Reichardt also noted that analysis of covariance does not control for all relevant internal validity threats— only for those selection and selection-maturation patterns where the within-group growth mirrors the between-group.[32] While such data patterns probably constitute the single most important class of internal validity threats, biases can still arise from local history (one-time events that happen to one group more than another between the pretest and posttest), and from selection-instrumentation (differences in scaling between conditions at different measurement points). Thus, even if the problem of initial selection on unobserved attributes could be solved soon, this would still not guarantee causal inference. Statistical adjustments provide no free lunches, which may be why mathematical statisticians are keen to advocate improving causal inference through design rather than statistical adjustment!

Describing internal and external validity. There is widespread evidence that, despite decades of use, Campbell's concept of internal validity has been misunderstood. To correct matters he published a clarification in which he relabeled internal validity as Local Molar Causal Validity.[33] With this relabeling he hoped to emphasize that internal validity is concerned with whether a relationship between two observed variables was causal in the particular settings and with the particular human populations sampled in the research demonstration. In this regard, the meaning of cause is the traditional molar counterfactual one: Would the same change in the outcome have been observed had there been no treatment? No necessity exists in this formulation for the cause and effect variables to be specifiable in a general abstract way that is free of the particulars of the research operations actually used in a study. Nor is there any necessity to identify either the causally efficacious components of the molar independent and dependent variables or any processes that might have mediated the relationship between them. To justify such a retrospective, contextually embedded conception of causation, Campbell leaned heavily on the manipulability theory of causation, rejecting those theories of causation that aspire to total prediction, full explanation, or complete control. Campbell asks: "Was the relationship between X-as-manipulated and Y-as-measured presumptively causal in the study under review?" This is not the same as the more prospective and hence general question: "Is the relationship between X and Y causal?"

To some who finally understood Campbell's explication of internal validity, it seemed narrow, if not trivial. Cronbach attacked its retrospective and local nature, its obliviousness to issues of causal mediation, and its neglect of factors that might statistically interact with the treatment to enhance outcome prediction.[34] These sins of omission made internal validity largely irrelevant to his conception of the major task of evaluation—promoting practical methods of program improvement from which many sites could benefit and perhaps even programs other than the one under evaluation. Cronbach used the term "internal validity," but in a quite different sense from Campbell. He used it to refer to how well a causal connection can be generalized to particular populations of persons and settings and to particular cause and effect constructs—usually those specified in the guiding research question. A study is internally valid for Cronbach if particulars of the study's measurement and sampling plans can be used to justify inferences of the form: "Television violence (the abstract treatment) causes aggression (the abstract effect) among five-year-olds (the population) in California (the setting)." Yet for Campbell a study is internally valid if it justifies more sample-bound inferences like: "Television violence of the types witnessed by children in the particular study under review caused aggression of the type measured." In Campbell's formulation no reference is made to general cause and effect constructs or to specific populations of settings or persons. Thus, by 1982 there were two competing descriptions of internal validity in the field of evaluation.

To make matters worse, Cronbach's conception corresponded with Campbell's understanding of "external" validity. Campbell's earlier theoretical work did not treat external validity as comprehensively as internal validity. This may be because nothing in the philosophy of science provides as clear a theoretical rationale for external validity as the manipulability theory of causation provides for internal validity. It may also be because external validity does not have as clear and as obvious an exemplar in research practice as the randomized experiment provides for internal validity. In publicizing the question: To which populations of persons, settings, times and operational manipulations and measures can an internally valid conclusion be generalized? and in labeling the concerns behind the question as "external validity," Campbell acknowledged the importance of causal generalization. Moreover, his major early theoretical paper on the topic contained an argument based on practice in the natural sciences which held that causal relationships should be assumed to be general after a few demonstrations, however particularistic these demonstrations might be.[35] The generalizations in question might subsequently have to be abandoned if disconfirming evidence accumulates, but for the present a replicated causal relationship should be assumed to hold more generally. We judge that this argument will not convince those who believe that the social world is so complexly determined that causal contingencies are the norm rather than the exception.

Campbell later argued that external validity should be relabeled as "proximal similarity."[36] This emphasizes that the generalization of causal connections depends on the extent to which an achieved sample of manipulations, outcome measures, persons or settings overlaps in its prototypical observables with the attributes ascribed to cause and effect constructs and to populations of persons and settings. Such proximal similarity is best achieved by sampling with known probability from clearly designated universes. But this is never possible with future time, rarely feasible when selecting manipulations and measures, and, even though people or settings can be selected at random, resource constraints limit this to highly circumscribed contexts relevant to few consumers of research.

Fortunately, purposive sampling techniques are also relevant to proximal similarity since the theoretical requirement is that the achieved samples of measures, units, etc. should resemble their target population on all the attributes that common language use, current theory, and experience suggest are prototypical, that uniquely identify the construct or population to which generalization is sought. For Cronbach, such pattern matching is part of internal validity rather than Campbell's external validity, for proximal similarity deals with the correspondence between samples and populations, between operations and constructs. For Cronbach, external validity entails going beyond the achieved sampling and measurement design in order to draw inferences about treatments and outcomes with attributes different from those observed to date, and about populations of persons, settings, and time other than those represented in past empirical research. Campbell's external validity has to do with generalizing to universes and constructs achieved in research, while Cronbach's has to do with extrapolating to universes and constructs that have not been represented in the sampling particulars.

Cronbach assumes that extrapolation is best achieved through causal explanation rather than sampling theory. He wants evaluators to learn *why* a treatment is or is not effective rather than identifying *whether* it is effective. He seeks explanation through several different mechanisms, including: decomposing macro-level variables to identify their causally efficacious components; learning which molar forces statistically interact with the treatment; and identifying those forces that temporally mediate between when a treatment is manipulated and when an effect is observed. In Cronbach's conception, understanding external validity as proximal similarity is counterproductive. It focuses attention on superficial correspondences rather than generative causal processes; and it defines external validity in terms of generalizing to particular constructs and populations rather than extrapolation beyond the constructs and population already studied. The possibility for terminological confusion is great here. Two great theorists of social science method use the same label, external validity, but imbue it with different meanings that are even partially contradictory in that Cronbach's internal validity seems equivalent to Campbell's external validity!

It seems sensible to us to retain Campbell's retrospective, local, and imperfectly predictive conception of internal validity. Otherwise, there is no way of focusing attention on the crucial issue of whether the relationship observed in a study is causal in the manipulability sense. Identifying manipulanda that can make a difference is of great potential practical benefit and closely overlaps with ordinary language usage of "cause." But it also seems sensible to us to promote Cronbach's distinction between generalizing *to* planned target constructs and populations (his "internal validity") and extrapolating *beyond* the studied targets (his "external validity"). Sampling theory is germane to the first, and causal explanation is one type of method germane to the second. In any event, conceptual understanding of external validity is now progressing. While it is still in many ways the "ugly sister" to internal validity, the profile of external validity is on the rise, fuelled by two other related developments to which we now turn.

The priority of validity types. Campbell has always argued the priority of internal over external validity. It makes little logical sense to him to assess the reach of a causal connection if there is doubt about the connection itself. Cronbach's counterargument is that Campbell has adopted a standard about the degree of uncertainty reduction required for drawing useful conclusions that is unduly scholarly and is at odds with the different standards of the policy-shaping community to which evaluators should be particularly responsive. Social research is looked to for uncertainty reduction in both the academic and policy worlds, but Cronbach contends that the scholarly world demands compulsively more. To buttress this, he cites Moynihan's claim that little need exists in government to rule out every last—and often highly marginal—source of uncertainty; action is the policy watchword, and not truth.[37]

On this particular issue, Cronbach's position is not very convincing. Senior evaluators within the federal government claim that standards there are not different from academe.[38] Moreover, we have personally witnessed instances in the policy world where the standards are even more rigorous than those of the academic world, e.g., in debates about television violence. The issue of the scholarly and policy communities having different standards for acting on caus-

132   QUASI-EXPERIMENTATION

al claims is important, but we would caution evaluators against blanket judgments which assume that many stakeholders in the formal policy world are more willing than academics to adopt lower technical standards for molar causal connections.

Campbell's second argument for the primacy of internal validity is that incorrect inferences about descriptive causation are likely to be especially costly. Effective components may wrongly be judged to be ineffective, while ineffective ones may be judged effective and promoted as worthy of transfer. Incorrect inferences about external validity (in either Campbell's or Cronbach's sense) are presumed to have less serious consequences, especially if the inaccuracy stems from contextual differences in the strength rather than the direction of a causal connection. Campbell believes that the policy world is so coarsely grained that few possibilities exist to implement one policy or program in one context and another in a different context. The political need to treat people equally is strong, he believes, and local discretion in providing services is deeply entrenched in American practices of public administration. Hence, the central government's power to use differentiated information for differentiated purposes is restricted. The argument, then, is that fine-grained information about causal contingencies that limit external validity can rarely be used in the course-grained world of public policy, so that errors in over-generalizing a descriptive causal finding are not likely to be as costly as errors in identifying a causal connection.

Though Campbell is pessimistic about how much can be done with statistical interactions that limit the generalizability of a causal connection, Cronbach aspires to just such differentiated knowledge. He believes that elucidating the contingencies on which a causal connection depends will help local decision makers and other practitioners decide whether a causal relationship is likely to hold in the contexts where they work—contexts where the relationship itself may never have been tested. Cronbach is less willing than Campbell to assume that what has been shown to be internally valid in a few contexts, or even across a wide range of contexts, will likely be valid in any one particular local context. He prefers to forego some uncertainty reduction about a causal connection in order to learn more about specific causal contingencies.

This disagreement about priorities is not resolvable. It can perhaps be clarified a little, though, by noting that Campbell's priorities give more weight than Cronbach's to the views of central decision makers. Also, Cronbach has had considerable experience in education, a sector where adults have enough control over students that they can sometimes implement different procedures with different subgroups, whereas in other sectors the service deliverer's control is less. Clarification of the priority issue would also be enhanced if we knew more from meta-analyses about how often negative—and not just null—results are attained in particular research areas. If negative results are widespread, then Campbell's assumptions about the generally benign consequences of assuming too much generalization would be problematic. Finally, clarification would also be promoted if we could better judge the extent to which the technical quality of claims about average causal effects would be diminished if more study resources were devoted to the study of treatment interactions or causal processes. As things now stand, there has been no systematic probe of Campbell's assertion about the differential consequences of being wrong about internal and external validity as he understands them. This issue deserves more attention.

Campbell's third reason for prioritizing on internal validity is circular, but not for that reason undeserving of commentary. He claims that quasi-experiments were developed to promote descriptive causal conclusions in open-system contexts. Hence, anyone choosing to implement a quasi-experiment should already have decided that a causal question is paramount, but cannot be resolved in the laboratory. In this formulation, avoiding the laboratory has implications for generalization, but causation is still the essence. If it were not, quasi-experiments would not be the method of choice. Surveys or ethnographies might be.

The debate between Campbell and Cronbach is not just about the priority of two types of validity; it is also about the relative priority of experimental and nonexperimental methods in evaluation. Cook and Campbell have acknowledged that individual quasi-experiments are mute about many evaluation issues,[39] such as the relevance of the guiding research question, the nature of causal mediating processes, the generalizability of causal connections, and the utilization of research results. In stressing molar causation so heavily, the experiment or quasi-experiment is basically mono-purpose, not multi-purpose as Cronbach and others want evaluation to be. Experiments can be adapted at the margin to fulfill additional purposes, but their major function is to test causal connections. The challenge to Campbell's assumption about the priority of internal validity has reminded all those involved in evaluation that quasi-experiments were developed for cause-probing reasons that do not correspond with *all* the reasons why evaluations are conducted.

Methods for increasing generalizability. Campbell and Cronbach agree on one important point about validity matters. Campbell worries lest emphasizing external validity (in the sense of generalizing to target populations) will induce researchers to conduct single large studies with carefully selected samples. With the same resources he would prefer to see several smaller, independent studies. He opposes large studies because the quality of program implementation is likely to suffer and because any biases are likely to be constant across the sites and persons examined. He believes that smaller, independent studies will produce higher quality implementation and greater cross-site heterogeneity in the biases inadvertently built into the research— a heterogeneity that should permit analysts to probe whether similar results occur when the direction of bias varies. Cronbach agrees with these arguments and adds that synthesizing results across multiple sites is also likely to promote aptitude-treatment interaction conclusions that better describe the complex ways in which molar causal forces operate in the real world. Since Cronbach expects treatments to be differentially rather than universally effective, his rationale for many smaller studies has more of a causal contingency flavor than Campbell's, whose emphasis is more on identifying robust, replicable main effects.

The 1980s witnessed other concerns about promoting external validity in all its meanings. For Campbell, the key to external validity lies in the correspondence between the samples and populations in entity-defining attributes, provided that irrelevant attributes are heterogeneously distributed across the sample cases. When carefully conducted, meta-analyses conform with this conception of external validity. Across all the studies examined there are usually multiple versions of each target cause and effect construct and many different types of persons, settings, and times. The operations and samples are usually imbued with considerable heterogeneity of irrelevancies, making it possible to test whether the average effect size differs from zero despite such irrelevancies. When sample sizes and measures permit, the meta-analyst can go one important step further to examine whether effect sizes depend upon particular attributes of respondents, settings, and times (as well as on irrelevant methodological characteristics at the study level). Any general causal claim that persists across these sources of heterogeneity is presumptively robust, while any claim that is shown to depend on specific third variables alerts potential users of the data to circumstances where negative side effects or null effects are possible. Given Campbell's understanding of external validity, meta-analysis would seem to be the method of preference. It aspires to identify effects that are robust across multiple irrelevancies, and it can help identify a few large statistical interaction effects.

Cronbach takes a less benign view of the potential of meta-analysis. It is too coarse-grained for him, being unable to support the fine conclusions about causal contingency and mediation that correspond with his complex ontology. Moreover, it speaks more to internal than external validity as he understands the terms. That is, it helps identify the particular constructs and populations to which a causal relationship can be generalized, but it gives no basis for generalizing to unobserved constructs and populations. In this last regard, Cronbach never explicitly examines either the inductivist argument or the Bayesian argument that the more often—and the more heterogeneous—the attributes across which a causal relationship has been demonstrated in the past, the more likely it is that the relationship can be generalized to unexamined contexts in the future. To promote external validity and the transfer of research findings, Cronbach seems to prefer the theoretical route of causal explanation over the more brute empirical route of meta-analysis, though we guess he would find some merit in each of them.

But being mindful of the problems of model specification and measurement quality that beset traditional causal modeling in the social sciences, Cronbach does not look to these techniques (and the computer programs like LISREL that embody them) for help with causal explanation. Instead, he looks to the more qualitative methods of the ethnographer, historian, and journalist. His operating assumption is that their methods are more practical than those of the causal modeler, more honed in the crucible of experience, and capable of reducing enough uncertainty about causal explanation to be useful. Few practicing social scientists would agree with him; but increasing numbers of evaluators might, especially in education. These evaluators see in the methods of the ethnographer, journalist, and historian, not only ways of achieving explanatory knowledge, but also ways of meeting multiple evaluative purposes within the same data collection effort. Knowledge can be gained about program design, program implementation, descriptive causal effects, as well as causal explanatory processes. To anyone who believes evaluation should be multifunctional, the flexible methods of the journalist, ethnographer, and historian have considerable advantages over more monofunctional techniques like the experiment. On the other hand, to anyone who believes that information is more useful the more certain it is, the methods of the journalist, ethnographer, and historian will seem too prone to bias. Thus, a debate about methods for promoting external validity has now been opened, at least among evaluators in education. It is a serious debate, and the methods that Campbell and Cronbach prefer for causal generalization are quite at odds.

To summarize, we have discussed three validity debates: (1) about the nature of internal and external validity; (2) about their priority ordering; and (3) about methods to promote external validity understood as generalizing both to and beyond sampled populations and contexts. None of these debates has been resolved. Still, the terms of each debate are clearer now than before, even if some of them are more complicated. External validity has now been brought out of the closet, and it cannot be put back. How the notion will be developed is not yet clear. But we consider it to be an achievement that it can no longer be ignored by evaluators like it was until the early 1980s. Causal generalization deserves the same effort as causal identification.[40]

The "Special Role" for Quasi-Experimentation within Evaluation

One of the first systematic expositions of evaluation was by Suchman.[41] He argued that quasi-experimental methods were central to evaluation because: (1) evaluation should be primarily concerned with establishing the molar-level causal consequences of social programs and their constituent parts; (2) evaluation should use the best feasible "scientific" methods available for testing causal connections; (3) randomized experiments, though the best scientific method for causal purposes, could not become standard in evaluation because they can only be rarely implemented in the complex, politicized field settings where social program services are delivered, (4) nonexperimental methods are rarely definitive for causal identification and are sometimes even downright misleading; so that (5) quasi-experiments with control groups and pretest observations provide the most feasible, fall-back option for a practical cause-centered science of evaluation. In line with this reasoning, Suchman advocated Campbell and Stanley as *the* Bible for evaluation.

Campbell was not happy with this status and message. Though he never lost faith in the strongest quasi-experimental designs like the interrupted time series and regression discontinuity, he maintained that most quasi-experiments lead to more ambiguous causal conclusions than Suchman had portrayed and that random assignment was more desirable and feasible than Suchman had implied.[42] Campbell's preference was to make evaluation even more "scientific" and to this end he ceaselessly advocated randomized experiments over quasi-experiments. He even went so far as to lament that his own work on quasi-experiments might have legitimated second-class designs!

Campbell's regrets notwithstanding, a 1986 survey of practicing evaluators showed that his writings on quasi-experimentation are still seen as more influential than any other evaluation-relevant work.[43] Nevertheless, our impression is that quasi-experiments played an even more dominant role in evaluation in the 1960s and first half of the 1970s than today. If we are correct in this, we can easily understand why its hegemony has slipped by considering reactions to the four preceding assumptions on which Suchman built his argument.

The assumption that evaluation should prioritize on molar causal connections came under fire because this type of question neglects obviously important issues—about sampling and generalization, about causal mediation and the transfer of study findings, and about social values and the political interests that are inadvertently smuggled into the framing of evaluation questions. Concerns were also raised about whether the priority accorded to molar causal connections might lower the quality of inferences about noncausal questions. The presumption here is that factors promoting strong quasi-experimental designs might consume study resources that are needed for examining issues of generalization, transfer, and value analysis. Thus, the argument went beyond whether quasi-experiments were irrelevant to many important evaluation tasks; it also included the proposition that quasi-experiments might be detrimental to fulfilling these tasks well!

The assumption that evaluation should be scientific (i.e., based on quantitative hypothesis testing) was attacked on many grounds: that the quantitative tradition is insensitive to the discovery of unanticipated processes and outcomes; that its structures are so rigid that guiding research questions cannot be changed as new issues emerge and old ones lose their importance; that the use of evaluative evidence depends on incidental knowledge accumulated during a study as much as from its quantitative results; that "scientific" evaluations rarely, if ever, result in the clear and uncontroversial conclusions; and that the policy-making community is less interested than the more conservative academic world in reducing all uncertainty about a causal hypothesis. Why then should the conservative standards of academic science be imposed on the policy world of practical action? Though these attacks on "scientific" evaluation differ considerably in validity, it is clear that by 1980 an influential group of education evaluators (but not evaluators in public health or social welfare, say) was writing about "the art" rather than "the science" of evaluation. They were also writing in the same spirit about evaluation as a form of "social inquiry" as distinct from evaluation as social research. Indeed, by 1982 the term "evaluation *research*" has nearly disappeared from the vocabulary of education, being replaced by the less scientific label of "evaluation."

The foregoing criticisms were not specifically targeted at quasi-experimentation. But others were. Campbell himself argued that most quasi-experiments fail to reduce enough uncertainty about descriptive causal corrections to be useful. He forcefully represented this case,[44] even for the most frequently used design with nonequivalent groups and pretest and posttest measures collected on the same scale. Six sources of equivocality in causal inference were detailed, including the inability to adjust away all selection artifacts and ceiling and basement effects. One could not come away from the paper convinced that the most frequently used quasi-experimental design was capable of high quality descriptive causal inferences. Suchman's assumption about the "scientific" quality of inferences from quasi-experiments did not seem well supported.

Nor did his third assumption that randomized experiments are rarely feasible. Lists were published of randomized experiments that had actually been carried out,[45] and many solvable problems besetting the successful implementation of such experiments were identified.[46] Also, details were published about the conditions under which these ameliorative methods might be most effectively used.[47] Throughout the 1970s and 1980s more and more randomized experiments were successfully conducted. While they received a mixed press in education, which had been at the forefront in introducing them and so was probably the sector where most mistake-learning took place, they received a much more favorable reaction in public health and labor economics. The argument for a special role for quasi-experiments lost its force as evidence accumulated about the feasibility of randomized experiments. The argument for quasi-experiments had always been that they were pragmatically but not logically superior. Now it was not clear whether they were even pragmatically superior.

The final Suchman assumption that came under attack was that nonexperiments produce misleading inferences about molar causal connections. Proponents of causal modeling techniques like LISREL argued that maximum likelihood factor analytic methods eliminated the problems associated with the unreliable measurement of selection processes and produced less biased answers than models with observed variables.[48] As regards specification of the selection process itself, proponents of nonexperimental methods claimed that these limitations could be mitigated through more developed instrumental variable techniques.[49] At issue here is not the validity of these causal modeling techniques, but rather the undeniable growth in their influence during the 1970s and 1980s.

Actually, the advocacy of nonexperiments for purposes of descriptive causal inference was not restricted to causal modeling. The 1970s witnessed a surge of interest in qualitative methods, primarily by education evaluators who argued that the cause-probing role of qualitative methods had been slighted. They often cited Campbell's own cautious advocacy of qualitative methods,[50] though a careful reading of his work suggests a more complex opinion, viz., that while qualitative methods can *in principle* rule out all threats to internal validity, particularly when a causal hypothesis has many unique implications, it is rare to achieve such definitiveness in practice. Nonetheless, the case was made that causal description does not even require quantified measurement let alone complex designs or statistical analyses. When linked to the argument that the public policy world does not require the same degree of uncertainty reduction about causal connections as academic scholarship, it was difficult to defend Suchman's proposition that quasi-experiments should enjoy a special compromise position between the often infeasible true experiment and the usually uninterpretable nonexperiment.

What remained of Suchman's case by 1990? Should evaluation be predominantly concerned with molar causal connections, as he had argued? In education the brief consensus on this score had evaporated by about 1975. Should evaluation be "scientific"? In education the early consensus on this score evaporated by the late 1970s, though it did not in other sectors. Do quasi-experiments produce causal findings definitive enough to be useful? Active disagreement exists about this, though less when rarer quasi-experimental designs like the interrupted time series and regression-discontinuity analysis are being considered than when the more common designs with a single control group and a single pretest measurement wave are under analysis. Are randomized experiments as infeasible as Suchman asserted? The existing lists of completed and carefully conducted experiments strongly suggest that Suchman's view was overstated. Are nonexperiments, whether quantitative or qualitative, as unclear in the causal inferences they promote as Suchman claimed? Again, the early consensus had evaporated by the late 1970s in education, though not in medicine or labor economics. The upshot of all this ferment is that it is now less easy to argue that quasi-experiments represent the sole realistic compromise capable of generating high quality inferences about the molar causal connections presumed to be central to program evaluation.

What remains in 1990 as the consensually validated realms of application of quasi-experiments, the realms where they are uniquely suited to evaluation? One is when few units can be assigned to the various treatments, as happens in community studies of, say, health promotion and disease prevention where it is prohibitively expensive to achieve enough units to make the Central Limit Theorem applicable. A second area is when ethical or political factors proscribe random assignment, as happens in many areas of research on AIDS. A third context is where random assignment has been attempted and has failed because of treatment-correlated refusals to participate in a study or treatment-correlated attrition from it. The available data then have to be analyzed as coming from some form of quasi-experiment, an implication of which is that no randomized field experiment should be conducted unless it also has pretest measures. A fourth context of application is where the evaluation is causal but retrospective, as when one asks after the fact what a program or program component has achieved. If high quality archives and exact knowledge of treatment onset are available, this is where quasi-experiments like the interrupted time series are feasible and where ambiguity about causal inferences is likely to be lowest. A final context is where a nonexperiment has been carried out and where the application of quasi-experimental principles to the conceptualization of measurement waves, differences in treatment implementation and mode of treatment assignment can support an analysis of internal validity threats within the framework of Campbell and Stanley.[51]

There is still a unique role for quasi-experiments. But it is much more circumscribed than the role explicit in Suchman[52] and implicit in the special dominance of Campbell among evaluation theorists and practitioners in the 1960s and 1970s. In 1986, Campbell's work on quasi-experiments was still the most widely acknowledged method source among evaluators. However, our impression is that by then it had lost the hegemony it had once enjoyed. It is now among the methods to be used when descriptive causal questions can be justified as the centerpiece of an evaluation design. But it is definitely not the sole method of choice.

FOOTNOTES

1. Donald T. Campbell, "Factors Relevant to the Validity of Experiments in Social Settings," *Psychological Bulletin* 54 (1957): 297-312; idem, "Relabeling Internal and External Validity for Applied Social Scientists," in *Advances in Quasi-Experimental Design and Analysis*, New Directions for Program Evaluation, no. 31, ed. W. M. K. Trochim (San Francisco: Jossey-Bass, 1986), pp. 66-77; Donald T. Campbell and Julian C. Stanley, *Experimental and Quasi-Experimental Designs for Research* (Chicago: Rand McNally, 1966); Thomas D. Cook and Donald T. Campbell, *Quasi-Experimentation: Design and Analysis Issues for Field Settings* (Chicago: Rand McNally; Boston: Houghton Mifflin, 1979).

2. Edward A. Suchman, *Evaluative Research: Principles and Practice in Public Service and Social Action Programs* (New York: Russell Sage, 1967).

3. Campbell, "Factors Relevant to the Validity of Experiments in Social Settings"; Campbell and Stanley, *Experimental and Quasi-Experimental Designs for Research.*

4. Campbell, "Factors Relevant to the Validity of Experiments in Social Settings"; Campbell and Stanley, *Experimental and Quasi-Experimental Designs for Research*; Cook and Campbell, *Quasi-Experimentation.*

5. Thomas S. Kuhn, *The Structure of Scientific Revolutions* (Chicago: University of Chicago Press, 1962).

6. Cook and Campbell, *Quasi-Experimentation.*

7. Donald T. Campbell, "Pattern Matching as an Essential in Distal Knowing," in *The Psychology of Egon Brunswick*, ed. Kenneth R. Hammond (New York: Holt, Rinehart and Winston, 1966), pp. 81-106.

8. Cook and Campbell, *Quasi-Experimentation.*

9. Ibid.

10. Campbell, "Pattern Matching as an Essential in Distal Knowing."

11. Paul E. Meehl, "Theoretical Risks and Tabular Asterisks: Sir Karl, Sir Ronald and the Slow Progress of Soft Psychology," *Journal of Consulting and Clinical Psychology* 46 (1978): 806-834.

12. W. G. Cochran, "The Planning of Observational Studies of Human Populations" (with Discussion), *Journal of the Royal Statistical Society*, Series A, 128 (1965): 234-266; George E. P. Box and Gwilym M. Jenkins, *Time-Series Analysis: Forecasting and Control* (San Francisco: Holden-Day, 1970).

13. For example, see Paul W. Holland and Donald B. Rubin, "On Lord's Paradox," in *Principles of Modern Psychological Measurement*, ed. Howard Wainer and Samuel Messick (Hillsdale, NJ: Erlbaum, 1983); Paul W. Holland, "Statistics and Causal Inference," *Journal of the American Statistical Association* 81 (1986): 945-959; Paul R. Rosenbaum, "From Association to Causation in Observational Studies: The Role of Tests of Strongly Ignorable Treatment Assignment," *Journal of the American Statistical Association* 79 (1984): 41-48; Paul R. Rosenbaum and Donald B. Rubin, "The Central

Role of the Propensity Score in Observational Studies for Causal Effects," *Biometrika* 70 (1983): 41-55; idem, "Reducing Bias in Observational Studies Using Sub-classifications on the Propensity Score," *Journal of the American Statistical Association* 79 (1984): 516-524; idem, "Estimating Causal Effects of Treatments in Randomized and Nonrandomized Studies," *Journal of Educational Psychology* 66 (1974): 688-701; idem, "Assignment of Treatment Group on the Basis of a Covariate," *Journal of Educational Statistics* 2 (1977): 1-26; idem, "Bayesian Inference for Causal Effects: The Role of Randomization," *Annals of Statistics* 7 (1978): 34-58; idem, "Which Ifs Have Causal Answers?" *Journal of the American Statistical Association* 81 (1986): 961-962.

14. For example, see Arthur S. Goldberger, *Selection Bias in Evaluating Treatment Effects: Some Formal Illustrations*, Discussion Paper 123-72 (Madison, WI: Institute for Research on Poverty, University of Wisconsin, 1972); Burt S. Barnow, Glen G. Cain, and Arthur S. Goldberger, "Issues in the Analysis of Selectivity Bias," *Evaluation Studies Review Annual 5* (1980): 42-59; Burt S. Barnow, "The Effects of Head Start and Socioeconomic Status on Cognitive Development of Disadvantaged Students" (doct. diss., University of Wisconsin, 1974).

15. Orley Ashenfelter, "Estimating the Effect of Training Programs on Earnings," *Review of Economics and Statistics* 60 (1978): 47-57.

16. For example, see James J. Heckman, "Sample Bias as Specification Error," *Econometrica* 47 (1979): 153-162; James J. Heckman and R. Robb, "Alternative Methods for Evaluating the Impact of Interventions," in *Longitudinal Analysis of Labor Market Data*, ed. James J. Heckman and Burton S. Singer (New York: Cambridge University Press, 1985); idem, "Alternative Identifying Assumptions in Econometric Models of Selection Bias," in *Advances in Econometrics: Innovations in Quantitative Economics*, Vol. 5, Essays in honor of Robert L. Basman, ed. Daniel Slottje (Greenwich, CT: JAI Press, 1986); James J. Heckman and V. Joseph Hotz, "Choosing among Alternative Nonexperimental Methods for Estimating the Impact of Social Programs: The Case of Manpower Training," *Journal of the American Statistical Association* 84 (1989): 862-874; idem, "Rejoinder," *Journal of the American Statistical Association* 84 (1989): 878-80.

17. Karl G. Joreskog and Dag Sorbom, *Advances in Factor Analysis and Structural Equation Models* (Cambridge, MA: Abt, 1979).

18. Peter M. Bentler, *Theory and Implementation of EQS: A Structural Equations Program* (Los Angeles: BMDP Statistical Software, 1986).

19. Jay Magidson, "Toward a Causal Model Approach for Adjusting for Preexisting Differences in the Nonequivalent Control Group Situation," *Evaluation Quarterly* 3 (1977): 399-420.

20. Peter M. Bentler and J. Arthur Woodward, "A Head Start Reevaluation: Positive Effects Are Not Yet Demonstrable," *Evaluation Quarterly* 2 (1978): 493-510.

21. Thomas D. Cook, "Postpositivist Critical Multiplism," in *Social Science and Social Policy*, ed. R. Lance Shotland and Melvin M. Mark (Beverly Hills: Sage, 1985); C. S. Reichardt and S. H. F. Gollub, "Taking Uncertainty into Account When Estimating Effects," in *Multiple Methods in Program Evaluation*, New Directions in Program Evaluation, No. 35, ed. Melvin M. Mark and R. Lance Shotland (San Francisco: Jossey-Bass, 1987); William R. Shadish, "Critical Multiples: A Research Strategy and Its Attendant Tactics," in *Health Services Research Methods: A Focus on AIDS*, DHHS Pub. No. PHS-89-3439 (Rockville, MD: NCHSR and HealthCare Technology Assessment, PHS, USDHHS, 1989), pp. 5-28.

22. Cook and Campbell, *Quasi-Experimentation*, pp. 54-55.

23. Rosenbaum and Rubin, "The Central Role of the Propensity Score in Observational Studies for Causal Effects."

24. Robert J. LaLonde, "Evaluating the Econometric Evaluations of Training

Programs with Experimental Data," *American Economic Review* 76 (1986): 604-620; Robert J. LaLonde and Rebecca Maynard, "How Precise Are Evaluations of Employment and Training Programs? Evidence from a Field Experiment," *Evaluation Review* 11 (1987): 428-451.

25. Thomas Fraker and Rebecca Maynard, "Evaluating the Adequacy of Comparison Group Designs for Evaluations of Employment-Related Programs," *Journal of Human Resources* 22 (1987): 194-227.

26. Heckman and Hotz, "Choosing among Alternative Nonexperimental Methods for Estimating the Impact of Social Programs"; idem, "Rejoinder."

27. Robert Moffitt, "Comment," *Journal of the American Statistical Association* 84 (1989): 877-78.

28. Paul W. Holland, "Comment: It's Very Clear," *Journal of the American Statistical Association* 84 (1989): 875-877.

29. Cook and Campbell, *Quasi-Experimentation*.

30. Holland, "Comment: It's Very Clear."

31. Donald T. Campbell and Robert F. Boruch, "Making the Case for Randomized Assignment to Treatments by Considering the Alternatives: Six Ways in Which Quasi-Experimental Evaluations Tend to Underestimate Effects," in *Evaluation and Experiment: Some Critical Issues in Assessing Social Programs*, ed. Carl A. Bennett and Arthur A. Lumsdaine (New York: Academic Press, 1975).

32. C. S. Reichardt, "The Statistical Analysis of Data from Nonequivalent Group Designs," in *Quasi-Experimentation: Design and Analysis Issues for Field Settings* (Chicago: Rand McNally, 1979).

33. Campbell, "Relabeling Internal and External Validity for Applied Social Scientists."

34. Lee J. Cronbach, *Towards Reform of Program Evaluation: Aims, Methods, and Institutional Arrangements* (San Francisco: Jossey-Bass, 1980); idem, *Designing Evaluations of Educational and Social Programs* (San Francisco: Jossey-Bass, 1982).

35. Donald T. Campbell, "Prospective: Artifact and Control," in *Artifact in Behavior Research*, ed. Robert Rosenthal and Ralph L. Rosnow (New York: Academic Press, 1969).

36. Campbell, "Relabeling Internal and External Validity for Applied Social Scientists."

37. Daniel Moynihan, *Maximum Feasible Misunderstanding: Community Action in the War on Poverty* (New York: Free Press, 1969).

38. Eleanor Chelimsky, "The Politics of Program Evaluation," *Society* 25 (1987): 24-32.

39. Cook and Campbell, *Quasi-Experimentation*.

40. Thomas D. Cook, "The Generalization of Causal Connections: Multiple Theories in Search of Clear Practice," in *Strengthening Causal Interpretation of Nonexperimental Data*, PHS Publication No. 90-3454, ed. L. Sechrest, E. Perrin, and J. Bunker (Rockville, MD: Agency for Health Care Policy and Research, Public Health Service, 1990).

41. Suchman, *Evaluative Research*.

42. Campbell, "Prospective: Artifact and Control"; Campbell and Boruch, "Making the Case for Randomized Assignment to Treatments by Considering the Alternatives."

43. William R. Shadish and Robert Epstein, "Patterns of Program Evaluation Practice among Members of the Evaluation Research Society and the Evaluation Network," *Evaluation Review* 11 (1987): 555-590.

44. Campbell and Boruch, "Making the Case for Randomized Assignment to Treatments by Considering the Alternatives."

45. Robert F. Boruch, "On Common Contentions about Randomized Field Experiments," in *Experimental Testing of Public Policy: The Proceedings of the 1974 Social Science Research Council Conference on Social Experiments*, ed. Robert F. Boruch and Henry W. Riecken (Boulder, CO: Westview Press, 1975), pp. 107-142.

46. Henry W. Riecken, Robert F. Boruch, Donald T. Campbell, N. Caplan, T. K. Glennan, J. Pratt, A. Rees, and W. Williams, eds., *Social Experimentation: A Method for Planning and Evaluating Social Intervention* (New York: Academic Press [for the Social Service Research Council], 1974).

47. Cook and Campbell, *Quasi-Experimentation.*

48. Bentler and Woodward, "A Head Start Reevaluation."

49. Heckman and Robb, "Alternative Identifying Assumptions in Econometric Models of Selection Bias"; Heckman and Hotz, "Choosing among Alternative Nonexperimental Methods for Estimating the Impact of Social Programs."

50. Donald T. Campbell, "Qualitative Knowing in Action Research" (Kurt Lewin Award Address, Society for the Psychological Study of Social Issues, New Orleans, September 1974).

51. Campbell and Stanley, *Experimental and Quasi-Experimental Designs for Research.*

52. Suchman, *Evaluative Research.*

Randomization and Comparison

Robert Boruch has been a long-standing advocate of the use of randomized true experiments in evaluation. In the chapter that follows he describes the conditions under which they would be useful in the decade of the 1990s. His argument sets out from the need to obtain policy-relevant data about programs, especially the need to determine what programs or approaches work better than others. Here comparison is required, and he argues that it is possible more often than evaluators commonly assume.

In the 1970s and 1980s, when government agencies funded pilot or demonstration projects, too often the evaluation of these projects was limited. The focus of evaluation tended to be on whether or not the program's services were adequately delivered to the target population—a matter of nontrivial importance as there had been many instances of programs that had faced extraordinary problems in becoming operational. But having this specific focus, evaluators sometimes downgraded other questions such as: Did the program actually have a beneficial, or even a harmful, effect? Which particular variants of the program were the most effective? To answer such questions comparative studies were required. But the centrality of comparison in the logic of evaluation was questioned by some during this period, including Lee J. Cronbach, and defended by others, such as Michael Scriven and Robert Boruch. During this period, too, many evaluators had bad experiences with large-scale experimental evaluations, which proved difficult if not impossible to carry out effectively. Those writers who disagreed over the emphasis that should be given to comparison reached agreement that whatever studies were done should be modest enough in scale to allow work of highly professional quality to be carried out. It became a canon of evaluation theory that more could be learned from a series of small studies than from a single large one.

Rigorous comparative studies, using random assignment and true experimental designs, seemed possible to perform when a program was new. For at first (for logistical reasons) the program would not be deliverable to all people who required its services, so those who were

145

not covered by it could constitute the control group. It seemed more difficult to organize a comparative study when the program was well established, and when it was the only one servicing a particular domain of need.

Robert Boruch revisits these issues, in a spirit typical of his work of the past two decades.

CHAPTER VI

The President's Mandate: Discovering What
Works and What Works Better

ROBERT F. BORUCH

In considering how to enhance the quality of education in the United States, President George Bush said: "There must be an emphasis on accountability—setting goals, objectively measuring progress toward these goals, changing what doesn't work, and rewarding what does. It seems like common sense, but it is too seldom done."

In this chapter, I translate the President's mandate into evaluation strategies that generate evidence about what works and what works better. In doing so, I rely substantially on the efforts of the U. S. Department of Education to clarify the presidential initiative and to assure that evaluative evidence is available to make decisions about education projects and programs. I also rely on the U. S. General Accounting Office as counsel to the U. S. Congress on related matters.

The Policy Context

President Bush's directive can be put in the form of plain questions: (1) What is the state of students, teachers, or administrators? Are there problems? How do we know? (2) What activities can be or have been undertaken? How do we know? (3) Do the activities make a difference? How do we know? (4) What works better to resolve problems? How do we know?

An early version of this paper was presented at the U. S. Department of Education Conference on the Presidential Mandate for Accountability in Education (February 25, 1989) in Washington, DC. Work on the paper has been supported by the Department. Earlier research on the topic has been supported by the National Science Foundation, the U. S. Department of Education (including the National Institute of Education), and the National Institute of Mental Health.

Answering the first question requires depending on high-quality monitoring systems at the local or state level. Absent such systems, the information is obtained at best through high-quality probability sample surveys, coupled with a small number of qualitative investigations that are usually supported by the federal government and occasionally by states with both capacity and interest. Addressing the second question implies investing in local or regional demonstration projects or making surveys of such projects to learn about their feasibility.

Addressing the third and fourth questions implies estimating project effects, that is, generating understanding beyond a description of the problem or of how a project was implemented. These more difficult and often controversial questions are the focus of this paper.

Framing questions this way is also compatible with the efforts of the Department of Education to understand how to implement the President's mandate. In a draft memorandum on *Guidance*,[1] for instance, the Department emphasized monitoring systems that bear primarily on the question "What activities have been undertaken?" The memorandum contained a catalog of desirable features of such systems, including timeliness, usefulness, reliability of the information they produce, *and* mechanisms for assuring that the information gets used. In this chapter, I go beyond the Department's memorandum in addressing the questions about "effects."

The questions also accord with executive-level activity designed to improve and revitalize evaluation policy at the U.S. Department of Education. Ginsberg's paper,[2] for example, focuses on weaknesses of evaluation in the Department and on corrective action.

A Little History

The public servant who is sensitive to history recognizes that a government program often develops from an idea that is eventually translated into law. The law, in turn, often leads to the implementation of an array of new projects that are designed to actualize the ideas that public representatives seek to encourage. Such demonstration projects have often been used as a political device to fund services rather than to learn whether the idea actually works.[3]

This sequence of events, in many arenas, is followed by a period in which thoughtful questions emerge about the actual effects of the policy, programs, or projects so implemented. This stage is usually characterized by efforts to understand how well the projects worked, relative to some standard. The relevant evidence is useful, in principle at least, for legislative or administrative decisions about whether to continue the support of the endeavor, truncate support, redirect support, or enlarge it.[4] Consider three contemporary illustrations of the sequence of events.

The Centers for Disease Control (CDC) have been responsible since 1988 for allocating over $200 million each year to AIDS-prevention projects including local education efforts and media-based public education campaigns. Almost all these efforts were initially designed and executed as old-time demonstration projects. That is, a school district, a community-based organization, or government agency proposed an idea for an AIDS-prevention project to the CDC. The projects were screened and the worthiest of them were funded under the assumptions that projects (a) could be put into the field and (b) would have an effect.

Any serious requirement by the CDC to evaluate the program, in the sense of either attentively documenting activities or estimating the relative effects of the projects, was absent initially. Pressure to evaluate in either sense has been evident only recently.

For instance, the Committee on AIDS Research of the National Academy of Sciences urged the CDC to get beyond the puny products usually generated in such demonstration projects, i.e., to document the activities of some projects well and to estimate the effects of a few projects, using controlled field tests where possible.[5]

Consider another example. The National Institute of Justice provided technical support to the Milwaukee Public School System's implementation of a monitoring facility, the SMART System, for monitoring criminal and noncriminal disorders in high schools. SMART (School Management and Resource Team Program) was installed by Milwaukee as a demonstration project. The object was to see *if* such a system could be installed and, more important, if it would be used in some thirty large high schools.

No formal evaluation plan was laid out to estimate the effects of SMART on the incidence of school disorders. Despite this, and because the project appeared promising enough to export to other school districts, the Milwaukee Public School System offered some evidence on the worth of the project to the Joint Dissemination and Review Panel (JDRP) of the U.S. Department of Education.[6] The JDRP's acceptance of such evidence would have (a) recognized the effects of the project and (b) positioned the project's participants to receive assistance from the National Diffusion Network for installing the system in other districts. The evidence offered initially for the system's effectiveness was judged inadequate because the evidence

150   DISCOVERING WHAT WORKS

was too ambiguous. Consequently, SMART is not yet being disseminated through the Network.

As a final example, consider the "evaluations" of large-scale manpower training programs. The Youth Employment Development Program Act (YEDPA) led to over 300 projects designed to alleviate the problems of unemployed young men and women. Less than a dozen of these projects produced interpretable evaluative evidence, defensible in scientific forums, that the projects actually reduced unemployment or increased wage rates.[7] All evaluative evidence is not equally good despite claims to the contrary.

The independent reviews of the evidence on the effects of such training programs and the lack of evidence resulted in a shift in policies of organizations whose stewardship includes ameliorative human resources projects.[8] In particular, more resources for designing better evaluations, notably resources for controlled field experiments, were developed by the Department of Labor, the Rockefeller Foundation, and the Ford Foundation for the production of credible evidence.

What Demonstrations and Experiments Teach Us

Experiences such as these are common, and the U. S. Department of Education has had similar ones. More important, such experience invites inventing evaluation policy for the Department of Education that facilitates better exploitation of demonstration projects and experiments and, as a consequence, produces better evidence about what works, what works better, and why.

DEMONSTRATION PROJECTS AT THEIR BEST

Demonstrations of the 1970s and 1980s usually involved trying to put a project into the field. The best of such efforts, a small fraction of the total, produced good evidence about the project's implementation. That is, they produced defensible data on: (a) *how* to specify goals and actualize plans; (b) *whether* a plan can be actualized, e.g., whether services can be delivered efficiently; and (c) client flow, e.g., the pipeline on number served, dropouts, and so forth. For example, the Rockefeller Foundation's field tests of programs for minority female single parents included serious attention to these aspects of the project. Ethnographic and management studies were undertaken early to understand the problems of recruiting women into the project, to understand women's views of their experience, and other implementation issues. The major benefits of well-done implementation studies, to judge from McLaughlin's review, are substantial: sophisticated understanding of variability in implementation, the tension between micro and macrolevel implementation issues, the systemic and contextual influences on implementation, and the critical need for negotiation.[9]

Despite their merits on these grounds, demonstration projects as they have usually been designed do *not* give answers to two important questions: What was the project's (or program's) effect? And what approach or project variation is more effective?

As they were implemented during the 1980s, demonstration projects did not answer the question "Does it work?" because they commonly included no provision for a credible control condition. One could not then determine whether the activity had an effect regardless of its ostensible success. Put in other words by an able scholar: "A qualitative researcher who seeks causes thus has to become an experimenter—a matter that those in the anthropological tradition have long recognized."[10]

To reiterate, this criticism of the old style demonstration project does not mean it is worthless. Demonstrations produce useful evidence about program implementation. Indeed, such evidence is commonly in demand and used in policy forums.[11] But the thoughtful public servant, practitioner, bureaucrat, or scholar need not be content with demonstration projects which at their best have involved no systematic attempt to estimate effects. This leads us to the comparative test generally, and in particular to the controlled randomized field experiments considered later.

WHAT COMPARATIVE TESTS, ESPECIALLY RANDOMIZED FIELD EXPERIMENTS, TEACH US

Well designed comparative tests address one of two questions: (a) What was the project's (or program's) relative effect? That is, what difference does it make? and (b) What approach is more effective? That is, what works better? The statistical technology available to answer either question, notably for design of randomized experiments, is dedicated to producing an estimate of relative difference that is as unequivocal as possible. Exploiting the technology leads to unbiased estimates of the project's effect relative to a control condition (Does it work?) or an unbiased estimate of the differences among project regimens (What works better?), and to a credible statistical statement of one's confidence in the results.

Determining whether a drop-out prevention project has an effect on its target individuals, for example, requires understanding how the adolescents would have behaved in the absence of the project. This understanding comes about by assuring that we can either (a) predict adolescents' behavior in the absence of the program or (b) represent adolescents' behavior well in the absence of the program by using an equivalent comparison group. The prediction of adolescents' behavior is usually difficult or impossible. The representation of adolescents' behavior in the absence of the project is difficult but possible. We cannot predict behavior well, but we know how to construct a fair comparison group, notably by randomly assigning individuals to alternative regimens.

The most credible representative of behavior by an equivalent comparison group involves a randomized experiment. Consider a contemporary example. In testing new variations on Head Start during the 1970s, various researchers initiated efforts to learn whether programs for new home environments could be introduced to and would be used by the parents of high-risk children.[12] The researchers also thought it was important to produce high-quality evidence on effectiveness of the new programs especially in view of the low quality of evidence on effectiveness of earlier related Head Start projects. Longitudinal studies were undertaken in seven sites. In one site, the project was evaluated using an experimental design in which half of each of six cohorts were randomly assigned to the new program versus conventional services.

The random assignment of individuals to alternative regimens assures that there are no systematic differences between the groups receiving special services and those receiving conventional ones. The procedure also permits one to exploit available technology to generate a legitimate statistical statement of one's confidence in the results.

Evaluation designs of kinds *other* than randomized tests can, at times, yield credible estimates of the effects of new regimens. But they require more assumptions. The assumptions are often heroic and untestable.[13] This, and evaluations that had arguably invidious statistical biases,[14] led during the 1980s and early 1990s to considerably more sophisticated randomized field experiments.

Ellickson and Bell, for instance, randomly assigned schools to a special drug prevention program versus control conditions. They found that the program did indeed reduce the likelihood that students would start to use marijuana but that the program's effect on their initiating use of alcohol was short-lived.[15] This experiment builds on earlier tests of risk reduction regimens for adolescents.[16] It extends recent policy emphasis on randomized tests for planning and evalua-

tion in AIDS education and prevention programs,[17] youth employment programs,[18] drop-out prevention programs,[19] and others.

During the 1970s, randomized field tests of social and education
programs usually did *not* focus heavily on the content of programs
being tested, i.e., on the implementation evidence that a high-quality
demonstration project might generate.[20] During the 1980s, the best of
field experiments attended to both the controlled randomized test for
outcome differences *and* the implementation issues.[21] Further, the best
of federal evaluation policies during the 1990s, including those of the
U.S. Department of Education, make attention to each a sine qua non
for good work.[22]

Elements of Evaluation Policy for
Education Projects and Programs

The experience, then, of the last two decades is that the best of
demonstration projects answer well such implementation questions as
"What is going on?" The best of controlled field experiments address
questions about both implementation *and* the project's effect.

How might this understanding be incorporated into evaluation
policy that meets the directive of President Bush's administration?
How do we exploit this experience to assure that education programs
can be improved?

The hard lessons of evaluation in education, civil and criminal
justice, human resources, and health services suggest the importance of
the elements of an evaluation policy discussed in the following
paragraphs.[23]

DO FEWER BUT BETTER EVALUATIONS

Considerable resources are necessary to design, execute, and educe
policy implications from evaluations of a project's effect or the relative
effectiveness of alternative interventions. Well-designed randomized
experiments to estimate the effects of manpower training programs in
five sites supported by the Rockefeller Foundation, for instance, cost
nearly $1 million per year excluding program costs.[24] Well-designed
experiments in five police jurisdictions, designed to test ways of
handling domestic violence better, required about the same level of
support from the National Institute of Justice. Both efforts required
experienced, technically competent researchers who were well informed about local conditions and sensitive to national needs in order
to assure that the research was relevant to local and federal policy.

One of the consequences of trying to do too many demonstrations or evaluations is that money is wasted in supporting work of dubious value. For instance, over 80 percent of YEDPA projects produced evaluation results that were not credible in demanding public policy forums.[25] Only a few conscientiously designed efforts were sufficiently good to justify relying on them in planning new evaluation and research policy at the U.S. Department of Labor.

The implication of all this is that undertaking a small number of good evaluations of program effects is sensible and ought to be a part of any evaluation policy. Such an element of evaluation policy, put in other words by Boruch and Wortman and by Campbell,[26] runs against the practice in the 1970s and early 1980s of mounting a single "national program evaluation." The latter strategy does not comport well with scientific standards of understanding. Campbell, for example, argues that evaluations of selected projects, replicated in diverse settings instead of uniform national efforts, are far more likely to "resemble hard science . . . (and be) regarded as more complete if confirmation (of evaluative results) comes under differing instrumentation that is theoretically equally relevant."[27]

EVALUATE THE PROUDEST OR MOST PROMISING

It is important to develop sensible selection criteria for choosing which demonstrations to evaluate, in the sense of gauging effects. Campbell advises us to evaluate only the projects that are proudest of (or most likely to be proud of) their work. The advice is sensible. For Campbell, the element of pride is determinable partly from statements like "We've got something special that we know works and think others ought to borrow."[28]

This criterion, evaluating the proudest, arguably involves some abrogation of responsibility. Government also needs to know what projects are not proud. And why. This, in turn, argues for augmenting Campbell's advice. It implies a responsibility to search for failure. *How* to do this effectively and productively is not clear. But thoughtful bureaucrat-scholars and public servants are likely to be able to invent ways to handle this responsibility. That is part of their job.

ASK "WHAT WORKS BETTER?" MORE OFTEN THAN "DOES IT WORK?"

Answering the question "Does it work?" requires that a new program or project be compared against a control condition in which only ordinarily available services are provided to an equivalent group. At best, each group is a randomly constituted sample of eligible target individuals. This control condition is, at times, politically or ethically unacceptable.

The obstacles to a "no-program" control are especially great for ongoing programs and entitlement programs. As a consequence of this and as a consequence of the need to improve, the policy question for such programs must be shifted.

In particular, asking "What works better?" will often be more interesting for society and science. It will often be more feasible than a question such as "Does it work?" that requires a "no-program" control group. It invites us to learn by comparing different ways of doing things. A statement that "A produces a higher achievement level than B" is more palatable than "B does not work." This perspective drives the advice of the National Academy of Sciences to the Centers for Disease Control on evaluation policy for AIDS education programs.[29]

ENCOURAGE COMPETITION

Serious peer review is difficult for a government agency or private foundation to actualize. It is nonetheless worthwhile in the sense that it arguably produces a higher-quality product. The implication is that evaluation proposals ought to be reviewed in a competitive peer review process.

It is not always possible to have competing proposals, of course. Nor is it always desirable. This argues for learning how to exploit competition better when regular competition is not possible.

So, for example, both Northwestern University and the National Academy of Sciences (NAS) were awarded sole source contracts by the U.S. Department of Education some time ago to assess the quality of educational evaluations produced during President Carter's administration. The NAS is distinctive in its ability to bring together a prestigious, visible, and influential blue ribbon panel to review research. For this reason, NAS was a viable candidate for a sole source contract and indeed did receive such a contract.[30]

Northwestern University's faculty members were among a list of researchers who were sufficiently outside the educational evaluation industry *and* well enough informed about evaluation to justify being considered for a sole source contract for reviewing the industry's products.

After the contracts were awarded, both groups competed vigorously, in the sense of acquiring and analyzing information and in attempting to produce usable research. Other indicators of competition include the fact that (a) the NAS Committee was not entirely comfortable with the arrangement and (b) the hungry young

Northwestern evaluators were eager to get beyond what a NAS committee could produce. Both reports were arguably better than they would have been in the absence of the competition, although both were sole source awards.

USE HIGH-QUALITY CONTROLLED FIELD TESTS

The failure to capitalize on evaluation designs of sufficiently high quality is evident in a variety of areas. Estimates of Head Start's effects, for instance, produced results that were arguably misleading at worst, and ambiguous at best.[31] Imperfect evaluation designs for estimating project effects or relative effectiveness have led to similarly misleading or ambiguous results in evaluation of manpower training projects,[32] medical interventions,[33] pregnancy prevention efforts,[34] and other areas.[35]

The implication is that evaluation designs that produce the least equivocal and least biased estimates possible ought to be used. The technology of high-quality designs for comparative tests for determining what works or what works better is well understood. The designs include randomized field experiments of the sort stressed here. The suitability of other designs, notably quasi-experiments, usually depends heavily on theory and the availability of evidence that help rule out competing explanations for the effect that is found.[36]

The benefits of high-quality designs for comparative tests of projects are, as Bangser suggested,[37] that policy arguments will revolve around implications of the evaluation and *not* around whether the results are scientifically credible. The use of high-quality randomized experiments in tests of High/Scope, "Sesame Street," Middle Start, Supported Work, and so forth, were, in fact, credible relative to scientific standards. The results are often cited and have been used despite their imperfections.

REPLICATE THE SINGLE RESULTS IN
OTHER SETTINGS

A single well-designed experiment can be informative and useful. Witness the extent to which the High/Scope experiment on education for preschoolers has been cited.[38] Consider also that the arrest policy shown to be effective in the Minneapolis Domestic Violence experiment was adopted by nearly a third of the nation's 120 big-city police departments.

Relying on a single, well-controlled experiment, however, is risky. The cultural, ethnic, and income characteristics of High/ Scope's sample of mothers and children are different from what one would find among families eligible for special programs in Tucson and New Haven, for example. The cultural and ethnic context and the criminal justice system in Minneapolis differ appreciably from the contexts in Miami and Omaha.

The important implication for science and policy is that what works better in site A, to judge by excellent evidence from an experiment at the site, may *not* work in site B. In fact, reversals do occur. An early experimental test of pretrial hearings, for example, produced evidence that the hearings did not reduce court time. Subsequent tests, which modified the system thoughtfully, showed that pretrial hearings work in the sense of producing higher rates of settlement and settlements that are less time consuming than the conventional appeals court regimen.[39]

Assuring that we know how results might vary across sites in a multisite sequence set of comparative tests is a major justification for the Spouse Assault Replication Program of the National Institute of Justice (NIJ).[40] The interest of NIJ lies in understanding whether how police handled domestic violence in Minneapolis will work, or make no difference, or have a negative effect in Miami, Omaha, and other sites.

Campbell pushes this policy element a step further in advising us to evaluate only the proudest programs that can be disseminated, i.e., put into place somewhere else.[41] His line of argument is that evaluating a program conscientiously in settings *other* than the one in which it first seemed to be, or was shown to be, successful is essential to building scientific understanding in the social sector. Evaluations of "voluntary borrowing" build science in the education arena as in the physical domain.

The policy implication is that replicative evaluations ought to be supported. That is, government should fund controlled tests of projects transported from other settings to determine how, and how well, they work in the new settings.

Field Testing New Programs and Purported Improvements to Ongoing Programs

DEMONSTRATION PROJECTS: DOES IT WORK?

Recall that the major virtue of demonstration projects during the 1970s and 1980s has been that they have usually been designed to produce only one kind of accountability evidence, i.e., data bearing on provision of service. Their major failure during the same period was to give short shrift to the question "Did it have an effect?" Consider the following, then, as a strategic rule: *For any given program area, some demonstrations must employ a randomized controlled experiment that produces unbiased estimates of the project's effects.* There is ample evidence from field testing in this and other arenas that such randomized experiments are often, if not always, feasible when *new* projects are tested. Consider some examples.

Jason and his colleagues at DePaul University undertook randomized experiments to prevent or ameliorate the problems of children at high educational risk.[42] The children were third, fourth, and fifth graders from impoverished families. The program focused on tutoring and other intensive in-school support. The children's educational disadvantage was sufficient to justify augmenting the program during the third year with biweekly parent education.

The project introduced something new to the schools. As a consequence it was easier to introduce the idea of a randomized "no-program" control. In these experiments, twenty schools were randomly assigned to the special regimen and twenty were randomly assigned to serve as controls.

In Houston, Johnson and others mounted randomized tests of a parent education project for parents of young Mexican-American children at high risk.[43] This involved assigning half of each annual cohort of parents to the new program and the other half to the control condition. The program services were well beyond ordinary ones and consequently the control condition was feasible.

The recent history of field experiments in the social sector and education suggests that requiring randomized experiments of *all* new projects, even where projects are uniform in character, is not sensible. Sample sizes in some projects may be too small to exploit, except perhaps in a cooperative multischool effort. Many schools or districts will not have the capacity even with technical support, or the willingness even with incentives. Further, not all projects (e.g., statewide initiatives) have activities and purposes that lend themselves to comparative tests. Finally, not all projects will be important enough to evaluate this way. That is, the investment of evaluation resources is not justified given the size, replicability, or nature of the project.

All this argues for a procedure proposed in Coyle, Boruch, and Turner's *Evaluating AIDS Prevention Programs:*

1. Identify the new projects that are important enough to justify experiments and lend themselves technically to comparative randomized tests that involve a control group.

2. Develop incentives, notably funding, to provide to the selected

schools or districts in return for their cooperation in comparative randomized tests.

3. Employ an *independent* evaluation team to design the experiments, execute randomized assignment, monitor integrity and maintenance of assignment, and analyze results. The evaluators must be able to work with schools or districts and be technically able. The evaluation group would also be responsible for analyzing data, estimating relative effects, and reporting to the Department.

4. Employ an advisory board that oversees the multisite experiments and does cross-site analyses and simultaneous secondary analysis. This is likely to be essential given the diversity of even ten to twenty projects.[44]

The feasibility of a similar strategy has been demonstrated in a variety of areas. The cross-site oversight approach to independent projects has been used in the experiments of the National Institute of Justice on police handling of domestic violence.[45] The single evaluation team approach to design, execution, and interpretation has worked well in recent evaluations of training programs for a variety of vulnerable populations, e.g., Rockefeller Foundation's randomized field experiments for estimating the effect of training programs for poor minority mothers.[46]

EXISTING PROGRAMS: WHAT WORKS BETTER?

In the preceding section, I proposed that a small sample of the *new* projects be tested against control conditions. That is, the object was to understand whether the project "makes a difference" relative to ordinary conditions. In this section, I propose a procedure for determining which of two or more approaches to a problem works better. The procedure is most relevant to improving *ongoing* programs rather than new programs. Consider the following strategic rule: *Some programs must do comparative randomized experiments to determine which of two or more approaches works best.* Only a few school districts or community-based organizations are likely to be suitable for comparing different approaches to a problem. Not all are capable of inventing potentially better approaches than what they have developed already. This leads to the consideration of the following procedural strategy:

1. Select candidate projects on the basis of project importance, pride in the project, project capacity, and program transportability.

2. Develop a system and incentives for encouraging projects to determine what works better, i.e., employing at least two approaches within a site, and testing using randomized experiments. Such a

system might involve a request for a proposal to replicate approaches found elsewhere. The incentives may include providing money for the program replication (i.e., the new variation) and further money for participating in the experiment.

3. Obtain or support an *independent* evaluation team to design the experiment, do random assignment and monitor its integrity, collect data, analyze results.

4. Develop or support an advisory board that does cross-site analyses in the interest of controlling the evaluation and representing a coherent set of findings.

Some problems in executing such studies will be very difficult, so we should expect to fail in one out of five attempts to execute a field test.

Appropriateness and Feasibility of Randomized Field Experiments

The policy elements given earlier encourage the use of randomized tests to estimate the effects of projects *where appropriate and feasible*. This phrase needs definition, of course.

APPROPRIATENESS

The Federal Judicial Center (FJC) proposes at least four critical threshold conditions for deciding whether randomized tests need to be considered seriously. Put simply, they are: (1) there is need for important improvement in practice or policy; (2) the effectiveness of proposed approaches to improvement is uncertain, and relative certainty is important; (3) methods other than randomized tests, will not, in the particular context, yield estimates of effectiveness that are as good as those yielded by experiments; (4) the results will be used.[47]

Bangser's discussion of strategies in successful manpower experiments and Ambach's discussion of education make plain the importance of getting results of the evaluation used.[48] The implication is that there must be a considerable investment of resources in publishing readable reports for a lay public, in providing testimony to the Congress, and so on.

Bangser puts considerable emphasis on determining whether proposals and possible improvements are important enough to test using a randomized field experiment: some experiments are avoided simply because the proposal is not sufficiently important.[49] The weaknesses of evaluation designs other than randomized tests, implied by the third FJC criterion, has been considered deeply and routinely in discussions to mount randomized tests of programs in the manpower arena,[50] in vocational rehabilitation,[51] in Chapter I,[52] and in methodological work by scholars such as Campbell.[53]

Bangser added to these four another condition that is sensible.[54] He maintains that government changes in *systems*, alterations of entire state organizations do not lend themselves well to controlled comparative tests. Variations on multiple units within a system can, however, lend themselves well to comparative tests, for example, of reduced reporting requirements in the 400 school districts of a state such as Pennsylvania.

FEASIBILITY

Randomized experiments designed to gauge what works or works better may be "appropriate" relative to the conditions just described. But they may not be feasible. Criteria for judging and enhancing the feasibility of controlled randomized field experiments or high-quality quasi-experiments have been developed over the past decade for educational evaluation and in other arenas. Put briefly, tactics for enhancing feasibility include:

1. Assuring that standards of propriety (for example, the standards of the Federal Judicial Center discussed earlier) are met;

2. Providing incentives for school districts or education-related and community-based organizations to cooperate in comparative tests (e.g., scientific, social, managerial, professional, or financial gratification);

3. Building on precedent (i.e., exploiting others' experience);

4. Mounting pilot tests to enhance feasibility of a controlled experiment;

5. Assuring that the size of the target group is large enough to generate precise estimates of effect and sensitive comparisons among regimens;

6. Developing clear and effective ways to explain and justify random assignment to stakeholders (parents, teachers, etc.) in the context;

7. Tailoring the experimental design to suit the setting;

8. Working with teachers, parents, administrators, etc. to improve the evaluation design and to actualize it.[55]

Summary

To make President Bush's accountability mandate for education a material enterprise rather than a virtual one, consider the following.

First, the hard experience of the last decade or two of evaluations in education and other arenas must be exploited. Second, we must get beyond that experience to assure that future successes are easier to detect and easier to capitalize on.

The experience of special concern here lies in how to address two questions about an educational intervention: Does it work? And what works better? These questions are important. They are implicit in the President's directive and in some of the activities of some state departments of education and some components of the U.S. Department of Education. How to answer the questions is important, but not so obvious.

The strategy proposed here reiterates and augments strategy exploited well at times in education and in other arenas such as medicine and health services, civil and criminal justice, and therapy. It puts special emphasis on the questions "Does it work?" and "What works better?" and recognizes that antecedent questions such as "What is the problem?" must be addressed earlier. It depends also on a question that is a sequel to each of these: "How do we know?" (i.e., What is the evidence?).

Consider the question "Does it work?" for *new* government initiatives at the local, state, or federal level. Demonstration projects have been fine vehicles for political initiative and learning whether or not an idea can be translated into program activity. Historically, however, such projects have usually avoided the question of effects or have not had the capacity to determine whether the demonstration had a remarkable effect on its targets.

The better capitalization on demonstration projects, if Bush's directive is taken seriously, involves assuring that some demonstrations are evaluated relative to a randomized control condition. That is, eligible individuals are randomly assigned to either the project or to a control condition (already existing services) in the interest of determining whether the demonstration's effect on children (or teachers or administrators) is positive, negligible, or even negative. The determination, when groups are randomly assigned, produces a more defensible estimate relative to scientific standards and a statement of one's certainty in the results that is legitimate on statistical grounds, relative to other approaches.

Demonstrations are usually undertaken under the assumptions that (a) the project is "new," (b) the services already available to ameliorate a problem are not entirely adequate, and (c) the demonstration's effectiveness is not known, despite rhetoric, fashion, or popular appeal. I concur with these assumptions in recommending a strategy that requires *some* demonstration projects to involve randomized control groups.

For ongoing projects, rather than new ones, the question "Does it work?" is usually unanswerable or difficult to answer. When the program is well in place, for instance, when no suitable (fair) control conditions can be found, and when there are no base line data, no answer is possible.

For ongoing programs, the strategy recommended here is to address the question "What works better?" using randomized field experiments in *some* projects. That is, children, schools, or teachers are randomly assigned to alternative regimens in the interest of learning which new regimen improves on the current program. Again, the random assignment produces groups that can be compared fairly on scientific grounds. The comparison yields statements of certainty about the results that are legitimate on statistical and scientific grounds.

The strategy recommended for demonstrations cannot be applied to all demonstrations. Nor should it be. In some sites, a randomized experiment may be inappropriate on account of local standards, small client flow, low technical capacity, or other reasons. Similarly, the strategy recommended for learning what works better in existing programs, i.e., that individuals or groups be randomly assigned to one or two or more regimens in order to learn which regimen works better, cannot be applied to all ongoing programs in all areas. In some areas, professionals may be willing and able to participate and conditions at the site are appropriate. Other sites may not be appropriate or professionals may not be capable or willing.

Deciding whether a randomized field experiment is appropriate relative to ethical and legal standards and feasible relative to experience is important in the context of the proposed strategy. A decision about appropriateness can rely on standards developed by the Federal Judicial Center. The Center's criteria include questions of the following sort for which positive answers imply determined and thoughtful consideration of a randomized experiment: (a) Is there a need for improvement? (b) Is the effectiveness of proposed solutions uncertain? (c) Will the results of the tests be used and therefore be subject to harsh scrutiny in public, scientific, and professional forums? (d) Will evaluation designs other than randomized tests yield remarkably more debatable results? and (e) Will the rights of individuals be protected?

A positive response to each question invites running a controlled randomized test whether the issue concerns a new initiative or an existing program. A negative response means that either a randomized test is impossible, in which case nonrandomized tests may be acceptable, or that no reasonable estimate of a demonstration's effect or of the relative effects of variations on an ongoing program is likely to be possible.

Determining whether a randomized test of a demonstration project is feasible or whether a randomized test of new variations on an existing program is feasible also demands attention to criteria. The practitioner-scholar, bureaucrat-scholar, and politician-scholar, and scholars have made the following criteria important: (a) assuring that standards of ethical and legal propriety are met; (b) providing incentives for practitioners, bureaucrats, and politicians to collaborate in controlled randomized tests; (c) recognizing precedent (what has been done well before can arguably be done again); (d) exploiting conventional statistical methods (e.g., statistical power analysis) to assure evaluations that are sensitive, and orthodox statistical methods (e.g., pilot tests of experiments and pipeline studies) to assure that flops are less frequent; (e) tailoring the experiment to suit the setting (e.g., by depending on local practitioner, bureaucrat, politician, and scholar).

Much of the strategy offered so far is based on technological criteria (e.g., statistical design of randomized experiments) and on the evaluative experience at the micro and intermediate levels over the last two decades. The strategy is suspect, and ought to be suspect, because it is parochial relative to federal standards. To meet these standards, we might take the advice of wise colleagues and wise enemies over the last ten years on evaluation policy generally:

1. Do few evaluations but better ones to understand what works and what works better.

2. Try to estimate the effects of only the promising ones; evaluate the proud.

3. Address the question "What works better?" far more often than the question "Does it work?"

4. Encourage competition, even in sole source arrangements.

5. Reanalyze each important evaluation and ask that each major experiment be replicated.

FOOTNOTES

1. U. S. Department of Education, *Guidance on Implementing President Bush's Accountability Mandate* (Washington, DC: U. S. Department of Education, 1989).

BORUCH 165

2. Alan L. Ginsberg, "Revitalizing Program Evaluation: The U. S. Department of Education Experience," *Evaluation Review* 13, no. 6 (1989): 579-597.

3. Ibid.

4. U. S. General Accounting Office, *Educational Issues* (Transition Series), GAO OCG-89-8TR (Washington, DC: U. S. General Accounting Office, 1988); idem, *Program Evaluation Issues* (Transition Series), GAO OCG-89-8TR (Washington, DC: U. S. General Accounting Office, 1988).

5. Charles F. Turner, Heather G. Miller, and Lincoln E. Moses, eds., *AIDS: Sexual Behavior and Intravenous Drug Use* (Washington, DC: National Academy Press, 1989); S. L. Coyle, Robert F. Boruch, and Charles F. Turner, eds., *Evaluating AIDS Prevention Programs* (Washington, DC: National Academy Press, 1989).

6. Milwaukee Public School System, "Evidence on the Effectiveness of the SMART System" (Milwaukee, WI: Milwaukee Public School System, 1988).

7. Charles L. Betsey, Robin Hollister, Jr., and Mary Papageorgiou, eds., *The YEDPA Years: Report of the Committee on Youth Employment Programs* (Washington, DC: National Research Council, 1985).

8. Ernst W. Stromsdorfer and George Farkas, eds., *Evaluation Studies Review Annual* (Beverly Hills, CA: Sage Publications, 1980); Phoebe H. Cottingham and Aida Rodriguez, "The Experimental Testing of the Minority Female Single Parent Program," in *Proceedings of the American Statistical Association: Survey Research Methods Section* (Washington, DC: American Statistical Association, 1987). pp. 114-121.

9. Milbrey W. McLaughlin, "Learning from Experience: Lessons from Policy Implementation," *Educational Evaluation and Policy Analysis* 9, no. 2 (1987): 171-178.

10. Denis C. Phillips, "Validity in Qualitative Research: Why Worry about the Warrant Will Not Wane," *Education and Urban Society* 20, no. 1 (1987): 17.

11. See Ginsberg, "Revitalizing Program Evaluation," and references therein.

12. Allen W. Gottfried, ed., *Home Environment and Early Cognitive Development: Longitudinal Research* (New York: Academic Press, 1984); Dale L. Johnson, James N. Breckinridge, and Ronald J. McGowan, "Home Environment and Early Cognitive Development in Mexican-American Children," in *Home Environment and Early Cognitive Development*, ed. Gottfried, pp. 151-196.

13. Donald T. Campbell and Julian C. Stanley, *Experimental and Quasi-Experimental Designs for Research* (Chicago: Rand McNally, 1966). (For Danish, Spanish, and German Versions, see E. S. Solomon, ed., *Evaluating Social Action Projects: Principles, Methodological Aspects, and Selected Examples* [Paris: UNESCO, 1980]). See also, Robert E. Barnes and Alan L. Ginsberg, "Relevance of the RMC Models for Title I Policy Concerns," *Educational Evaluation and Policy Analysis* 1, no. 2 (1979): 7-14; Donald T. Campbell et al., "Quasi-Experimental Designs," in *Methodology and Epistemology for Social Science: Selected Papers*, ed. E. Samuel Overman (Chicago: University of Chicago Press, 1988); Paul Meier, "The Biggest Public Health Experiment Ever," in *Statistics: A Guide to the Unknown*, ed. Judith M. Tanur et al. (San Francisco: Holden-Day, 1972).

14. Donald T. Campbell and Robert F. Boruch, "Making the Case for Randomized Assignment by Considering the Alternatives: Six Ways in Which Quasi-Experimental Evaluations in Compensatory Education Tend to Underestimate Effects," in *Evaluation and Experiment: Some Critical Issues in Assessing Social Programs*, ed. Carl A. Bennett and Arthur A. Lumsdaine (New York: Academic Press, 1975).

15. Phyllis L. Ellickson and Robert M. Bell, "Drug Prevention in Junior High: A Multi-Site Longitudinal Test," *Science* 247 (1990): 1299-1306.

16. Reviewed in Turner, Miller, and Moses, eds., *AIDS: Sexual Behavior and Intravenous Drug Use.*

17. Coyle, Boruch, and Turner, eds., *Evaluating AIDS Prevention Programs.*

18. Betsey, Hollister, and Papageorgiou, eds., *The YEDPA Years.*

19. Ginsberg, "Revitalizing Program Evaluation."

20. Henry W. Riecken et al., *Social Experimentation* (New York: Academic Press, 1974).

21. For example, see Broward County School District, *Achievement through Instruction and Motivation: Program Evaluation Report for 1986-87* (Fort Lauderdale, FL: Research Department, School Board of Broward County, 1987).

22. Ginsberg, "Revitalizing Program Evaluation."

23. The elements considered here build on the earlier work of Campbell, of Boruch and Wortman, and of Ginsberg. See Donald T. Campbell, "Reforms as Experiments," *American Psychologist* 24 (1969): 409-429, also in *Handbook of Evaluation Research*, ed. Elmer L. Struening and Marcia Guttentag (Beverly Hills, CA: Sage, 1975); Robert F. Boruch and Paul M. Wortman, "Implications of Educational Evaluation for Evaluation Policy," in *Review of Research in Education*, vol. 7, ed. David Berliner (Washington, DC: American Educational Research Association, 1979), pp. 309-361; Ginsberg, "Revitalizing Program Evaluation."

24. Cottingham and Rodriguez, "The Experimental Testing of the Minority Female Single Parent Program."

25. Betsey, Hollister, and Papageorgiou, eds. *The YEDPA Years.*

26. Boruch and Wortman, "Implications of Educational Evaluation for Evaluation Policy"; Donald T. Campbell, "Problems for the Experimenting Society in the Interface between Evaluation and Service Providers," in *America's Family Support Program*, ed. Sharon Lynn Kagan, Douglas R. Powell, Bernice Weissbourd, and Edward Zigler (New Haven, CT: Yale University Press, 1987), pp. 345-351.

27. Campbell, "Problems for the Experimenting Society in the Interface between Evaluation and Service Providers," p. 347.

28. Ibid.

29. Coyle, Boruch, and Turner, *Evaluating AIDS Prevention Programs.*

30. Senta A. Raizen and Peter H. Rossi, eds., *Program Evaluation in Education: When? How? To What Ends?* (Washington, DC: National Academy Press, 1981).

31. Campbell and Boruch, "Making the Case for Randomized Assignment by Considering the Alternatives."

32. Robert J. LaLonde, "Evaluating the Econometric Evaluations of Training Programs with Experimental Data," *Ameican Economic Review* 76, no. 4 (1986): 604-620; Thomas Fraker and Rebecca Maynard, "The Study of Comparison Group Designs in Evaluation of Employment Related Programs" (Princeton, NJ: Mathematics Policy Research, 1987).

33. Katherine Gray-Donald and Michael S. Kramer, "Causality Inference in Observational versus Experimental Studies," *American Journal of Epidemiology* 127 (1988): 885-892; Committee for Evaluating Medical Technologies in Clinical Use, National Academy of Sciences, *Assessing Medical Technologies* (Washington, DC: National Academy Press, 1985).

34. U. S. General Accounting Office, *Teenage Pregnancy: 500,000 Births but Few Tested Programs* (Washington, DC: General Accounting Office, 1986).

35. Riecken et al., *Social Experimentation.*

36. Campbell and Stanley, *Experimental and Quasi-Experimental Designs for Research.*

37. Michael Bangser, "Manpower Experiments" (Paper presented at the U.S. Department of Education Conference on Educational Accountability and the Bush Mandate on Education, Washington, DC, February 24, 1989).

38. Gordon Ambach, "Political Perspectives on Accountability in Education" (Paper presented at the U. S. Department of Education Conference on Educational Accountability and the Bush Mandate on Education, Washington, DC, February 24, 1989).

39. E. Allan Lind, "Randomized Experiments in the Federal Courts," in *Randomization and Field Experimentation*, ed. Robert F. Boruch and Werner Wothke, New Directions for Program Evaluation, No. 28 (San Francisco: Jossey-Bass, 1985), pp. 73-80.

40. National Institute of Justice, *The Spouse Assault Replication Program* (Washington, DC: National Institute of Justice, 1989).

41. Donald T. Campbell, "Guidelines for Monitoring the Scientific Competence of Prevention Intervention Research Grants," *Knowledge: Creation, Diffusion, Utilization* 8, no. 3 (1987): 389-430. See also, K. F. Watson, "Interview with Donald T. Campbell," *Canadian Journal of Evaluation* 1, no. 1 (1986): 83-86.

42. Leonard A. Jason et al., "Developing, Implementing, and Evaluating a Preventative Intervention for High Risk Transfer Children," in *Advances in School Psychology*, ed. Thomas R. Kratochwill (Hillsdale, NJ: Erlbaum, forthcoming).

43. Johnson, Breckinridge, and McGowan, "Home Environment and Early Cognitive Development in Mexican-American Children."

44. Coyle, Boruch, and Turner, *Evaluating AIDS Prevention Programs.*

45. National Institute of Justice, *The Spouse Assault Replication Program.*

46. Cottingham and Rodriguez, "The Experimental Testing of the Minority Female Single Parent Program."

47. Federal Judicial Center, *Experimentation in the Law* (Washington, DC: Federal Judicial Center, 1981).

48. Bangser, "Manpower Experiments"; Ambach, "Political Perspectives on Accountability in Education."

49. Bangser, "Manpower Experiments."

50. Cottingham and Rodriguez, "The Experimental Testing of the Minority Female Single Parent Program"; Stromsdorfer and Farkas, *Evaluation Studies Review Annual.*

51. Diane C. Pelavin and Sol H. Pelavin, eds., *Evaluating Vocational Education/ Rehabilitation Projects: Report to the U. S. Department of Education* (Washington, DC: Pelavin Associates, 1989).

52. Elizabeth Reisner, ed., *Briefings on Evaluation of Chapter 1 Programs: Report to the U. S. Department of Education* (Washington, DC: Studies Associates, 1989).

53. Donald T. Campbell, "Guidelines for Monitoring the Scientific Competence of Prevention Intervention Research Grants," *Knowledge: Creation, Diffusion, Utilization* 8, no. 3 (1987): 389-430.

54. Bangser, "Manpower Experiments."

55. For examples of the application of these criteria and fuller explanation, see Coyle, Boruch, and Turner, *Evaluating AIDS Prevention Programs*, and Robert F. Boruch, "The Propriety and Feasibility of Testing Vocational Rehabilitation Programs Using Randomized Experiments" (Paper presented at the U. S. Department of Education Conference on Evaluating the Impact of Vocational Rehabilitation Programs, Washington, DC, November 3-4, 1988). The criteria presented here go well beyond those found in Robert F. Boruch et al., "Randomized Experiments for Evaluating and Planning Local Programs: A Summary on Appropriateness and Feasibility," in *Program Evaluation: Patterns and Directions*, ed. Eleanor Chelimsky (Washington, DC: American Society for Public Administration, 1985), pp. 165-175.

Connoisseurship

In its earliest days, educational and program evaluation was both measurement and science oriented. Evaluators thought of themselves as a species of social scientist (or psychologist), the true experiment was the favored design, and measurement of carefully stated objectives was the favored activity. During the decade of the 1970s, there were many criticisms of this general orientation to evaluation, and a variety of other approaches or orientations were developed. (These were sometimes misleadingly known as alternative "models." However, they are best not seen as models, for none of them was so tightly specified, in cookbook fashion, that it dictated the precise steps that should be followed in an evaluation.)

In 1976, Elliot Eisner, Professor of Education and Art at Stanford, published the first of a number of papers and books supporting the "connoisseurship and criticism" orientation. The gist of his argument was as follows: In many important areas of human activity, the judgment of experts is relied upon because the features that matter in those fields cannot be quantified or dissected "scientifically." In fact, often the qualities that evade measurement are those that are key. This is particularly the case in the arts, but it is also the case in many areas of social life, including education. The educational connoisseur has a broad background of experience in his or her field of expertise, and also has a depth of theoretical understanding and educated taste. The judgments of connoisseurs can be relied upon, and can be a guide to others about what factors ought to be attended to in particular situations. Connoisseurs convey their judgments in evocatively (and powerfully) written descriptions or criticisms. In the chapter that follows, Professor Eisner describes the assumptions underlying the approach he has advanced, and he discusses the structure of educational criticism.

CHAPTER VII

Taking a Second Look: Educational Connoisseurship Revisited

ELLIOT W. EISNER

It is rare for scholars to be invited to take a second look at work considered influential when it was first published. Milbrey McLaughlin and Denis Phillips have given me the opportunity to do so in the context of this yearbook. How could anyone pass up the opportunity?

The ideas that they invited me to reexamine were first published in the October 1976 issue of the *Journal of Aesthetic Education*,[1] a journal of admirable quality, but on no one's list of academic best sellers. Indeed, I was surprised but gratified that among my various publications McLaughlin and Phillips selected "Educational Connoisseurship and Criticism: Their Form and Functions in Educational Evaluation." As much as any of my early writing, that piece perhaps develops most clearly my discomfort with then prevailing models of evaluation. In that article I described a different model, one rooted in the arts, and provided an example of what work using this model would look like. In addition, I described what I thought its special utilities in education might be.

Because I have no reason to believe that readers of the NSSE *Yearbook* also read the *Journal of Aesthetic Education* (and every reason to believe that they do not), I will describe the main lines of argument in my earlier essay and then take a "second look."

Educational Connoisseurship Revisited

The argument I advanced began by pointing out that the field of educational evaluation had been significantly influenced by the field of educational psychology and that the field of educational psychology was significantly influenced by the desire of its most influential early leaders (E. L. Thorndike, for example) to create a science of education.

Aligned with the efficiency movement in education, Thorndike believed that a scientifically developed curriculum, scientifically managed, would eventually make it possible to assure the results desired from the schools. Measurement of achievement was not only possible; it was the only way to determine objectively if schools were productive. Taken in concert with curriculum development, educational management and the measurement of performance would provide a technology of practice that would take the guesswork out of teaching.

The results of this aspiration for children, teachers, and schools were not, I said, always helpful. Indeed, the evaluation practices they encouraged, largely through the tests and measurement movement, often interfered with the more important aims of education. The problems with the technological model, I argued, were fourfold.

"First, because scientific assumptions and scientifically oriented inquiry aim at the search for laws or law-like generalizations, such inquiry tends to treat qualities of particular situations as instrumentalities."[2] My point was that the unique qualities of *this* particular classroom, *that* particular child, *this* particular teacher are more likely to be neglected or regarded as "noise" if one treats such qualities as data for saying something about features that are common to a sample of children, a population of classrooms, or a group of teachers. When you look for commonalities and do so through a standardized set of categories or a quantitatively scored set of descriptors, whatever is not included in the categories tends to fall out. Furthermore, the quantification of qualities transforms the distinctive features of the particular into matters of magnitude. Yet what we seek to know about performance is not only how much, but what it is like. Just what is the quality of this child's thinking as displayed in his essays or in mathematics? Just what is this teacher like when she works with these particular children? A number or even a set of numbers is clearly unlikely to reveal what an enlightened eye can see and what a rich, literary form of narrative is able to disclose. I made this case in 1976, and I see no reason to believe that the problems I identified then have been eradicated. But this is only the first of four such problems.

A second problem I had with the technological assumptions directing educational research and evaluation in 1976 was that the aim of educational practice was to achieve specific, measurable goals and that as educational research got better and better, it would be possible not only to specify behaviorally defined objectives for each student, but to implement scientifically tested teaching procedures through which those objectives could be achieved. This model led to a conception of educational practice that was means-ends oriented, concerned with efficiency, and standardized.

There are, of course, not a few who still embrace this model of educational practice. Recent discussions at the Education Summit of September 1989 echo such beliefs. A standardized national curriculum is not far from a standardized national approach to educational accountability. Also associated with the model is the view that the job of the university researcher is to do the basic research, to pass along his or her findings to the educational equivalent of an agricultural extension worker who then disseminates the results to eagerly awaiting teachers. Like the farmers interested in increasing yield per acre, eager teachers would embrace the newly discovered information with alacrity and the yield per acre in schooling would rise as a result.

The problems that concerned me then concern me now. When objectives dominate a teacher's activities, the present is likely to be sacrificed for the future: objectives are by definition always out of reach. This is not to say that teachers or curriculum developers should have no aims; it is to say that a model of evaluation or educational practice built upon the assumption that the quality of education is determined by measuring the achievement of prespecified objectives is one that is far too limited. Teachers pay attention to much more than any set of objectives can specify. Decision making "on the wing" is necessary in any classroom and one of the features that distinguishes the merely competent from the artistic teacher is the skill, grace, and appropriateness of decisions made "in flight." A model that purports to be rational and yet neglects the critical features of genuinely excellent teaching is less rational than it purports to be. I believed this in 1976, and I believe it now.

My third discomfort with the technological model was its preoccupation with objectivity. "Intimation," I wrote, "metaphor, analogy, poetic insight have little place in such a view."[3]

The ramifications of that poorly understood notion we call objectivity led to a sense of detachment. One wrote about subjects in research, treatments given to them, one spoke of "we," or "the researcher," never I. The irony was that these prescribed locutions were (and still are) rhetorical devices designed to persuade the reader that the person doing the research has no personal stake in the way conclusions are derived or how the data are interpreted. Happily, far fewer people believe this today than they did then. Indeed, the most recent edition of the *Publication Manual of the American Psychological*

Association[4] gives psychologists permission to use the first person singular—no small victory.

I say no small victory because the change in language from the third person singular in 1976 to the first person singular in 1983 reflects a broadened, and in my opinion, a more enlightened epistemology. The prevailing view in 1976 was that we lived in a world that was, in principle, discoverable and that the aim of social science was to tell it like it is, that is, to create a representation of reality that is isomorphic with its real features. For a description or explanation of reality to be real, it had to correspond to the reality it purported to represent. Knowledge was produced as the features of reality were discovered and revealed.

This conception of knowledge, long dominant, pays inadequate attention to the human contribution; the contributions that are made by the ways in which we have been socialized, by the language we use, by the theories we employ to guide perception and which we use to account for what we have seen.[5] It fails to acknowledge that the worlds we see and explain are those that we construe and that what we are able to tell others about what we have construed is influenced by the forms of representation we use and the skills we possess in their application. Immaculate perception and ontologically objective description are impossible. Indeed, if there is anything we have learned from the history of science it is that what we believe to be true at any particular period is likely to change.[6] Although there are some, like Denis Phillips,[7] who regard scientific knowledge as the model toward which all who claim to create knowledge should aspire, who believe that the arts have no legitimate claims to the enlargement of understanding, and who believe that propositions that correspond to reality are the ultimate test of truth, insofar as truth can be determined, most of those working in the field of evaluation hold more liberal and, I believe, more liberating views. The entire field of cultural anthropology is a kind of encomium to the ways in which culture shapes the ways humans experience their worlds.

A fourth discomfort I had with the technological scientism that dominated evaluation in the mid-1970s is directly related to the three concerns I have already described. It is this. As tests are developed to provide objective information about the achievement of common objectives for students, they ineluctably control the content and form of the curriculum, influence the ways in which teachers teach, and drive the priorities teachers establish in their classrooms.

It should not be surprising that tests should have such influence.

Teachers, like the rest of us, cannot long remain immune to the ways
in which our work is assessed and when the results of testing get front
page space in local newspapers, the pressure is on for teachers to
address whatever it is those in Princeton, New Jersey, and Iowa City,
Iowa, have included on the standardized tests they have designed.

The old homily that if the tests were really good ones, teaching to
them does not really matter, will not stand up under scrutiny. In the
first place, we do not have "really good" standardized achievement
tests. In the second place, multiple choice tests, the kind that the
Educational Testing Service creates, are designed to provide
procedural objectivity by eliminating the possibility that judgment
might be used in scoring student responses. When there are five
alternatives for the student to select and only one correct response
among the five, scoring can be handled by an optical scanner; no one
needs to exercise any judgment whatsoever.

Although such procedures are efficient, they prohibit test makers
from asking the kinds of questions that give students opportunities to
respond in ways that do not fit a predetermined correct answer. The
provision of such opportunities would make scoring less efficient; it
would also make the tests less objective and since we seek procedural
objectivity in scoring, we design instruments that possess features that
appear objective. In doing so we limit what we teach and what we can
learn about what students know.

Toward an "Alternative" Paradigm

The aim of my earlier work was not primarily to express my
discomfort with prevailing evaluation practices and the assumptions
upon which they were built, but to provide another way to look at the
process and aims of educational evaluation. Since this view is one that
was derived from the arts, I should tell the reader that my proclivity
for an artistic paradigm is something deeply rooted in my early career
as a painter, not from my ignorance of social science. I was trained in
the social sciences at the University of Chicago and my doctoral
dissertation (a factor analytic study of children's artistic creativity[8])
received the Palmer O. Johnson Memorial Award from the American
Educational Research Association. If reinforcement theory was right,
I should have continued to do factor analytic research in education
after I received that award. Alas, I was guided by other lights.

The model I proposed was called then, as it is called now,
educational connoisseurship and educational criticism. My aim here is to

describe the basic features of this model, to discuss the assumptions upon which it is built, and then to address the questions Milbrey McLaughlin and Denis Phillips posed to me: "How do matters stand on this general issue today? What would you write now, if you were re-doing your earlier work? Can you see if you would rephrase your argument or push it to new depths? How do you feel your contribution has influenced the practice of evaluation?"

OPERATING ASSUMPTIONS

As I said, the ideas underlying educational connoisseurship and educational criticism emanate from long-standing practices in the arts. Connoisseurship in art, or music, or literature, is essentially the art of appreciation. The connoisseur is someone who knows what he or she is looking at, or listening to, or reading. The connoisseur is someone whose ability to notice the subtleties that count in some domain, to experience nuance, to recognize the import of a painting, a poem, or a symphony is highly refined. Connoisseurship does not just happen, even though there are some who are naturals. In virtually all cases it requires time, experience, and an ability to surrender oneself to a work of art in order to let it speak. This does not mean emptying one's head and coming to a work as an empty vessel waiting for an inanimate object to fill it. On the contrary, it requires an active intelligence and the application of refined schemata. It requires knowing which schema is appropriate for which work of art. Tone poems are not to be listened to with the expectations appropriate to the music of Antonio Vivaldi. A connoisseur is someone who has worked at the business of learning how to see, to hear, to read the image or text and who, as a result, can experience more of the work's qualities than most of us.

It should be noticed that in this broad sense any coach or teacher, say of literature, is something of a connoisseur within his or her specialization. It is the achievement of connoisseurship that provides the content for a heightened consciousness and the ability to assess its significance. Without such abilities both coaching and teaching are not likely to be handled with competence. Thus one might say that connoisseurship is related to the possession of perceptivity and perceptivity is as important in appreciating the significance of the students' comments, the quality of their essays, the performance of a teacher, and the character of a school as it is in the fields of art, music, and literature. It is our connoisseurship, at whatever level it might be, that yields the experience with which we come to know an object or performance.

Connoisseurship, however, is a private affair, that is, it is a process that lives in the experience of individuals. To make experience public requires the use of some symbolic form, some form of representation. Criticism performs this function.

Critics talk and write about things. Film critics write about movies, social critics about societies, art critics about painting and sculpture, food critics about restaurants, food, and wine. Educational critics talk and write about teaching, classrooms, schools, school districts, textbooks, school architecture, and students. Educational critics, in fact, can talk and write about anything that they believe has educational significance.

The aim of criticism is the enlargement of perception. Dewey put it this way: "The function of criticism is the re-education of the perception of the work of art."[9] The critic, in this sense, functions as a midwife to perception. The offspring is the achievement of a new consciousness. It is worth noting that Dewey says *re*-education of perception. I believe he emphasizes *re*-education because at one level we all can perceive classrooms, students, and teachers. Most of these perceptions are not particularly perceptive. By re-education I believe Dewey meant that criticism is aimed at helping us *re*-see, that is, to see in a new way. The critic's function is to replace the stock response with a keener, more acute sense of the object of his or her attention. De Tocqueville did this for nineteenth century America. Pauline Kael does it for today's films. Sigmund Freud did it for anxious Victorians and Clifford Geertz for Indonesian cock fights. What all of these critics have in common, whether they work as Kael does for the *New Yorker* or as Geertz does for the Institute for Advanced Study at Princeton University, is their penchant and skill in helping the rest of us to see and understand. This achievement requires first, a level of connoisseurship that locates the subtle, often unnoticed yet significant aspects of a situation and, second, the ability to use language to make public what connoisseurship has revealed. Connoisseurship provides criticism with its subject matter and critics provide the rest of us with a bridge with which to get into the work. Educational criticism, or forms close to it, is being done by people like Philip Jackson, Sara Lawrence Lightfoot, Thomas Barone, and Maxine Greene.[10] I will not create a roster of names here; there are many.

When I wrote "Educational Connoisseurship and Criticism: Their Form and Function in Educational Evaluation" in the mid-1970s, I described three dimensions or aspects of educational criticism. These were: *description, interpretation,* and *evaluation.* The descriptive function employed by the critic is to enable others to secure a vivid picture of the scene and in some sense to participate in it vicariously. Scientific description is often so detached, so operationalized, so formalized, so denuded of the qualities from which the data were derived that it is impossible for a reader to reconstruct the scene: only God knows what happened.

Good criticism puts you there. Elie Weisel's *Night*,[11] for those who have the stomach to experience Buchenwald through literature, puts you there. The affect you experience is a part of what it means to know the camp. Indeed, without affect what is learned is only a small part of the story; at worst it is a kind of lie.

The second dimension of educational criticism is interpretation, the process of accounting for what one has given an account of. Why does this teacher function the way he does? How can I explain the influence of testing on the values children are being taught in this classroom? What role does the teacher's planning perform in helping her keep things running smoothly? What problematic, covert function does continuous positive reenforcement have upon children in this classroom? What are the lessons it teaches? To answer these questions it is necessary to go beyond the description of events and to explain how these events function in the lives of students.

Interpretation also refers to the meaning of an event. It should be recognized that there is no clear line to be drawn between description and interpretation. The description of lips that are turned up at each end can signify a smile or a smirk. What is it? It all depends. Notwithstanding the difficulty in saying just how we know, more often than not, we know. And the ability to distinguish the difference is critical for both students and teachers. Interpretation was important in 1976, it is important in 1990.

The third aspect of educational criticism pertains to evaluation. It has always been puzzling to me why the idea that evaluation was a critical element in any set of observations was not obvious to everyone. The essence of perception is its selectivity; the connoisseur is as unlikely to describe every thing in sight as a gourmet chef is to use everything in his pantry. The selective process is influenced by the values one brings to the classroom. What the observer cares about, she is likely to look for. The individual who values academic rigor, the presence of the classics, and hard work for children will look for those things. Making value judgments about the educational import of what has been seen and rendered is one of the critical features of educational criticism, as it also must be in the conduct of conventional *educational* research. The prospects of value free inquiry are about as promising as the correspondence theory of truth.

The three dimensions or aspects of educational criticism that I described in 1976 provided the structure of the model I advanced. When the results of their application were appraised through a set of criteria called *structural corroboration* and *referential adequacy*, the merits of the critic's work could be appraised.

I do not wish to provide a further exegesis of educational connoisseurship and criticism; I have already used more space than I intended. Several of my works can be referred to for those interested in more.[12] I turn now to a dimension of educational criticism I had not conceptualized in 1976. I call it *thematics*.

Thematics

Everyone who has been through graduate school in education or in any of the social sciences knows full well that the business of generalization is one of the essential aims of social science inquiry. They also know that in order to generalize you need to draw a random sample from a population and apply inferential statistics to the data to determine the levels of probability that pertain to future expectations. Most of the readers of this chapter were introduced to these notions early in their academic career. Thematics is a part of a conceptual structure that says that random selection *is not* the only way to generalize.

You will recall that the leads for educational connoisseurship and criticism emanate from the arts. Do works of art generalize? If so, how?

It takes no Socrates to realize that great works of drama and literature, from Aristophanes' *Clouds* to Tennessee Williams's *A Street Car Named Desire* are works that are by no means only about the central characters of these plays. What Aristophanes has to teach goes well beyond the confines of fifth-century B.C. Greece, and the relevance of Tennessee Williams's story about the delicate flower of southern womanhood called Blanche DuBois and her raucous opposite Stanley Kowalski is not limited to New Orleans—or to America. The themes of these works extend over time because they embody features of life that have not paled. Both Aristophanes and Williams help us see our own lives more clearly and in so doing they enlarge our understanding. What does all of this have to do with educational evaluation?

Simply this. Good educational criticism of teaching, classrooms, schools, and even textbooks has lessons to teach that go well beyond their particular subject matters. We have something general to learn by reading Lightfoot's accounts of particular schools in *The Good High School* or Jackson's *Life In Classrooms*. Elie Weisel's *Night* is not only about his personal experience in 1939, but about hell itself and how man creates it. "Concrete universals," philosophers call it. Others call it art. While the work addresses a particular, its meanings transcend any particular classroom. This transcendence allows us to learn from particular experiences. And it is learning from particular experiences that constitute our most useful generalizing capacities.

It is curious, in a way, that this account of generalization from individual cases through the processes of analogy should rankle some of those committed to social science. Almost all research conclusions in the social sciences are "applied" by analogy; after all, the contexts to which findings are applied are never the same; teachers never know if the results reported in journal articles will hold in their particular situation. What teachers do (when they read research) is to *think with* those generalizations rather than to apply them. Replication is possible in the physical sciences: a vacuum, is a vacuum, is a vacuum. It is not in the social sciences, an observation that led Lee Cronbach to quip, "All studies in the social sciences are case studies."

Thematics is that aspect of educational criticism that provides readers with the moral of the story. This can be done explicitly in a concluding set of remarks or it can be provided throughout the course of the criticism itself. Thematics represents the formal acknowledgement of a practice that permeates our daily lives and which has been, de facto, the way we use a part of social science inquiry in the context of schools. That acknowledgement also leads to the realization that generalizing is an inherent aspect of all learning. We would be reluctant to say someone had learned if he could not use ideas learned in one context in another; this process is an ongoing part of the way we negotiate our worlds each day. Hardly anyone I know randomly selects his experiences or depends upon randomization as a condition for generalization.

I do not want to get into an extended discussion of how humans generalize. We all generalize in order to survive. We all modify what we have learned from the past and select those aspects of it that are relevant for dealing with the present. We all consider aspects of the new situation in light of past experience and modify prior experience in light of the immediate context. Both classical research as it is used by practitioners and educational criticism as it is formally rationalized display such features in practice. Thematics represents the explicit acknowledgement of such practices and makes it clear that the lessons to be learned by studying cases pertain to cases beyond those studied.

How Do Matters Stand Today?

How *do* matters stand today? I would say that interest in qualitatively oriented research and evaluation has become one of the most significant developments to emerge in the field of education since the turn of the century. The reason for its significance is not primarily due to the growing numbers of scholars who have been attracted to it, but because qualitative inquiry has made problematic the epistemological hegemony that science has held in the educational research and evaluation communities. Even former hard liners such as Philip Jackson, Donald Campbell, Egon Guba, Robert Stake, and Lee Cronbach have shifted perspectives. There is a change in the nature of the conversation, not simply a refinement of the existing one. There are some, like Denis Phillips, who worry about what he calls the perils of a "tower of Babel."[13] (He is concerned that if we use more than one language, we will not understand each other.) There are others, like Miles and Huberman,[14] who do qualitative work as soft positivists. But most of those attracted to qualitative work display a more generous and, I believe, a more courageous view of method.

This willingness to explore ideas that run counter to accepted methodological canons was not common in the late 1960s. Jackson's *Life in Classrooms* and Louis Smith's *Complexities of an Urban Classroom*[15] provided very important moves in qualitative directions, but, in the main, the strictures of Campbell and Stanley[16] were taken as near gospel in most research centers. At my own institution, Stanford's School of Education, even correlational studies were thought at that time to be merely reconnaissance efforts; *real* research required the "true" experiment, or something close to it. Times indeed have changed. Stanford's School of Education now has a sequence of courses in qualitative methods that parallel those in statistics, and textbooks in qualitative methods have proliferated the educational shelves of university bookstores: Guba and Lincoln's *Naturalistic Inquiry*, Miles and Huberman's *Qualitative Data Analysis*, Patton's *How to Use Qualitative Methods in Education*, are only a few.[17] In 1990, Eisner and Peshkin's *Qualitative Inquiry in Education* was published by Teachers College Press. And in 1991, Macmillan will publish Eisner's *The Enlightened Eye: Qualitative Inquiry and the Enhancement of Educational Practice.*[18] There is no question that during the past fifteen years the context for the conduct of educational research and evaluation has changed.

Books are not the only indices. In the American Educational Research Association, a special interest group in qualitative methods was started in 1985. Its membership has more than doubled since then. In my 1983 AERA vice-presidential address, I spoke of the need for philosophical and political space for those who do educational criticism and other qualitatively oriented studies.[19] This space has continued to grow. In 1987, the *International Journal of Qualitative Studies in Education* was created and even the *American Educational Research Journal*, that bastion of quantitative research, invited Mary Lee Smith to prepare an article intended to signal readers that that journal was receptive to qualitative work. The editor said: "We hope that these steps [the publication of Smith's article and two others] will encourage those of you who may have felt that your manuscripts were inappropriate for *AERJ* to reconsider your judgments and submit them forthwith."[20]

As promising as these developments are, the current situation is not all sweetness and light. Although qualitative research and evaluation are far more acceptable now than they were in the mid-1970s, qualitative research and evaluation are too often defined as essentially a kind of educational ethnography. This conception is limiting and sets unwarranted constraints on method. There are two points I wish to make about the nature of qualitative research and evaluation. First, scholars in any social science—sociology, psychology, political science—can do research and evaluation that is qualitative in nature. Interpretive sociology from Georg Simmel to Erving Goffman is fully qualitative in character.[21] The scholarship in political science represented in the work of David Kretzer is fully qualitative in character.[22] The psychology of Sigmund Freud and that of Bruno Bettelheim and Harry Stack Sullivan are fully qualitative in character.[23] Anthropology has no monopoly on qualitative inquiry and qualitative inquiry should not be defined by anthropological methods alone.

My second point is that qualitative inquiry has no obligation— moral, epistemological, or otherwise—to be scientific in character. Perhaps the primary contribution of my earlier work is its effort to free inquiry from the restrictions of a scientific model, not in order to reject science but to make it possible for scholars to work with other assumptions about the nature of human understanding and the conditions that enlarge it. Educational connoisseurship and criticism, as I have said, is rooted in the arts. It has a long and distinguished history. What I believe we need in education is a bit more space for artistically grounded inquiry to emerge rather than to assume that if one is going to do qualitative research or evaluation, it must be ethnographic and its epistemology scientific.

I predict that acceptance of the diversity of types of scientifically oriented qualitative inquiry will precede acceptance of the artistic model. The former constitutes less of a break with tradition than the latter. Nevertheless, acceptance of the latter will occur. It is already adumbrated in the work of Madeline Grumet, Maxine Greene, Thomas Barone, and though her views on method are a bit ambivalent, in the excellent work of Sara Lawrence Lightfoot. Even, or should I say especially, in anthropology and history artistically rooted work appears. Renato Rosaldo, for example, referring to the work of historian J. H. Hexter writes:

The concept of suspense, for example, pertains to the skills of the former, but not the craft of the latter. "Unless the writer," Hexter says, "has the outcome in mind as he writes the story, he will not know how to adapt the proportions of his story to the actual historical tempo, since that is knowable only to one who knows the actual outcome." Far from being in suspense, writers of history use their knowledge of how the narrative will end to decide how vividly and at what length to portray particular episodes. These features of narrative require conceptual analysis, Hexter says, "if one accepts the view that such attributes of historiography as accessibility, force, vividness, and depth are not merely decorative but have true noetic value." In his view, narrative is a cognitive instrument, not a mere condiment designed to make historical knowledge more palatable.[24]

Carol Stack's *All Our Kin* and Nancy Scheper-Hughes's *Saints, Scholars, and Schizophrenics: Mental Illness in Rural Ireland* also bring an artistic perspective to bear upon their anthropological efforts.[25] Sociologist Barry Schwartz builds his analysis of the social ideals of American society by examining the ways in which visual images reveal social values and reflect social ideals at different points in the history of America.[26] In philosophy even so staunch a philosopher of science as Stephen Toulmin recognizes that, in his words, "episteme was always too much to ask. Instead, the operative question is, Which of our positions are rationally warranted, reasonable, or defensible?"[27]

Scholars in fields such as sociology, education, and anthropology are making significant contributions to a more pluralistic conception of method. In this newfound pluralism artistically based approaches will eventually have their appropriate acceptance. In short, although the fastest growing edge of qualitative methods in education has been in fields closest to those most familiar (they are, after all, members of the same church), other assumptions about method and knowledge are increasingly being recognized.

What are these other assumptions about method and knowledge? What do they portend for the future?

First, the form of representation that is used to convey one's experience to others both constrains and makes possible what one is able to represent.[28] In more prosaic terms this means that poetic language allows us to say what literal language cannot express, and vice versa.[29] Pictures can display what words and numbers cannot describe (something that Apple computer has long recognized). Numbers can symbolize what metaphors cannot indicate. And so it goes. Forms of representation are not indifferent to the content of expression. But even further, the forms of representation one knows how to use and believes to be legitimate for evaluation influence the data one seeks or the qualities one is likely to experience. What we intend to represent with the forms we know how to use interacts with what we are likely to see.

Consider the difference between temperature and the sensation of heat. Temperature is a measurement of heat standardized according to a conventionally defined scale. Heat is the quality of experience. If we believe descriptions of heat to be untrustworthy or imprecise, we turn our attention to temperature. When we turn to temperature we measure. In the process we turn away from matters of sensation and the personal experience of heat. In artistic approaches to evaluation, attention to the personal and social equivalent of heat is crucial; we want to know what the world is like to those in it or how it seems to us. For this we need to pay attention to the subtle qualities individuals and situations display so that we can make justifiable inferences about their experience. Counting and measuring are not precluded in such inquiry; they simply are not central to it.

A second assumption upon which artistic approaches to evaluation rest is that the observer is the primary instrument in what is euphemistically called "data collection." I use quotations around the phrase data collection because it implies that data are out there to be plucked like peonies in a field; the image is of someone carrying a wicker basket walking through a great meadow collecting flowers.

Data are not out there; they are events interpreted. What constitutes data and what constitutes garbage depends upon frame of reference, aim, and method. Furthermore, data are not collected, they are constructed. Data require interpretation and represent the results of a construal, not simply a discovery. To make this construal, the observer needs to have refined sensibilities and a sufficiently differentiated array of schemata to be able to experience and make sense of a small piece of the world. That piece might be a classroom or an essay written by a particular student. The fact that an essay is put into your hands does not guarantee that you can read it anymore than your presence in an art museum guarantees you will be able to read the images of deKooning or Rothko. The physical presence of the subject matter is necessary, but not sufficient.

A third assumption underlying artistic approaches to evaluation is one that I identified earlier: generalization does not require random sampling. Cases provide insights and understanding that can function as a map for examining the future. What one learns about a particular teacher in action can be looked for in other teachers one observes. What one finds in one school, one can seek in others. What generalizes is the generic idea, what Arnheim calls the canonical image,[30] and this idea makes the search more effective and efficient because it alerts one to what counts and to what one might find elsewhere.

But generalizations work in other ways as well. I call it *retrospective generalization*.[31] The usual model of generalization is that of an ideational structure employed to make predictions. What we learn about X, we expect to be true about Y. Retrospective generalization is a process of checking out a new insight against past experience rather than upon experiences yet to be secured. The middle school principal who once commented to me, "Schools are places that have very few soft surfaces" gave me an idea whose validity I determined by consulting my memory, not by searching for hardness in other schools. I did not need to go into other schools to realize that what he said about schools was on the mark. What is puzzling is why I had not thought about it myself. The narrative of educational criticism is often "verified" by relating it to a backlog of experience, not only by looking ahead. Referential adequacy can be determined by checking the past, as well as by checking the future. Indeed, on a broader base, revisionist historians provide a wholly different view of the past which, for those who find it acceptable, provides a more coherent and credible account of a particular period than the work of their more conventional brethren.

A fourth assumption in artistic approaches to evaluation is that knowledge (a) is a verb, not a noun, and (b) is rooted in experience, and experience is, at base, qualitative. Words are *one* of the means we use to create knowledge; they provide cues for its recovery by evoking the experience that gives words meaning. Without a semantic we can experience, words reduce to noise. The implications of the foregoing are significant for our view of the role of language in human understanding. When we limit knowledge to words—propositions at that—we limit our conception of knowledge to what words can convey. Yet who among us is willing to say that everything he or she knows can be put into words—even poetic words?

Humans have the capacity to experience the world in a multitude of ways and the inventiveness to represent their experience in forms that do them justice. To take this idea seriously, and scholars from Cassirer to Langer, from Goodman to Polanyi, from Rorty to Arnheim take it seriously,[32] is to recognize that cognition is wider than language and that restricting research methods to the measurement of variables or to propositional description is to limit understanding. Educational connoisseurship and criticism was intended to drive this point home. It has not as yet reached home, but we are farther along the journey than we were in 1976 and the momentum achieved during the past five years suggests to me that we may double the rate of progress in the next five.

In Retrospect

What have I learned in the past fifteen years and what difference has it made? One of the things I have learned in the past fifteen years is that you can't move into the future if you are always looking back at your behind. If you believe in a set of ideas, it is important to stay with them even when the company is scarce. The field of education has moved in the direction that my work helped develop, and as I stated earlier, I expect the momentum to continue.

I have also learned that ethical matters in qualitative evaluation can be ignored only at one's peril. When you get into schools and classrooms and stay for a long time you get to see things that touch the most personal aspects of teaching. Evaluators have a profound obligation not to hurt and to take those steps necessary to insure appropriate confidentiality.

I have also learned that this is harder to do than it seems. Consider for a moment the matter of informed consent. How does one secure informed consent from a teacher or principal on matters you cannot anticipate will emerge when you begin? And how do you balance your obligations to students with your commitments to teachers? And under what circumstances, if any, are you justified in violating your commitments to the person you observe? These questions are more complex than they first appear and this is not the place to try to formulate answers. It is the place to say that I have become ever more sensitive to these considerations. The field of education has a long way to go in this arena. In how many graduate schools of education are courses being taught in educational ethics?

I have also learned that the ideas that emanated from my work as a painter and my immersion in the field of art have had a long and distinguished history in philosophy and that many of our best social scientists have been experiencing similar trepidations about conventional assumptions employed in research in their own fields. My year as a fellow at the Center for Advanced Study in the Behavioral Sciences in 1987-88 made it possible for me to discover through conversations with other scholars that they had similar concerns about method and that corresponding developments were occurring in their own fields. In fact, the interest among fellows at the Center in qualitative methods was sufficiently large and widespread that we created a special interest group for purposes of discussion and debate.

Finally, Milbrey McLaughlin and Denis Phillips asked in their invitation whether or not I thought my "contribution has influenced the practice of evaluation?" I suppose it has. I suppose it contributed to the growing legitimacy that qualitative evaluation now enjoys. One never really knows the extent to which one's work makes a difference. An occasional letter appears, a student writing a dissertation in this institution or that writes to seek advice, people comment about your work at conferences. It is information such as this that provides the basis for inference.

I would like to think that my contributions were important, but I know very well that they have been a part of a more general movement. I also know that the kind of work that I have advanced is difficult to do well. It is a form of work that cannot be standardized or rule driven. It depends on insight, perceptivity, and not the least, the ability to write in ways that illuminate rather than obscure the delicate phenomena that constitute educational practice. Nevertheless, invitations such as the one extended to me provide reassurance that my work has been consequential, and that realization is both satisfying and motivating.

. FOOTNOTES

1. Elliot W. Eisner, "Educational Connoisseurship and Criticism: Their Forms and Functions in Educational Evaluation," *Journal of Aesthetic Education* 10, nos. 3-4 (1976): 135-150.

2. Ibid., pp. 136-137.

3. Ibid., p. 138.

4. American Psychological Association, *Publication Manual of the American Psychological Association*, 3d ed. (Washington, DC: American Psychological Association, 1983).

5. Nelson Goodman, *The Languages of Art* (Indianapolis: Hackett Publishing Co., 1976); idem, *Ways of Worldmaking* (Indianapolis: Hackett Publishing Co., 1976); Richard Rorty, *Philosophy and the Mirror of Nature* (Princeton, NJ: Princeton University Press, 1979).

6. Arthur Koestler, *The Sleepwalkers* (New York: Macmillan, 1959).

7. Denis C. Phillips, "Validity in Qualitative Research: Why the Worry about Warrant Will Not Wane," *Education and Urban Society* 20, no. 1 (1987): 9-24.

8. Elliot W. Eisner, "Children's Creativity in Art: A Study of Types," *American Educational Research Journal* 2, no. 3 (1965): 125-136.

9. John Dewey, *Art as Experience* (New York: Minton Balch and Co., 1934), p. 324.

10. Philip W. Jackson, *Life in Classrooms* (New York: Holt, Rinehart and Winston, 1968); Sara Lawrence Lightfoot, *The Good High School* (New York: Basic Books, 1983); Thomas Barone, "Things of Case and Things of Beauty: The Story of the Swain Country High School Arts Program," *Daedalus* 112, no. 3 (1983): 1-28; Maxine Greene, *Landscapes of Learning* (New York: Teachers College Press, 1978).

11. Elie Weisel, *Night* (New York: Discus Books, Avon Publishing Co., 1969).

12. Elliot W. Eisner, "Emerging Models for Educational Evaluation," *School Review* 80, no. 4 (1972): 573-590; idem, "Alternatives to Quantitative Forms of Educational Evaluation," *Thrust for Educational Leadership* 5, no. 2 (1975): 13-15; idem, "Educational Connoisseurship and Educational Criticism: Their Forms and Functions in Educational Evaluation"; idem, "On the Use of Educational Connoisseurship and Educational Criticism for Evaluating Classroom Life," *Teachers College Record* 78, no. 3 (1977): 345-358; idem, "The Use of Qualitative Forms of Evaluation for Improving Educational Practice," *Educational Evaluation and Policy Analysis* 1, no. 6 (1979): 11-19; idem, "Toward a Conceptual Revolution in Evaluation," *Educational Forum* 44, no. 3 (1980): 373-374; idem, "The 'Methodology' of Educational Connoisseurship and Educational Criticism," *California Journal of Teacher Education* 8, no. 1 (1981): 82-96; idem, "On the Differences between Artistic and Scientific Approaches to Qualitative Research," *Educational Researcher* 10, no. 4 (1981): 5-9; idem, *Cognition and Curriculum: A Basis for Deciding What to Teach* (New York: Longman, 1982); idem, "Anastasia Might Still be Alive, But the Monarchy Is Dead," *Educational Researcher* 12, no. 5 (1983): 13-14, 23-24; idem, "Can Educational Research Inform Educational Practice?" *Phi Delta Kappan* 65, no. 7 (1984): 447-452; idem, "Aesthetic Modes of Knowing," in *Learning and Teaching the Ways of Knowing*, ed. Elliot Eisner, Eighty-fourth Yearbook of the National Society for the Study of Education, Part 2 (Chicago: University of Chicago Press, 1985): idem, *The Art of Educational Evaluation: A Personal View* (London, England: Falmer Press, 1985); idem, *The Educational Imagination: On the Design and Evaluation of School Programs*, 2d ed. (New York: Macmillan, 1985); idem, "A Secretary in the Classroom," *Teaching and Teacher Education* 2, no. 4 (1986): 325-328; idem, "The Primacy of Experience and the Politics of Method," *Educational Researcher* 17, no. 5 (1988): 15-20.

13. Denis C. Phillips, "After the Wake: Postpositivistic Educational Thought," *Educational Researcher* 12, no. 5 (1983): 4-12.

14. Matthew Miles and A. Michael Huberman, *Qualitative Data Analysis* (Beverly Hills, CA: Sage Publications, 1984).

15. Louis Smith and William Geoffrey, *Complexities of an Urban Classroom: An Analysis toward a General Theory of Teaching* (New York: Holt, Rinehart and Winston, 1962).

16. Donald Campbell and Julian Stanley, *Experimental and Quasi-Experimental Designs for Research* (Chicago: Rand McNally, 1966).

17. Yvonna Lincoln and Egon Guba, *Naturalistic Inquiry* (Beverly Hills, CA: Sage Publications, 1985); Miles and Huberman, *Qualitative Data Analysis*; Michael Patton, *How to Use Qualitative Methods in Evaluation* (Newbury Park, CA: Sage Publications, 1987).

18. Elliot Eisner and Alan Peshkin, eds., *Qualitative Inquiry in Education* (New York: Teachers College Press, 1990); Elliot Eisner, *The Enlightened Eye: Qualitative Inquiry and the Enhancement of Educational Practice* (New York: Macmillan, 1991).

19. Eisner, "Can Educational Research Inform Educational Practice?"

20. Virginia Richardson-Koehler, "Editor's Statement," *American Educational Research Journal* 24, no. 2(1987): 171.

21. George Simmel, *On Individuality and Social Forms* (Chicago: University of Chicago Press, 1971); Erving Goffman, *The Presentation of Self in Everyday Life* (New York: Doubleday, 1959).

22. David Kretzer, *Ritual, Politics, and Power* (New Haven, CT: Yale University Press, 1988).

23. Sigmund Freud, *Interpretation of Dreams* (Leipzig and Vienna: Deuticke, 1900); Bruno Bettelheim, *Children of the Dream* (New York: Macmillan, 1969); Harry Stack Sullivan, *The Interpersonal Theory of Psychiatry* (New York: W. W. Norton, 1953).

24. Renato Rosaldo, *Culture and Truth: The Remaking of Social Analogies* (Boston: Beacon Press, 1989), p. 134.

25. Carol Stack, *All Our Kin* (New York: Harper and Row, 1975); Nancy Scheper-Hughes, *Saints, Scholars, and Schizophrenics: Mental Illness in Rural Ireland* (Berkeley: University of California Press, 1979).

26. Barry Schwartz, "The Icon and the Word: A Study in the Visual Depiction of Moral Character," *Semiotica* 61 (1986): 69-99.

27. Stephen Toulmin, "The Construal of Reality: Criticism in Modern and Postmodern Science," in *The Politics of Interpretation*, ed. W. I. T. Mitchell (Chicago: University of Chicago Press, 1983).

28. Eisner, *Cognition and Curriculum.*

29. Goodman, *The Languages of Art*; idem, *Ways of Worldmaking.*

30. Rudolf Arnheim, *Visual Thinking* (Berkeley, CA: University of California Press, 1969).

31. Eisner, *The Enlightened Eye.*

32. Ernst Cassirer, *The Philosophy of Symbolic Forms*, tr. Ralph Manheim, 3 vols. (New Haven: Yale University Press, 1961-1964); Suzanne Langer, *Philosophy in a New Key* (Cambridge, MA: Harvard University Press, 1942); Goodman, *The Languages of Art*; Michael Polanyi, *Personal Knowledge: Toward a Postcultural Philosophy* (Chicago: University of Chicago Press, 1958); Rorty, *Philosophy and the Mirror of Nature*; Arnheim, *Visual Thinking.*

Cost-Effectiveness

In 1975, Elmer Struening and Marcia Guttentag edited a two-volume *Handbook of Evaluation Research*. Sponsored by a subgroup of the American Psychological Association, the volumes were a landmark. They were encyclopedic in scope, and painted an authoritative picture of the state of program evaluation at about the time of its tenth birthday. One of the *Handbook* articles was written by Henry M. Levin, the Stanford economist and educational researcher; together with one other contribution to the *Handbook*, it was the first time that serious recognition had been granted to economic factors within the evaluation literature.

Levin's article focused on the importance of cost-effectiveness data. He pointed out that program evaluations often compare the effectiveness of several treatments, but do this without taking the costs of each into account. Using the well-chosen hypothetical example of a prison-reform experiment involving alternative treatments given to prisoners (psychological counseling, vocational guidance, a combination treatment, and no treatment), Levin showed that the conclusion reached about which program was the most effective—and which, therefore, ought to be recommended for broad implementation—changed dramatically when economic data were taken into account. The most effective program (the mixed treatment) had a much higher cost "per unit of success" (that is, it had a higher marginal cost), whereas one of the seemingly less effective treatments was so much cheaper that for the same dollar outlay as in the most effective case more prisoners could be successfully treated.

In 1983, Levin expanded upon his *Handbook* article, and produced a monograph that is still a key work on the principles of cost-effectiveness analysis in evaluation.

CHAPTER VIII

Cost-Effectiveness at Quarter Century

HENRY M. LEVIN

The purpose of this chapter is to explore some of the issues that have arisen over the last quarter of a century with respect to cost-effectiveness in educational evaluation. Cost-effectiveness analysis represents a policy-oriented dimension of evaluation in that it considers both the costs and educational merits of different alternatives in order to assist in selecting the one that has the lowest costs relative to results. Most evaluation techniques focus only on the effectiveness or process of implementation of alternatives without considering costs. Yet, decision makers are always faced with constrained resources. Cost-effectiveness analysis is designed to assist decision makers in obtaining the most favorable outcome for any given budget or other resource base.

It should be recognized explicitly that cost-benefit and cost-effectiveness analyses did not arise as parts of evaluation research. They emerged independently as tools that economists used to guide resource allocation in the public sector. Cost-effectiveness analysis was developed in the 1950s by the Department of Defense as a device for adjudicating among the demands of the various branches of the armed services for increasingly costly weapons systems with different levels of performance and overlapping missions.[1] Its close relation, cost-benefit analysis, was developed about two decades earlier. In the 1930s, the Congress was overwhelmed with demands for massive investments in water-resource projects (e.g., hydro-electric dams, deep-water harbors, major canals), which various regional interests viewed as panaceas for relieving the regional consequences of national economic depression. A bewildered Congress asked the Corps of Army Engineers to recommend only projects where benefits were at least equal to costs.[2]

By the 1960s, both cost-benefit and cost-effectiveness tools were being used widely by economists to assist in the search for efficiency in government spending. Before proceeding, it is useful to distinguish between these two closely related techniques. Both are used to inform decisions regarding alternative use of resources. Both assume that decision makers face alternatives from which choices must be made. Both also assume that the criteria for making the choice must include not only what will be gained—the benefits or effects—but the value of resources that will be sacrificed to achieve those gains—the costs.

Both cost-benefit and cost-effectiveness analyses measure costs in the same way. The resources or ingredients that are needed for each alternative are specified and assessed according to their market values or another technique that simulates their market values. But, benefits and effectiveness represent different approaches to the measurement of outcomes. Cost-benefit analysis compares the costs and outcomes of alternatives when the outcomes can be assessed in monetary terms.[3] It lends itself especially well to those alternatives or interventions in which the outcomes are market-oriented. For example, educational and training programs that are designed to improve employment and earnings or reduce poverty can be evaluated with a cost-benefit approach when the benefits are the additional earnings associated with the interventions.[4]

In these cases, both benefits and costs can be assessed in monetary units and compared to each other for each alternative. In general, decision makers would choose only among alternatives whose benefits exceeded costs. The most attractive alternatives would be those with the lowest cost-benefit ratios (or highest benefit-cost ratios) or that maximize net benefits (the difference between benefits and costs). The use of a cost-benefit guideline has two major advantages to decision makers. First, one can ascertain if the benefits exceed costs, the necessary criterion for considering an alternative. Second, one can compare the attractiveness of alternatives both within programs and among programs with different goals. For example, the fact that costs and benefits are both evaluated in monetary terms means that cost-benefit ratios or net benefits of a given investment can be compared among programs with similar or diverse objectives. Thus, cost-benefit analysis can be used to compare the efficiency of different educational alternatives as well as among investments in health, education, criminal justice, public assistance, transportation, and so on.

Many social interventions, however, are characterized by outcomes that cannot be converted acceptably into market outcomes. As illustrations, juvenile justice programs may be concerned with reductions in delinquency, school reading programs may focus on rises in reading proficiency, and preschool programs may address improvements in readiness for success in the primary grades. In each of these cases the outcomes of programs addressing a common goal can be evaluated in terms of effectiveness with relation to that goal, but they cannot be readily translated into monetary values or compared among programs with different goals. This is the typical situation for most program evaluations in education.

In these cases a cost-effectiveness analysis is undertaken.[5] Effectiveness is assessed by standard evaluation techniques for a common set of goals among the interventions that are considered as alternatives. For example, the effectiveness of educational programs may be evaluated by using achievement tests in the subjects that are being considered, if that is the goal, but evaluations might also be carried out of alternatives to increase student attendance, to reduce high school dropouts, or to address other educational goals. In these cases, alternatives with the same goals can be compared according to their costs and effectiveness. Those alternatives with the lowest cost-effectiveness ratios would be considered to be the most promising with respect to the use of an agency's or society's resources. Such interventions would use the least resources to achieve a particular program objective.

In some cases, attempts have been made to convert effects into economic measures of outcomes,[6] and in other cases utility scores have been used to place values on outcomes.[7] These approaches generally require the decision maker to make a range of subjective judgments about outcomes and their values.[8] The heavy reliance on subjective judgments makes them less attractive to evaluation experts who seek evidence that is publicly replicable when comparing alternatives. But they do address two of the major obstacles to more traditional cost-effectiveness and cost-benefit studies: (a) multiple objectives which cannot be converted into monetary benefits and (b) imperfect information.

A major theme of this chapter will be an understanding of past attempts to integrate cost-effectiveness into the more general evaluation research field as applied to education as well as future possibilities for doing so. The next section will provide a bit of historical background. This will be followed by the discussion of a set of issues that have arisen over these years as well as the insights that have been gained and some promising directions. Although the title of this chapter addresses cost-effectiveness analysis, I will refer often to its close neighbor, cost-benefit analysis, as well.

Some Background

The 1960s witnessed the establishment and remarkable growth of a new field in both economics and education, the economics of education. The pioneering work of T. W. Schultz, Gary Becker, Jacob Mincer, and Mary Jean Bowman viewed education as a form of human capital in which the productivity of and economic returns to investments in education could be compared with other types of social investments.[9] Moreover, different types of educational investments could be compared for their costs and benefits. Comparisons were made among rates of return on investments in all levels of education[10] and ultimately on vocational education[11] and on-the-job training.[12] This new body of literature demonstrated that cost-benefit studies could be initiated in education in order to choose among different educational investments or between further investment in education versus investments in other social programs or productive investments in the private sector.

By the mid-1960s, economists began to study the problem of how to improve efficiency within the educational sector, particularly with respect to student achievement.[13] The goal of these studies was to ascertain how education was produced through the estimation of educational production functions that relate changes in educational inputs to changes in educational outcomes. Such studies were stimulated both by the publication of and controversy over the Coleman Report as well as by the extensive set of data provided by that report.[14]

Economists, however, are concerned not only with the effects of particular interventions, but also with their costs. Even if a particular educational intervention is effective in some sense, it is not necessarily cost-effective. That is, its costs may be so high relative to its effectiveness that it does not merit policy consideration relative to other alternatives whose effectiveness in relation to cost is superior.

It is this preoccupation with efficiency of resource use that initiated cost-effectiveness studies in education. From the economics perspective, the resources that can be used for any endeavor are always limited. Accordingly, it is important to maximize the effectiveness of those resources, and this can be done by using strategies that promise the largest amount of effectiveness per unit of cost. For example, in the quest to raise student achievement, there are many alternatives, including better teacher selection, smaller classes, longer school days, peer tutoring, computer-assisted instruction, other educational technologies, staff development, and new curricula. Even if some version of each of these is found to provide higher achievement for students relative to students who lack the intervention, the issue is how we choose among such alternatives. By choosing the combination of interventions that provides the largest gains in achievement for any given resource base, resources will be used most efficiently.

EARLY STUDIES

Cost-effectiveness studies were slow to emerge in education for a variety of reasons. The obstacles were primarily the dearth of robust findings on what particular strategies or educational inputs were effective with students as well as the difficulty of identifying costs. With respect to the former, almost all studies of educational production functions were controversial with respect to their findings. In part, this was due to the problem of collinearity in which schools with more of one input, such as more experienced teachers, also have more of other inputs such as smaller class sizes and students from higher socioeconomic origins. Multivariate statistical techniques are often unable to separate out the unique effects of particular explanatory variables when all of them are intercorrelated.[15] Other obstacles to obtaining useful findings on effectiveness from educational production functions included the lack of a strong conceptual framework that guided researchers in specifying, measuring, and obtaining appropriate data that could connect student achievement with school and family variables.[16] The difficulty of obtaining cost data for many inputs—and especially teachers—was due to the apparent inextricability of the cost of a particular type of teacher input. That is, teacher salaries represent remuneration for the entire bundle of characteristics embodied in each teacher including their training, experience, abilities, attitudes, and so on. The problem is how to ascertain what it would cost to obtain more teachers with a given amount of each characteristic while holding the other teacher characteristics constant.

The first study to combine cost and effectiveness in an educational setting was a study of teacher selection.[17] Using Hanushek's multiple regression estimates[18] of educational production functions for achievement based upon Coleman data, I found that both teacher experience and teacher verbal score were related to the verbal achievement of sixth graders in the metropolitan North. Cost estimates of the teacher characteristics were obtained by estimating equations on teacher salaries (earnings functions) for a given metropolitan region in the North. The regression coefficients of these earnings functions provided estimates of the costs for obtaining a teacher with additional education, experience, verbal score, and so on. When the costs and effects for raising student achievement were compared between selecting teachers with higher verbal score or more experience, it was found that it was five to ten times more cost-effective to select teachers with higher verbal facility. That is, a given budgetary allocation for improving teacher quality would yield increases in student verbal achievement that were five to ten times greater for teachers with higher verbal scores than for more experienced teachers.

In the early 1970s, this type of analysis was followed by several studies of educational television.[19] In situations such as those in developing societies where trained teachers are unavailable—particularly in rural areas—or where populations are so sparse that there are not adequate numbers of students in school attendance boundaries to justify minimum personnel requirements, educational television was viewed as an alternative for delivering instruction. Studies were undertaken of educational television as a partial replacement for teachers, and such studies found that the television was relatively cost-effective.[20] However, such studies were considered to be controversial because assumptions were made in the analysis that generally biased the results in favor of the educational television.[21]

Over the same period, cost-benefit analysis became more prominent in education than cost-effectiveness. Economists found many situations in which the ostensible goal of educational interventions was that of raising earnings and productivity of students or trainees such as dropout prevention,[22] vocational education,[23] and job training.[24] In these cases, the costs of the programs were compared with their estimated benefits in generating additional earnings and productivity. Only programs with benefits exceeding costs were viewed as worthy of further consideration, and only those with the highest benefits relative to costs were viewed as promising.

Weisbrod compared the costs of a major attempt to reduce high school dropouts with the expected earnings and other benefits such as government revenues associated with the reductions in dropouts for that program.[25] He found that under a variety of assumptions, the costs always exceeded the benefits. This finding contradicted the conventional wisdom which suggested that investments in high school completion always paid off. Ribich's major work on education and poverty examined a wide variety of educational and training programs to reduce poverty and attempted to estimate their costs and benefits.[26] These programs included preschool interventions, compensatory education, and training programs. Only the training programs seemed to have benefits that exceeded costs. A number of researchers undertook studies of vocational secondary education to see if its higher cost per student was justified by higher benefits relative to the costs and benefits of general high school education.[27] The results were mixed. Finally, I found that a national investment in providing a minimum of high school completion would have benefits that were considerably in excess of costs.[28]

Integrating Cost Analysis into Educational Evaluation

The early works undertaken by economists showed promise in undertaking studies of educational benefits or results and combining them with costs. But, as the field of evaluation and its applications to educational evaluation developed, there was little recognition of the potential role that cost analyses might play. Early books on educational evaluation ignored the issues of costs in decision making. It was not until the publication of the *Handbook on Evaluation Research* that we saw such recognition conferred upon cost-benefit and cost-effectiveness analysis in the field of evaluation.[29]

The two-volume *Handbook* was based upon a vision of one of the pioneers in evaluation, the late Marcia Guttentag. Under the sponsorship of the Society for the Psychological Study of Social Issues (SPSSI) of the American Psychological Association, Guttentag assembled a committee of social psychologists and evaluators to plan and implement a major volume of essays that would define the field of evaluation research. Two chapters of the *Handbook* were devoted to cost analyses. Jerome Rothenberg of the Massachusetts Institute of Technology authored a chapter on "Cost-Benefit Analysis: A Methodological Exposition," and I prepared a chapter on "Cost-Effectiveness in Evaluation Research."[30]

The purpose of my chapter was to introduce to evaluation researchers the purpose and use of cost-effectiveness analysis as well as a method for estimating costs of interventions. As I reviewed the field of evaluation research in preparation for writing that chapter, I saw that evaluation research focused almost exclusively on "effectiveness" analysis. If I could set out a straightforward method of cost analysis that might be accessible to evaluators with only a minimal need for outside technical assistance, they might be able to combine their stock-in-trade on effectiveness with the cost dimension to create their own cost-effectiveness comparisons among alternatives.

The method that I proposed is based upon a fundamental

conception of what constitutes cost and its measurements. In economic analysis, the cost of an intervention represents the value of what is being given up or sacrificed by not using those resources in the best alternative use. If resources are used for one thing, they cannot be used for something else. The methodology that follows from this conception is straightforward and was explicated in my chapter in the *Handbook* and was subsequently expanded in my book-length treatment of the subject.[31]

The ingredients method, as it is called, of determining costs begins with an identification and specification of each of the ingredients required for each of the alternative interventions that are being compared.[32] The specification of personnel, facilities, and equipment must be sufficiently detailed in order to ascertain at a later stage the cost of each. Identification and specification of ingredients are derived from three sources: reports, observations, and interviews. The ability to draw upon three sources allows the type of verification that triangulation among such sources permits.

Once the ingredients are specified, there are fairly standard methods of ascertaining the costs of each.[33] In most cases, attempts are made to obtain the market price of each resource such as salaries and fringe benefits for specific personnel requirements. However, in some cases there does not exist a competitive market for a particular ingredient, so other methods must be used to obtain a "market equivalent" price or what economists call a "shadow price."[34] In the case of facilities, it is often necessary to use these methods. These separate ingredients costs can be summed to obtain the total cost of an intervention.

The third stage that was developed in my 1975 *Handbook* article entailed the development of a financial spreadsheet which paralleled the present use of electronic spreadsheet packages on microcomputers. The spreadsheet approach enables an analysis of the distribution of the cost burden among different entities including different levels of government, private agencies, voluntary contributions, and even user fees. There are two parts to this type of analysis: ingredients that are contributed in kind from one entity to another and cash subsidies through grants and user fees.

Taken together, these three steps enable the analyst to identify the resources or ingredients needed for alternative interventions, a valuable exercise in itself; to determine the overall costs of the alternatives; and to ascertain the distribution of costs among different constituencies. The overall costs can be linked to the effectiveness of alternatives in order to compare cost-effectiveness and rank the alternatives by this criterion. It is also possible to consider the cost-effectiveness of alternatives for different constituencies or stakeholders by comparing the specific costs and effects among alternatives for each constituency. Both costs by constituencies and effects or benefits received by them may vary among alternatives in ways that differ from the overall cost-effectiveness ratings.

I had hoped that the establishment and clarification of a methodology that would be accessible to evaluation researchers more generally would lead to an expansion of cost-effectiveness studies in the evaluation literature. While I have seen some excellent studies that have used this method in subsequent years (for example, the cost-effectiveness comparison of different mathematics curricula by Quinn, VanMondfrans, and Worthen) the expected expansion has not materialized to any major extent.[35] For example, fewer than 1 percent of presentations at the Annual Meetings of the American Evaluation Association over the last four years (1985-88) addressed cost-effectiveness analysis or included it as a component of evaluations. The proportion is even smaller among evaluative studies presented at the Annual Meetings of the American Educational Research Association. To my knowledge, only one of the leading texts on evaluation[36] includes as much as a chapter on cost analysis in evaluation, and virtually none on educational evaluation addresses the issue in any depth. The proportion of evaluations in the Educational Resources Information Center (ERIC) shows a similar pattern as does the Social Science Citation Index (SSCI) search of educational evaluations. A systematic survey of program evaluation units of the fifty state departments of education found almost no use of cost-effectiveness in evaluations, and it appeared that such units typically lacked the capabilities to do such analyses and were not called upon to do them.[37]

By virtually every standard, there is very little cost-effectiveness or cost-benefit analysis that is carried out in the evaluation arena. As I have pointed out, there are several reasons for this.[38] Few evaluation training programs provide training in cost analysis. Even at my own university, it is my economics students rather than those in the evaluation training program who seek out the development of competencies in this area. The evaluation training faculty in the Stanford School of Education thought that exposure to courses in cost-effectiveness should be an option rather than a requirement for a training program in evaluation.

Moreover, my experience tells me that decision makers are unfamiliar with the tool or how to use results from cost-effectiveness studies in making policy choices. Although the term "cost-effective" often arises in the policy arena, it is typically used in a hortatory way to assert how decisions should be made or an advocative one where it is suggested that a favored alternative is cost-effective with no systematic evidence. The decision makers themselves are rarely competent to interpret and evaluate cost-effectiveness studies. Without more and better training among both evaluators and decision makers, it is probably not likely that cost-effectiveness analyses will become more widely used.

Recent Developments

With the hope that better training and interest on the part of decision makers will generate better cost-effectiveness training and more demand for cost-effectiveness studies in education in the future, it is useful to address recent developments. Since my focus in this chapter is on integrating the missing dimension of cost analysis with the principal focus on effectiveness that tends to dominate the evaluation field, I have chosen three recent developments to discuss: meta-analysis; cost-effectiveness of secondary analyses; and cost-benefit insights.

META-ANALYSIS

One of the major developments in evaluation research over the last two decades has been the rise of meta-analysis. Meta-analysis represents the attempt to use various analytic techniques to generalize about a specific phenomenon that has been evaluated in a wide variety of independent and disparate studies.[39] Typically, a meta-analysis will collect all of the available studies on a particular phenomenon and estimate an effect size. The effect size will be a standard score such as a z-score on the criterion of effectiveness, a measure which can be derived from almost all studies of the phenomenon regardless of the metric that is used.

Meta-analysis in education has been carried out on a wide variety of topics including peer tutoring, computer-assisted instruction, and other educational interventions.[40] Most meta-analyses provide two types of outcomes. The first is an average effect size for a particular type of intervention. This result is interpreted as the average expected effect for a student who receives the intervention relative to a similar student who does not receive it. A second outcome of meta-analyses presentations (not always provided) is an attempt to assess the sources of variance in outcomes among the individual studies that comprise the meta-analysis such as differences in samples, methods, length of studies, variants of the intervention, and so on. For this purpose, the component studies of the meta-analysis are coded according to their features to enable a statistical search for differences in outcomes among these classifications.

Meta-analysis has been widely accepted in the evaluation literature, although it has also been criticized by highly regarded scholars.[41] Among these concerns are the issues of inclusion of studies that are based upon poor design and procedures, issues of how to average results among different studies, coding and classification aspects, and inappropriate statistical analysis and interpretation of results.

But, a different issue is the question of whether meta-analytic summaries—presumably ones of high quality—can be combined with cost-analyses to provide a cost-effectiveness comparison of different types of educational interventions. That is, why can't we take the meta-analyses of effect sizes of two different interventions such as peer tutoring and computer-assisted instruction and compare them relative to their costs to provide a meta, cost-effectiveness analysis? The basic flaw in this approach is that meta-analyses provide an effect size for an average of many different versions of a class of interventions, while decision makers are concerned with choices among concrete alternatives. This can be seen more clearly when examining a specific meta-analytic result.

A meta-analysis of peer tutoring obtained an effect size of .4 in student achievement in contrast to an effect size of .47 for a meta-analysis of computer-assisted instruction.[42] Why can't we just combine this information with the costs of the two alternatives to compare their cost-effectiveness? The problem is that there are no specific decision alternatives that can be derived and compared from these results. These effect sizes are based on averages of many different types of programs, each with different costs and different effects. For example, the peer tutoring programs whose effects are averaged to obtain an overall effect size include those that failed and those that succeeded, those that provide training for tutors and those that do not, those that monitor tutors and provide instructional materials, and those that simply tell some students to tutor others. There are enormous differences among the individual approaches that comprise the meta-analysis of computer-assisted instruction as well.

It is not possible to create a cost-effectiveness comparison from among such averages. Recall that cost-effectiveness analysis does not represent an academic exercise, but it is an attempt to provide concrete data on alternatives to be considered by decision makers in informing their choices. Decision makers are concerned with what results they are likely to obtain from a specific intervention, not what are the average effects from many different versions of that intervention—some that were poorly designed and implemented and others that were well-designed and implemented. Thus, the average effect size makes no sense to the informed decision maker who must consider the impacts of concrete interventions that can be clearly specified and considered for implementation.

Nor is it possible to provide a cost for a program that provides the average effect size. The costing of a program requires that there be a specific set of processes and resource ingredients to consider. But, the effect size from meta-analysis is based on a mixture of many different programs, precluding any conceptual or practical way to identify costs. The effect size simply does not refer to an implementable program alternative with specific resource requirements.

Further, because meta-analyses combine virtually all available studies on a particular phenomenon, they mix together wheat and chaff. Many of the studies captured by the meta-analyses are extremely poor in quality, drawing upon "in-house" documents of school districts and flawed dissertation research rather than carefully reviewed and refereed research studies. Three-fourths of the evaluations that were summarized in a particular meta-analysis showed serious flaws.[43]

The link between cost-effectiveness analysis and meta-analysis is tenuous at best. The two techniques were developed to address different purposes. Meta-analysis was developed to summarize the results of a large number of disparate studies on a single general subject. In doing so, it was never designed to identify exemplary practices that have been found to be replicable and that meet other standards for policy consideration. It combines the good and the bad in terms of both successful and unsuccessful interventions and low-quality and high-quality evaluations. Its value derives from its claims to summarize very diverse types of approaches and evaluations within a general rubric.

In contrast, cost-effectiveness analysis was designed to assist decision makers in choosing among *successful* practices on the basis of which ones would maximize the impact of available resources. In this vein the quality of existing evaluations and replication experience are crucial, as is the ruling out of those practices or interventions that have failed. An average effect for all evaluations of a particular class of interventions is not useful for this purpose, because the average is not embodied in any specific program. And the lack of a specific program means that what is embedded in the average effect size cannot be costed or implemented.

COST-EFFECTIVENESS AS SECONDARY ANALYSES

A second topic that has become more prominent in the last quarter century is that of secondary analyses.[44] In many cases, data are collected and evaluated in a primary analysis. For example, the initial wave of data from the High School and Beyond (HSB) survey of the U.S. Department of Education was evaluated to ascertain whether student achievement differs between public and private schools.[45] But, the data set was subjected to a secondary analysis by many other researchers in order to confirm or challenge the initial results.[46] The secondary analysis of a primary data source has become a fairly standard practice, with meta-analyses representing a particular version.

Since evaluators are unable or unwilling to build cost-analysis and cost-effectiveness analysis into their evaluation designs, cost-effectiveness analysis must typically take the form of a secondary analysis of a primary evaluation. That is, as primary evaluations of effectiveness of particular educational interventions are produced, it is possible to add the cost analysis later to create cost-effectiveness comparisons. But, in order to create cost-effectiveness studies as secondary analyses, it is necessary that certain conditions be met. These include replicability, availability of detailed information on interventions and ingredients, and good evaluations of effectiveness.

Since cost-effectiveness comparisons of alternatives are designed to assist decision makers in ascertaining how to obtain maximum effectiveness with available resources, it is important that the alternative interventions under consideration are replicable in the form that they were evaluated. Many evaluations of educational interventions are carried out under artificial conditions. For example, some educational evaluations refer to interventions carried out under laboratory conditions for a few weeks in order to gather experimental data. It is not reasonable to assume that similar results would obtain if the evaluation were implemented over an academic year in an actual school setting. A hint of the lack of replicability of brief interventions is the finding that computer-assisted instruction projects lasting less than four weeks showed an effect size of .56 in contrast with an effect size of only .20 for projects lasting more than eight weeks.[47]

A related issue is whether some special set of conditions existed for an intervention that was evaluated such as the involvement of universities in the intervention or the involvement of the evaluator in implementation. When universities are involved in the intervention, there may be influences that would not be replicated when a school undertakes the intervention on its own. One study found that when the evaluator is also the developer of the intervention, the effect size for computer-assisted instruction (CAI) is about half again as great as when the evaluation is done independently.[48] In general, we must pick evaluations of interventions in which the intervention is likely to be replicable with similar results in an actual school setting.

The costing procedure requires reasonable information on the details of the intervention and on ingredients. Most evaluation research reports lack sufficient detail. For example, they usually provide only a short description of the "intended" intervention and no systematic detail on ingredients. Of course, "intended" interventions are often modified by the realities of implementation.[49] The true description of an intervention is not what was intended, but what actually happened, on which details are only rarely provided. Moreover, the lack of details on ingredients means that evaluations of cost-effectiveness must look for multiple sources of information to identify ingredients for cost estimation. As I mentioned above, all pertinent forms of documentation beyond the final report should be examined as well as seeking information from participants in the intervention and from observations of the intervention or its replications. In some cases, an evaluation will be based upon a one-time implementation without adequate documentation. If the intervention is no longer functioning, it will not be possible to observe it; moreover, participants may be difficult to locate, and their memories may be subject to errors of retrospection. In those cases it is probably not possible to incorporate their results into a cost-effectiveness analysis.

Finally, the quality of evaluations is important. This point is underlined by the study cited above in which three-quarters of the individual studies used in a meta-analysis were found to be seriously flawed.[50] When the same teacher is used for both CAI intervention groups and controls—the best evaluation design—the effect sizes are considerably smaller than when different teachers are used.[51] Among eighty-three studies on the same subject, my research group found large numbers that had inappropriate research designs and lacked even basic statistical information such as standard deviations. When using primary evaluations as a basis for a cost-effectiveness analysis, it is important that the primary evaluations are of reasonable quality or that the original data are available to provide a secondary analysis.

When these conditions are met, it is possible to do cost-effectiveness studies as secondary analyses in which previous studies of effectiveness are combined with a cost-analysis of ingredients to provide comparisons of cost-effectiveness. One context that provided an opportunity for such analysis was the school reform movement of the middle 1980s. The various reports of the national commissions on educational reforms recommended large numbers of different interventions to improve student achievement.[52] Among those were recommendations to increase the length of the school day and to use more computer-assisted instruction. Since there existed good primary data and evaluations on each of these interventions, it was decided to compare the cost-effectiveness of computer-assisted instruction (CAI) and a longer school day with two other interventions for which primary data and evaluations were available, cross-age peer tutoring and reductions in class size.[53] Reading and mathematics achievement at the elementary level were selected as the criteria of effectiveness. The specific forms of the interventions were a standard peer tutoring program where fifth graders tutored second graders; the use of CAI for drill and practice; an extension of the school day by one hour of which half was devoted to reading and half to mathematics; and various reductions in class size in five student decrements from thirty-five students down to twenty students.

A range of additional interventions were considered, but we could not find evaluations that satisfied the criteria for inclusion in the cost-effectiveness comparison. These criteria included the availability of evaluations of reasonable quality to obtain estimates of effectiveness—evaluations that could be replicated in other settings with similar expected results; of adequate data on the interventions and their ingredients; and of a common set of effectiveness criteria—in this case, mathematics and reading achievement at the elementary level.

A comparison of effectiveness among the interventions showed that peer tutoring showed the largest effectiveness followed by CAI. Increases in the length of the school day and reductions in class size generally showed the smallest effects. With respect to costs, peer tutoring was the most costly because of its use of adult coordinators for training and supervision. CAI showed about half the cost of peer tutoring, with reductions in class size of five students and an extension of the school day costing about a quarter of the peer tutoring. When the cost and effectiveness data were integrated, the cross-age tutoring showed a cost-effectiveness ratio for increasing mathematics achievement that was nine times as great as extending the school day. This means that for the same resources peer tutoring would provide about nine times the effect of putting those resources into extending the school day by one half hour for mathematics. It is interesting to note that the national reform movement placed great emphasis on lengthening the school day and school year while saying little or nothing about peer tutoring. Differences in cost-effectiveness among the other interventions and for reading were also instructive.

A later study focused on different CAI interventions.[54] An extensive search process identified over eighty recent evaluations of CAI of which eight met all the criteria for cost-effectiveness comparison at the elementary level. Although large differences in cost-effectiveness among specific sites were found for the same ostensible curriculum and delivery of CAI, it was found that the differences were reduced considerably when adjustments were made for the degree to which the CAI was utilized. Average effects for the four sites that used the specific CAI approach evaluated in the earlier cost-effectiveness comparison found almost identical cost-effectiveness results with the earlier study of CAI.

The main lesson to be learned is that it is entirely feasible to do cost-effectiveness studies as a secondary analysis of primary studies or primary data sets. As emphasized above, it is important to select the particular primary studies with great care. Further, there seem to be large differences in cost-effectiveness among different interventions that are designed to accomplish the same goals. Thus, the potential impact on educational productivity of using cost-effectiveness results might be considerable when compared with using only the information from effectiveness evaluations or recommendations from national commissions.

COST-BENEFIT INSIGHTS

A final theme that has emerged in recent years are the insights that cost-benefit studies can yield. One of the most important of these addresses preschool enrichment for at-risk populations. Early studies of Head Start and similar programs found statistically significant gains in ability tests among students who were enrolled in the programs relative to similar children who were not. But, these differences typically evaporated by the second grade. Although there were many methodological critiques of this study, no reanalyses or new analyses produced results that differ in a major way from the initial findings.[55]

Thus, it was with some surprise that a follow-up of children from one of the major programs after which Headstart was patterned, the Perry Preschool in Ypsilanti, Michigan, found important longitudinal differences in favor of the children who received the intervention.[56] As with other studies, the Perry Preschool children had large gains in early IQ relative to similar children who were not in the program, but by age nine the differences between treatment and control groups had disappeared. The story did not end there. Careful follow-ups of treatment and control children to age nineteen revealed the following outcomes in favor of the students who had participated in the Perry Preschool: (1) higher achievement scores; (2) fewer years spent in special education; (3) higher graduation rates from high school; (4) greater participation in postsecondary education; (5) higher employment levels; (6) greater earnings; (7) lower probability of receiving public assistance; (8) fewer arrests; and (9) a lower probability of teen pregnancy.

These can be placed into a benefit-cost framework where the benefits are the reduction in costs of special education, higher earnings and employment, lower costs of public assistance and criminal justice, and so on. When the benefits and costs were calculated, it appears that the program provides benefits that are considerably in excess of costs, and about 80 percent of these net benefits are received by taxpayers and/or potential crime victims.[57] That is, the cost-benefit analysis has given a very different policy perspective to early childhood interventions than was yielded by the earlier studies that limited their focus to an evaluation of preschool gains in test scores and the retention of those gains in the primary grades. The cost-benefit analysis has focused not only on the longitudinal effects of the intervention, but has placed those effects in the framework of a social investment that can inform the stakeholders on what they might gain from such an investment. In a more general sense, this study has reminded us of how short-term studies of effectiveness might miss the more important long-term effects, effects that can often be summarized within a cost-benefit framework.

Future Trends

I have suggested that although some progress has been made, cost-effectiveness analysis is still not a standard part of educational evaluation or evaluation training. The need to maximize what can be accomplished with available educational resources is becoming more pressing over time for a variety of reasons. First, there is great pressure on the schools to improve educational outcomes in order to meet the needs for producing a labor force for an increasingly competitive world economic situation. Second, after a decline in enrollments in elementary and secondary schools, enrollments will be rising in the decade of the 1990s. This will put an increasing strain on educational budgets. Finally, a large and growing proportion of enrollments is comprised of at-risk students who require greater resources and more effective educational practices to enter the educational mainstream.[58]

All of these phenomena, taken together, suggest a greater need for concern about using educational resources productively, and cost-effectiveness analysis is a major tool for gathering the information to make informed decisions within this context. Although progress has been slow, I feel that there is an inexorable need to continue to push for an expansion of training and use of cost-effectiveness analysis in educational evaluations. I think that pragmatic pressures over the next quarter century brought about by intense educational demands with scarce resources will press educational evaluators to gain more fully the competencies used in cost-effectiveness analysis.

Finally, I believe that there will be a greater attempt to integrate decision approaches in education with cost analysis. One particular area that is deserving of greater development is that of cost-utility analysis.[59] I have suggested a scenario to make the application of cost-effectiveness and cost-utility analysis more user-friendly by using the capabilities of microcomputers to assist in structuring the framework and doing the calculations.[60] Such use of cost-utility and cost-effectiveness would become a decision tool that would expand the internal use of these tools by decision makers for their ongoing decisions in contrast to the emphasis on producing such studies for external audiences by evaluation researchers.

FOOTNOTES

1. Charles J. Hitch and Roland N. McKean, *The Economics of Defense in the Nuclear Age* (Cambridge, MA: Harvard University Press, 1960).

2. Otto Eckstein, *Water-Resource Development* (Cambridge, MA: Harvard University Press, 1958).

3. Ezra J. Mishan, *Cost-Benefit Analysis* (New York: Praeger Publishers, 1976).

4. Thomas I. Ribich, *Education and Poverty* (Washington, DC: Brookings Institution, 1968).

5. Henry M. Levin, *Cost-Effectiveness: A Primer* (Beverly Hills, CA: Sage Publications, 1983).

6. Stuart Nagel, "Nonmonetary Variables in Benefit-Cost Analyses," *Evaluation Review* 7 (1983): 37-64; Ribich, *Education and Poverty*, chaps. 4, 5.

7. Ward Edwards and J. Robert Newman, *Multiattribute Evaluation*, Quantitative Applications in the Social Sciences, No. 26 (Beverly Hills, CA: Sage Publications, 1982).

8. Ralph Keeney and Howard Raiffa, *Decisions with Multiple Objectives: Preferences and Value Tradeoffs* (New York: John Wiley and Sons, 1976).

9. Theodore W. Schultz, "Capital Formation by Education," *Journal of Political Economy* 68 (December 1980): 571-583; idem, "Investment in Human Capital," *American Economic Review* 51, no. 1 (March 1961): 11-17; Gary S. Becker, *Human Capital* (New York: Columbia University Press, 1964); Jacob Mincer, "On-the-Job Training: Costs, Returns, and Some Implications," *Journal of Political Economy* (Supplement) 70 (October 1962): 50-79; Mary Jean Bowman, "Schultz, Denison, and the Contribution of 'Eds' to National Income Growth," *Journal of Political Economy* 74 (October 1964): 450-464.

10. Giora Hanoch, "An Economic Analysis of Earnings and Schooling," *Journal of Human Resources* 2, no. 3 (Summer 1967): 310-329; W. Lee Hansen, "Total and Private Rates of Return to Investment in Schooling," *Journal of Political Economy* 71 (April 1963): 128-140.

11. Tei-wei Hu, Maw Lin Lee, and Ernst W. Stromsdorfer, "Economic Returns to Vocational and Comprehensive High School Graduates," *Journal of Human Resources* 6 (Winter 1971): 25-50.

12. Jacob Mincer, *Schooling, Experience, and Earnings* (New York: National Bureau of Economic Research, 1974).

13. Herbert J. Kiesling, "Measuring a Local Government Service: A Study of School Districts in New York State," *Review of Economics and Statistics* 49, no. 3 (August 1967): 356-367; Jesse Burkhead, Thomas G. Fox, and John W. Holland, *Input and Output in Large City High Schools* (Syracuse, NY: Syracuse University Press, 1967).

14. James S. Coleman et al., *Equality of Educational Opportunity*, U.S. Office of Education (Washington, DC: U.S. Government Printing Office, 1966); Alexander M. Mood, ed., *Do Teachers Make a Difference?* OE-58042, U.S. Office of Education (Washington, DC: U.S. Government Printing Office, 1970); Frederick Mosteller and Daniel P. Moynihan, eds., *On Equality of Educational Opportunity* (New York: Random House, 1972).

15. Samuel S. Bowles and Henry M. Levin, "The Determinants of Scholastic Achievement—A Critical Appraisal of Some Recent Evidence," *Journal of Human Resources* 3, no. 1 (Winter 1968): 3-24; idem, "More on Multicollinearity and the Effectiveness of Schools," *Journal of Human Resources* 3, no. 3 (Summer 1968): 393-400; Michael S. Lewis-Beck, *Applied Regression: An Introduction* (Beverly Hills, CA: Sage Publications, 1980).

16. Gary Bridge, Charles Judd, and Peter Moock, *The Determinants of Educational Outcomes* (Cambridge, MA: Ballinger Publishing Co., 1979).

17. Henry M. Levin, "A Cost-Effectiveness Analysis of Teacher Selection," *Journal of Human Resources* 5, no. 1 (Winter 1970): 24-33.

18. Eric Hanushek, "The Education of Negroes and Whites" (Doct. diss. Massachusetts Institute of Technology, 1968).

19. John Mayo, Emile McAnany, and Steven Klees, "The Mexican Telesecundaria: A Cost-Effectiveness Analysis," *Instructional Science* 4, nos. 3-4 (October 1975): 193-236; Dean Jamison, Steven Klees, and Stuart Wells, *The Costs of Educational Media* (Beverly Hills, CA: Sage Publications, 1978).

20. Mayo, McAnany, and Klees, "The Mexican Telesecundaria."

21. Martin Carnoy and Henry M. Levin, "Evaluation of Educational Media: Some Issues," *Instructional Science*, 4, nos. 3-4 (October 1975): 385-406.

22. Burton A. Weisbrod, "Preventing High School Dropouts," in *Measuring Benefits of Government Investments*, ed. Robert Dorfman (Washington, DC: Brookings Institution, 1965), pp. 117-48.

23. Arthur J. Corazzini, "The Decision to Invest in Vocational Education: An Analysis of Costs and Benefits," *Journal of Human Resources*, Supplement: Vocational Education 3 (Summer 1968): 88-120; Hu, Lee, and Stromsdorfer, "Economic Returns to Vocational and Comprehensive High School Graduates."

24. Ribich, *Education and Poverty*, chap. 3.

25. Weisbrod, "Preventing High School Dropouts."

26. Ribich, *Education and Poverty*.

27. Corazzini, "The Decision to Invest in Vocational Education"; Hu, Lee, and Stromsdorfer, "Economic Returns to Vocational and Comprehensive High School Graduates"; Michael K. Taussig, "An Economic Analysis of Vocational Education in the New York City High Schools," *Journal of Human Resources*, Supplement: Vocational Education 3 (Summer 1968): 59-87.

28. Henry M. Levin, *The Costs to the Nation of Inadequate Education*, Report prepared for the Select Senate Committee on Equal Educational Opportunity (Washington, DC: U.S. Government Printing Office, 1972). Summarized in Select Committee on Equal Educational Opportunity, U.S. Senate, *Toward Equal Educational Opportunity*, 92nd Congress, 2nd Session, Report No. 92-000 (Washington, DC: U.S. Government Printing Office, 1972), chap. 13.

29. Elmer L. Struening and Marcia Guttentag, eds., *Handbook of Evaluation Research*, 2 vols. (Beverly Hills, CA: Sage Publications, 1975).

30. Jerome Rothenberg, "Cost-Benefit Analysis: A Methodological Exposition," in *Handbook of Evaluation Research*, ed. Struening and Guttentag, vol. 2, pp. 55-88; Henry M. Levin, "Cost-Effectiveness in Evaluation Research," in *Handbook of Evaluation Research*, ed. Struening and Guttentag, vol. 2, pp. 89-122.

31. Henry M. Levin, *Cost-Effectiveness: A Primer*.

32. Ibid., chap. 3.

33. Ibid., chap. 4.

34. Mishan, *Cost-Benefit Analysis*, chaps. 13, 14.

35. Bill Quinn, Adrian VanMondfrans, and Blaine R. Worthen, "Cost-Effectiveness of Two Math Programs as Moderated by Pupil SES," *Educational Evaluation and Policy Analysis* 6, no. 1 (Spring 1984): 39-52.

36. Peter H. Rossi and Howard E. Freeman, *Evaluation: A Systematic Approach*, 3rd ed. (Beverly Hills, CA: Sage Publications, 1985).

37. Nick L. Smith and Jana K. Smith, "State-Level Evaluation Uses of Cost Analysis: A National Descriptive Survey," in *Economic Evaluation of Public Programs*, ed. James S. Cotterall, New Directions for Program Evaluation, no. 26 (San Francisco: Jossey-Bass, 1985), pp. 83-97.

38. Henry M. Levin, "Cost-Benefit and Cost-Effectiveness Analyses," in *Evaluation Practice in Review*, ed. David S. Cordray, Howard S. Bloom, and Richard J. Light, New Directions for Program Evaluation, no. 34 (San Francisco: Jossey-Bass, 1987), pp. 83-99.

39. Gene V Glass, Barry McGaw, and Mary Lee Smith, *Meta-Analysis in Social Research* (Beverly Hills, CA: Sage Publications, 1981); Fredrick M. Wolf, *Meta-Analysis: Quantitative Methods for Research Synthesis*, Sage University Paper 59, Quantitative Applications in the Social Sciences (Beverly Hills, CA: Sage Publications, 1986).

40. Peter A. Cohen, James A. Kulik, and Chen-Lin C. Kulik, "Educational Outcomes of Tutoring: A Meta-Analysis of Findings," *American Educational Research Journal* 19 (Summer 1982): 237-248; Robert L. Bangert-Drowns, James A. Kulik, and Chen-Lin C. Kulik, "Effectiveness of Computer-Based Education in Secondary Schools," *Journal of Computer-Based Education* 12, no. 3 (Summer 1985): 59-68; Herbert J. Walberg, "Improving the Productivity of America's Schools," *Educational Leadership* 41, no. 8 (May 1984): 19-27.

41. Larry V. Hedges and Ingram Olkin, *Statistical Methods for Meta-Analysis* (Orlando, FL: Academic Press, 1985); Robert E. Slavin, "Meta-analysis in Education: How Has It Been Used?" *Educational Researcher* 13, no. 8 (October 1984): 6-15, 24-27;

Robert E. Slavin, "Best-Evidence Synthesis: An Alternative to Meta-Analytic and Traditional Reviews," *Educational Researcher* 15, no. 9 (November 1986): 5-11.

42. Cohen, Kulik, and Kulik, "Educational Outcomes of Tutoring"; and Bangert-Drowns, Kulik, and Kulik, "Effectiveness of Computer-Based Education in Secondary Schools."

43. Richard E. Clark, "Evidence for Confounding in Computer-Based Instruction Studies: Analyzing the Meta-Analyses," *Educational Technology and Communication Journal* 33, no. 4 (Winter 1985): 249-62.

44. David J. Bowering, ed., *Secondary Analysis of Available Data Bases*, New Directions for Program Evaluation, no. 22 (San Francisco: Jossey-Bass, 1984).

45. James S. Coleman, Thomas Hoffer, and Sally Kilgore, *High School Achievement: Public, Catholic, and Private Schools Compared* (New York: Basic Books, 1982).

46. See articles published in *Sociology of Education* 55, nos. 2-3 (April/July, 1982).

47. James A. Kulik, Robert L. Bangert, and George W. Williams, "Effects of Computer-Based Teaching on Secondary School Students," *Journal of Educational Psychology* 75, no. 1 (1983): 19-26.

48. Bangert-Drowns, Kulik, and Kulik, "Effectiveness of Computer-Based Education in Secondary Schools."

49. Paul Berman and Milbrey McLaughlin, *Federal Programs Supporting Educational Change*, Vol. IV: The Findings in Review, R-1589/4-HEW (Santa Monica, CA: Rand Corporation, April 1975).

50. Clark, "Evidence for Confounding in Computer-Based Instruction Studies."

51. James A. Kulik and Chen-Lin C. Kulik, "Review of Recent Research Literature on Computer-Based Instruction," *Contemporary Educational Psychology* 12 (1987): 222-230.

52. For example, see National Commission on Excellence in Education, *A Nation at Risk: The Imperative for Educational Reform* (Washington, DC: U.S. Department of Education, 1983).

53. Henry M. Levin, Gene V Glass, and Gail R. Meister, "A Cost-Effectiveness Analysis of Computer-Assisted Instruction," *Evaluation Review* 11, no. 1 (February 1987): 50-72.

54. Henry M. Levin, "The Economics of Computer-Assisted Instruction," *Peabody Journal of Education* 64, no. 1 (Fall 1986): 52-66 (published in 1989).

55. W. Steven Barnett, "Benefits of Compensatory Preschool Education," (Philadelphia: Center for Research in Human Development and Education, Temple University, 1989), mimeographed.

56. John R. Berrueta-Clement, Lawrence J. Schweinhart, W. Steven Barnett, Ann S. Epstein, and David P. Weikart, "Changed Lives: The Effects of the Perry Preschool Program on Youths through Age 19," *Monographs of the High/Scope Educational Research Foundation*, No. 8 (Ypsilanti, MI: High/Scope Press, 1984).

57. W. Steven Barnett, "Benefit-Cost Analysis of the Perry Preschool Program and Its Long-Term Effects," *Educational Evaluation and Policy Analysis* 7, no. 4 (1985): 333-342.

58. Aaron M. Pallas, Gary Natriello, and Edward L. McDill, "The Changing Nature of the Disadvantaged Population: Current Dimensions and Future Trends," *Educational Researcher* 18, no. 5 (June-July 1989): 16-22.

59. Levin, *Cost-Effectiveness: A Primer*, pp. 116-127.

60. Levin, "Cost-Benefit and Cost-Effectiveness Analyses," 92-96.

Evaluation as a Political Activity

When evaluation began to flourish in the 1960s, evaluators of the period knew that evaluations were commissioned by political actors (e.g., members of legislatures, superintendents), but they had little awareness that evaluation itself was in some sense a political activity. Yet evaluators are not mere observers of the social and educational scene—they are not "innocent bystanders." Evaluators intervene, they ask questions, they collect data, they open up programs and subject things within them to scrutiny, and they make recommendations. All of these activities involve interaction with programs and program personnel, and of course with decision makers; and potentially, then, evaluators can have influence over people's professional and even private lives.

A related difficulty for evaluators was to appreciate the manner in which individuals who play political roles actually make decisions. The most widely held view was the "rational model" of decision making. According to this view a problem is identified, data are collected, and a decision is made more or less mechanically on the basis of the data. Thus, according to this model, a decision about the fate of a program would be made by identifying the goals, by gathering data to see if these goals were achieved, and if they were, the program would be continued, otherwise not.

Starting about 1970, Carol Weiss produced a series of influential papers that challenged this view. While not arguing that decision makers in politicized contexts were irrational, she argued that they had concerns and interests that made the rational model seem naive. She also sensitized the evaluation community to the political nature of their own activities.

CHAPTER IX

Evaluation Research in the Political Context: Sixteen Years and Four Administrations Later

CAROL HIRSCHON WEISS

When the editors invited me to review my 1973 paper on the politics of program evaluation, it sounded like an engaging idea. In the doing, it turned out to be much less fun. There were two possibilities: that I'd changed my mind considerably (which would make me look skittish and unreliable) or that I still believed the things I'd written (which would suggest I hadn't learned much). But I agreed to do the review, and I persevere. I want to consider the extent to which I still agree with what I wrote in 1973 and the extent to which greater wisdom or advancing years have altered my perceptions. I am also taking advantage of the occasion to muse about the differences between now and 1973 in the way in which political factors influence evaluation. I made a modest start on this review in a "Postscript" to the paper when it was reprinted in Dennis Palumbo's 1987 book,[1] but this is a chance to reexamine it in more leisurely fashion.

The paper made a splash (a splashlet, anyway) when it came out. It drew the largest number of requests for reprints of any paper I have written and has been reprinted over twenty times in at least three languages. What made it special, I think, is that I was saying out loud what a lot of people already knew but had never seen in print. I was saying that evaluation research was not only a technical and methodological exercise but also a political act. When evaluators undertook to examine the effects of social programs, they were making a statement that had political overtones. When they framed their questions and developed their measures and methods, they were making politically relevant choices. When they interpreted their data and chose which findings to highlight and which (if any) recommendations to make, they were intervening in affairs that had generally been the province of bureaucratic and political decision makers. Evaluation could have consequences for the fortunes of programs, agencies, budgets, and political actors.

Articles on evaluation at the time focused on methodological considerations, but I noted that evaluation was also relevant to prospects for services and client access, political reputations and careers, and public willingness to support social programs. I did not overstate the likely effects of evaluation results on program decisions, because I had already learned how erratic such effects could be. But I wanted to alert evaluators to the nature of the work they were engaged in, and to help them understand how other actors in agencies and legislatures reacted to them. If some people in an agency wanted them in and others did not, it was wise to find out what differences lay behind the disagreement; intraagency conflict was relevant to the evaluator's job. If they were not being greeted with welcome and cooperation, it was important to understand the reasons for the chill.

At the time I wrote the paper, most evaluators and policy researchers still seemed to regard program decision making as a rational enterprise. They expected program directors, agency officials, and legislators to define their goals for the program, to support evaluation to find out how well the program was operating and meeting its goals, and then to use the results of evaluation to fix things up. If the program was an outright failure, officials should close it down. If it was a roaring success, officials should expand it and institutionalize it as a permanent part of the system. If the program had some good results and some shortcomings, then officials should retain the good features and modify and improve the shortfall. That was presumably what evaluation was all about—to feed information into decision making to improve the caliber of social programs. And evaluators expected that that was the way it was going to be. For those who found that their evaluation results were being ignored or rejected, the assumption was that they had stumbled into a nest of particularly incompetent or venal operators. They tended to blame the individuals involved. Surely decision-making *systems* were rational; the problem had to lie with the peculiar individuals in the case.

The evaluator's job was seen as developing and reporting the best and most objective information possible. The evaluator's post was on some Olympian height well above the fray, untarnished by the squabbling down below among interests and factions. In fact, an implicit (sometimes explicit) goal of the evaluation enterprise was to "take the politics out" of program and policy decision making.

Gradually, of course, the larger context became obvious. I think that my 1970 paper, entitled "The Politicization of Evaluation Research,"[2] was the first to write in the professional prints that the game we had gotten involved in was not a rational game. It was a political game. If we wanted to survive and prosper in the game, we had better learn the rules. The 1973 paper elaborated the theme. It pointed out that politics intrudes on program evaluation in three ways: (1) programs are created and maintained by political forces; (2) higher echelons of government, which make decisions about programs, are embedded in politics; and (3) the very act of evaluation has political connotations. I still believe these statements are true.

Many people knew about the diversions and distractions for which agency people could use evaluation. Directors of programs could (and did) stave off demands for change with the rationale, "We're doing an evaluation of the program now and have to wait until the results are ready." Critics of a program could call for evaluation with the expectation that evaluation results would sink the program without a trace. Supporters of a program could help mount a cream-puff of a study that would show the program in the best possible light. But these were superficial indicators of political motives. My aim was to show that the very essence of evaluation research had a political dimension.

Political Interests at the Program Level

The first point of impact is at the level of the program being evaluated. Evaluators might think of the program as an "intervention," something purposely constructed so that they could study its effects, but to the director and staff running the program it is something else entirely. It is often their cause, something they believe in, something that they helped to develop and have a big psychological stake in. They may also see the program as a form of service to clients with whom they have a strong bond—special-needs children, frail elderly, victims of spouse abuse, schizophrenics. They have commitments to these people and to the services they give them. The program is also their job, their livelihood. If it were closed down, they would be out of work. If the whole class of programs of the same type were put out of business (e.g., individual casework), they would need job retraining. They do not think of the program as the "X" in Cook and Campbell's diagrams of experimental and quasi-experimental evaluation designs;[3] it is not the equivalent of a laboratory stimulus. This is real stuff.

Moreover, the programs did not just happen. Programs come into being through political processes, through the rough and tumble of political support, opposition, and bargaining. Because evaluations are more likely to be requested when programs are relatively new and dispensing innovative types of service, the political origins are fresh and warm. Legislative sponsors have attached their reputations to the program; opponents may be licking their wounds looking for ways to do the program in. Clients, some of whom may have been mobilized to help secure funding for the program, often have high expectations for what it will accomplish for them. A support structure coalesces around the program, composed of bureaucrats, program delivery staff, supportive legislators, and clients. But there remain in the wings a set of potential opponents, composed of the earlier foes, other agencies jealous of the new structure and its incursions on their turf or unsympathetic to the agency's mode of service, staff who had commitments to the old way of doing things and are now displaced, professional guilds whose members are not being employed, reporters looking for a muckraking story on waste and corruption, and perfectly good-hearted people who have other priorities for the money the program is spending.

In such an environment, it is small wonder that program directors came to view the evaluation process as more of a threat than a help. Once upon a time program people used to expect that evaluation would provide a glowing review of their program, which would be great public relations and would help them gain support. But by 1970 negative evaluation reports were pouring in, even of programs that had had fine reputations, and program people were becoming wary. A largely favorable evaluation might do them a little good; one that pointed out occasional weaknesses could give them a little help in making modifications. But the dangers of a basically negative report were overwhelming. Even if it did not lead to an early demise of the program, it could lower staff morale, reduce legislative or bureaucratic commitment to funding, and reopen struggles with contending agencies and alternative programmatic strategies.

The politics of organizational survival is an ancient art. From the time of the pharaohs, administrators have practiced techniques of insulating their organizations from scrutiny. They are in the business of safeguarding the organization's autonomy, mission, scope, and budgets, and they respond to sources of threat with well-practiced stratagems. When evaluation is perceived as potentially dangerous, they are ready to roll into place a battery of protective devices.

Administrators are not "irrational." They have a different model of rationality in mind. Their goal is not just to achieve immediate program targets, such as reducing carbon monoxide levels or school dropouts. Their longer range and more important goal is to maintain a viable organization. They need to be able to recruit good staff, motivate and retain them, keep the channels of communication open and functioning, help people work cooperatively and effectively, gain the support of the communities they work with, maintain good relations with collateral organizations, and maintain or, better yet, increase the organization's budget and scope of operations. Clients have to be attracted, constituencies have to be wooed, support has to be assured. For administrators, program goals are by no means irrelevant but they are embedded in a complex texture of operating concerns. The operating concerns inevitably take priority.

Evaluators tend to assume that accomplishing the objectives for which the program was established is the overriding imperative. But for program managers, the priority is usually to keep the agency going.

The disparity in viewpoint between evaluators and administrators has consequences for the kind of study that is done, or even whether an evaluation gets off the ground at all. The political sensitivies of administrators can lead them to block or delay the start-up of any study. Or they may want to dictate the kinds of questions that are asked and the kinds of people who respond. Or they can make life very difficult for the evaluator in petty things all along the way, by such tactics as limiting computer access, supplies, and paper clips, as in one study I know about, or restricting access to people and places. Again, when the study is completed, the manager's political sensibilities may get in the way of careful consideration of the evidence. The view some managers hold about their programs is "*nil nisi bonum,*" speak nothing but good; it is a phrase usually reserved for the dead.

One of the debates in the evaluation community has been whether evaluators should use official program goals as a basis for evaluating success. Some writers believe that official goals represent the best statement available about what society expects from the program and therefore the standards to which it should be held accountable. Others believe that official goals are often meaningless. They are either bland statements that paper over strong differences of opinion among program advocates or they are global and inflated promises, designed to win supporters to the program's side. At the extreme, some people believe that evaluators should purposely ignore official goals *because* they are official. The evaluator should not take the perspective of officialdom but of the people in need of program service. The evaluator should envision what clients' real needs are, and then evaluate the program against these criteria. It is an old debate, still interesting, because it is grounded in differing assumptions about how politics affects the statement of program goals.

My view in 1973 was, and is today, that the need to gather political support for passage of a program often leads to constructing an unrealistic set of goal statements, designed to win support and appease all factions. They are not clear, specific, or measurable, and people in different places in the program system will emphasize different elements. What the Secretary of Education says about Chapter 1 will differ from what the state director emphasizes, which will be different again from what the Chapter 1 coordinator and teachers in a local school are likely to put their energies to. Evaluators can not take official goals as the foundation of their studies without doing a lot of investigation to find out which goals are real and which are window dressing, which are public relations statements and which represent the direction that people are genuinely working toward. On the other hand, to substitute the evaluator's reading of people's "real needs" would merely substitute the evaluator's value judgment and political beliefs for officials' political statements. There are no objective "needs" irrespective of the criteria used to determine them. What is needed is a quest for what the program is really out to achieve. When the evaluator is astute enough to uncover the *operative* goals, overt or covert, that are genuinely setting the direction the program takes, the study is likely to look at the important things.

While an evaluation is in the field, political forces can alter or undermine it. Because of bureaucratic politics and legislative politics, programs undergo change over the months and years. They de-emphasize some activities, add others, change their target groups, alter the intensity or frequency of service, and so on. What brings about these changes is often a political event. Legislators cut the budget; top officials articulate new priorities; the program director resigns under political pressure and a new director with new ideas is appointed; rival agencies gain greater public support; the political winds shift toward—you name it—tougher prison sentences, privatization of public services, more stringent licensing requirements. Such events can alter not only what the program does but also what the program is.

The consequences for evaluation are dramatic. The evaluator can track what is happening, but if the study is designed to find out how good the outcomes are for program beneficiaries, he or she is in a quandary. Some of the things the evaluator was looking at under earlier conditions are no longer relevant; some outcomes now central to the program's expectations weren't examined at the start and there are no "before" data. Take a program that was originally developed to reduce the number of homeless people on the streets. Over time, political sentiment switched from support for shelters that simply provided a place to sleep to a demand for physical safety, a drug-free environment, and personal privacy for family units. The evaluator who had not paid attention to these factors in early data collection has no basis for comparing later conditions.

Even when indicators of effectiveness remain stable, the definition of "the program" has undergone significant change. Let's say the program is a counseling program for delinquents, where the desired outcome is a reduction in delinquent acts. The "program" has changed many times under budgetary pressures, change in departmental leadership, and day-to-day modifications by staff. When evaluation results come in, to what can they be attributed? Which version of the program is responsible for the effects observed? If the outcomes are good, which kind of counseling should be replicated? If the results are poor, which variation of the program was at fault? Because the program changed shape so often, the evaluation is unable to make causal interpretations.

This is pretty much what I said in the original paper. Recent studies of evaluation in action have elaborated the politics of the program level. For example, Farrar and House showed how the demands of evaluation pressed Jesse Jackson's charismatic PUSH/Excel program to become more organized and bureaucratic and faulted it when it failed to do so.[4] Stake found that evaluation of the Cities-in-Schools program "quieted" the reform effort.[5] Obviously

program-level politics not only *affect* the origin and conduct of
evaluation but are affected by it as well.

Politics of Higher-Level Policy Making

If the people who run a program are likely to be protective of it
and unresponsive to evidence about it, there is another set of actors on
the scene. These are the officials, both appointed and career, who
oversee a number of programs and the legislators who review, enact,
and fund them. Higher-level policymakers may be more likely to pay
attention. The Secretary of Labor, the state director of environmental
quality, and the city's superintendent of schools may have a greater
interest in evaluative evidence than operating staff for two reasons.
First, they have a wider set of options available to them than just the
one program under review. If one program is not functioning well,
they can more readily shift their allegiance to another. Second, by the
nature of their jobs, they are often more aware of public expectations
and more concerned with seeing that the public gets its money's worth
in program results. Legislators in particular may be attuned to the
needs and wants of voters.

But this does not mean that higher-level policymakers are
necessarily enthusiastic users of evaluative evidence. Although they
may have less commitment to the survival of a program than the staff
of the program, they respond to the imperatives of their own systems.
Their primary concerns are likely to be such things as: getting
reelected; maintaining the cooperation and support of the client group
with which the agency must constantly deal; negotiating a compromise among powerful competing factions; gaining prestige and repute
among members of their professional guild. How well a program is
doing may be less important than gaining the support of an influential
legislator. Tolerating an ineffective program may make sense if it
satisfies constituents or pays off political debts.

What evaluation can do is demonstrate just what the policymaker
is giving up when he or she settles for a poor program or fails to adopt
a successful one. Evaluation shows what social benefits are being
foregone, and policymakers can judge whether the political gains are
worth the social losses. In that event, evaluation serves a vital purpose
if it helps policymakers make such decisions with their eyes wide
open.

Evaluation will never be the sole basis on which policy decisions are made. Policymakers inevitably, and legitimately, take many other factors into account beyond the effects that programs have for their participants. But it has sometimes seemed as though evidence of program success has had little weight in policy deliberations. Observers have said that policy actors pay attention only to those results that fit with what they have already decided to do. They flourish reports that support their positions and use evaluations as a tactic in the play of power. According to this view, evaluation is employed not as illumination but as ammunition.

In my 1973 paper, I recognized that much experience supports this view. But I suggested that evaluation will be seriously considered not only by those for whom the results are congenial; evaluation will also get a hearing from those who share the values and assumptions on which the study is based.

Shortly after I wrote the discussion about what it takes to get evaluation findings used, I launched a series of studies of the uses of social science research—including but not limited to evaluations. At the start, I expected that potential users at federal, state, and local levels would pay attention to, and "use," studies that produced findings that were compatible with what they believed and with the values and assumptions embedded in the policies of their organizations. In a carefully designed study of the usefulness and usability of fifty social science studies supported by the National Institute of Mental Health (NIMH), we administered painstaking interviews to decision makers associated with local mental health programs, state departments of mental health, and officials at NIMH.[6] We didn't just ask them about the kinds of research they used, would use, or liked. Instead we gave them studies to read, had them rate the studies on a series of decriptive dimensions, and then asked them about the likelihood that they would take the findings of the studies into account in their work. Our analysis compared the ratings on the descriptors of the studies with the ratings on likelihood of use.

The results of that work were surprising. When we analyzed the data, we did not find the dimension of "political acceptability" that I had expected would characterize useful studies. Instead, there were two separate "political" dimensions, one of which had to do with whether the findings were congruent with the reader's *own* knowledge and beliefs, and the other dealing with whether the findings supported the *agency's* programs and policies. The first dimension, agreement with one's *own* beliefs, was positively related to the usefulness of research, but the other dimension, support for the agency's position, was negatively related to usefulness of research. It appeared that many people were ready to use research and evaluations that *challenged* the agency status quo. Evidently an underground already existed in many places composed of people who were skeptical of current programs (the research agreed with what they already knew) and who wanted to make use of the research as one basis for change. Our findings did not show that they were going to do anything right away with the research. But they thought the research that disclosed shortcomings in policy and practice was useful and likely to be used.

Now that I carefully re-read the 1973 paper, I realize that I should not have been surprised with these results. The paper had said:

It does appear that evaluation research is most likely to affect decisions when the researcher accepts the values, assumptions, and objectives of the decision maker. . . . But it suggests more than the rationalization of predetermined positions. There is a further important implication that those who value the *criteria* that evaluation research uses, those who are concerned with the achievement of official program goals, will pay attention as well. The key factor is that they accept the assumptions built into the study. Whether or not the outcome results agree with their own wishes, they are likely to give the evidence a hearing. . . . If a decision maker thinks it is important for job trainees to get and hold on to skilled jobs, he will take negative evaluation findings seriously [even if he is committed to the program].[7]

This is not exactly what we found, but it is close. We found that people were willing to pay attention to negative evidence, provided that it was in agreement with how they believed the world was working. It may also be true that they need to believe that the evidence, and the criteria, are relevant and important.

The other main thing we found in that study was that decisions are not the neat events that most of us had thought. Decisions do not generally emerge from a group of people sitting around a table at a certain time and place and deciding what to do. Rather decisions take shape in a disjointed series of amorphous steps.[8] Many people in many offices make small changes, and the end result is a decision that few of them anticipated. Often people do not realize until after the fact that a decision has been made. I called the process "decision accretion." If evaluation is to affect this kind of almost haphazard decision making, it has to get into the agency thought-stream. Its findings have to be known by many people in many different offices, all of whom have some say or do some thing that influences the shape of future action. I called the subtle percolation of evaluation findings into people's consciousness "enlightenment," or in a less value-laden term, "knowledge creep." I borrowed the latter term from Deborah Shapley who had written a piece in *Science* on "technology creep," the process by which weapons systems become more sophisticated. She said that rarely do top officials in the White House or the Pentagon deliberate and decide that the nation should move weapons up a notch in technical advancement. Rather it is the bureaucrats who manage each system who are responsible; on a day-to-day basis, they each keep up with the latest technology and make recurrent small improvements to keep the system they manage up to date. I believe that a similar kind of nondeliberative process occurs in the creep of research and evaluation findings into the policy arena. The information seeps in through a variety of uncoordinated channels and some of it affects the course of agency action.

In subsequent years I did further studies of the use and influence of research and evaluation—in education, criminal justice, alcoholism treatment, health care, and most recently in international development. I have looked at legislative and judicial, as well as executive, agencies. Nothing I have learned significantly challenges these basic insights. Some modifications are probably called for: legislatures, for example, seem to be less open to enlightenment and occasionally more receptive to instrumental uses of research and evaluation.[9] But the main theme holds.

The Political Stance of Evaluation

Evaluators take a political stand and make a series of political statements when they undertake to conduct a study. Just agreeing to do the study has political overtones. The message to the world at large is two-fold: (1) the program is problematic enough to need evaluating, and (2) the program is a serious enough effort to be worth the time and effort to evaluate.

A political statement is implicit in the selection of some programs to undergo evaluation and others to escape scrutiny. The evaluated program has all its linen, clean and dirty, hung out in public; the unanalyzed program can tuck its secrets away in the bureau drawers.

What criteria are used to select programs to evaluate? In the 1960s and 1970s it was the new and innovative program that was evaluated. The hardy perennials went on without cavil or question, whether or not they were doing much good. And since the new programs of the period were programs for marginal groups, such as poor children, juvenile delinquents, and released mental patients, these were the programs that were scrutinized. These programs are more frequent candidates for evaluation partly because there is so much uncertainty about how to serve the chronically unemployed or drug abusers, and agencies want to learn how different service modalities work. Partly, it may be that innovative nongovernmental funders take on programming for marginal groups, and they want to make sure that their limited resources are achieving progress. For example, foundations that are supporting educational, housing, and health programs for the black population of South Africa seem to want feedback that shows whether their funds are being well spent. In part, too, there is a political reason for evaluation. Programs with powerless clientele may lack the coalition of support that shields more mainstream groups. They may not have developed alliances of interest groups, professional associations, citizen representatives, and bureaucrats that will seek to reduce the intrusion of evaluation.

I noted in the paper that politically savvy analysts like Charles Schultze have recommended that analysts should pay more attention to programs that do not directly affect the structure of institutional and political power and less to programs that affect income distribution or impinge on the power structure. He also recommended that analysts study new and expanding programs rather than those with long traditions and well-organized constituencies.[10] There are good reasons for such advice. If evaluators get themselves entangled with programs that are protected by influential coalitions, they are asking for trouble. Information that finds such programs unsuccessful will do little good. When reported to decision makers, it will put them in an untenable position, and it will tend to call down the wrath of the mighty on the evaluation. Evaluation that finds such programs successful will be regarded as obvious and a thoroughgoing waste of money. Schultze's prescriptions have the virtue of practicality, but they have serious political implications. They lead to restricting evaluation to the unprotected program and the program that is marginal to the distribution of social and economic power.

The evaluator who agrees to study a new program for powerless clients in effect assents to defining the program as problematic. On the other hand, the evaluator is also saying that the program is plausible enough that the study is worth doing. For some programs, where experts know that the service is inappropriate, or when it is of insufficient intensity to make much headway, or when it is a replica of programs that have already been proved wanting, there is little point in undertaking another study. Yet the evaluator's willingness to sign on gives the program legitimacy.

Furthermore, the evaluator almost always limits the study to the effects of the few things that the program changes. He or she evaluates the introduction of housing vouchers or a new strain of rice, which suggests that all other elements in the situation are unimportant or that they are fixed and unchangeable. The program intervention is viewed as the key variable, and other conditions that may give rise to, sustain, or alter the problems facing the target population are given short shrift. By its very nature, evaluation tends to ignore the social and institutional structures within which the problems of the target group are generated and sustained. Although evaluation has the technical capacity to examine the effects of institution and context, most studies disregard critical structural variables in the lives of the client population.

In the specification of the evaluation questions, the sponsor of the study usually has the major say. Sponsors, of course, are almost always the organization that finances the program or the agency that runs the program. Almost never are they the clients of the program. If the youths enrolled in the job training program were in charge of the evaluation, they might ask different questions from those the operating agency asks. Yet their concerns and their perspectives rarely surface. Similarly, at the end of the study, when drawing implications from the results, the evaluator may consider only those next steps that are practical from the standpoint of the agency. If she or he wants the findings and recommendations to be "used," recommendations can be limited to those that are feasible within the agency's constraints. The evaluator is not likely to think long and hard about the practicalities of the trainees' lives or what makes sense in terms of the options that they see open to them.

Each study builds in certain values and assumptions of its own. In these postpositivist days we have all come to understand that there is no single perspective or mode of inquiry that will yield unvarnished truth. All truth is varnished; all inquiry takes on the coloration of its investigators' assumption. Values, including political values, are built into the study through the choice of questions to focus on, the types of measures used, the wording of questions, the choice of respondents, the choice of sites, even the selection of one methodological strategy rather than another. It makes a big difference whether the underlying question is: Is this agency running as good a program as it can given all its constraints? or Are the clients of the program getting all the help they need to lead constructive and satisfying lives?

Most of the political implications of evaluation have an establishment orientation. They accept—and bolster—the status quo. They take for granted the world as defined in the existing social structure, the way agencies are organized, official diagnoses of social problems, and the types of ameliorative programs that are provided. Writing about policy analysis, Aaron believes that all analysis has a conservative effect; because each study answers some questions only to raise new ones, analysis tends to slow the pace of reform.[11] But the basic tendency of evaluation is reformist. Its whole thrust is to improve the way that society copes with social and economic problems. At the same time that evaluation accepts program assumptions, it subjects them to scrutiny. It not only accepts, it tests and challenges.

Evaluation conclusions usually identify a gap between expectations and outcomes. Recommendations call for modifications to bring the program up to par. The assumptions are that relatively modest adjustments in what is already being done will be sufficient. Few recommendations look to basic changes in the pattern of the program. Existing goals tend to be accepted. The political stance of evaluation research is unremittingly incrementalist.

What's New

Probably the greatest change I would make in the paper now is to de-emphasize the goal orientation of evaluation. At the time I wrote, I considered that most evaluation studies would be asking "How well is the program meeting goals?"—funders' goals, operating agency goals, staff goals, clients' goals. That was the prevailing view in the early 1970s. Today evaluators ask a much broader array of questions. Many more evaluations look at the way that programs operate; they want to see what goes on and why. Evaluators are less concerned with pinning down goal statements before they launch the study. While goals still play a part in evaluations, explicitly or implicitly, they are not the centerpiece they once were.

Evaluators have learned that a major part of their craft is to understand the *process* of the program, how it takes shape over time, what kinds of activities it provides, to whom, under what conditions, with what witting or unwitting biases and emphases. Evidence about program process helps to enlighten people inside and outside the program about what the experience feels like and what meanings it has for occupants of different positions. This kind of information is often more useful to staff managers, planners, and policymakers than findings about how far the program fell short of its goals. They can use findings about activities directly to reshape the daily work and the long-term design of the program.

But process information has political overtones as well. Detailed evaluation data about what goes on inside the program give superordinate agencies the means for exercising greater control over the operating staff.[12] Having the knowledge to exercise control is particularly relevant when a federal department is in charge but operations are run by state or local agencies or by federal offices scattered across the country, or when a foundation in New York funds sites in ten states, or a state agency provides grants to local school systems. For good or for ill, evaluation findings give the higher echelon enough information to write new regulations, tighten reporting requirements, provide greater direction and control. We might call this the Haroun el-Rashid function of program evaluation, in honor of the Baghdad caliph who traveled incognito among his subjects to see how they were faring under his rule.

The other big change in evaluation practice in the intervening years has been the upsurge of qualitative methods of study—and their legitimation. I think that this is all to the good. Although it affects what I was writing about political influences only indirectly, in subtle ways the shift to qualitative methods makes the evaluator's job both easier and more difficult. Easier—because the evaluator is not bound to a set of measures that were developed in the "before" period when she or he knew less about the program and its context than she or he would know later. With qualitative methods, the evaluator can shift attention as she or he learns more. Qualitative methods also can provide richer and more relevant information, and they can enable the evaluator to analyze the link between what goes on in the program and the outcomes that ensue. But qualitative methods can also make things harder, because potential users of evaluation are often more skeptical of results; they are more likely to be aware that the evaluator's ideology, ideas, and interests affect the course of the study. Of course, the same is true of quantitative indicators too, but somehow audiences feel that numbers are hard and firm, and anything that comes out of computers must be true. Qualitative materials seem ordinary and familiar, not scientific, and readers lack a strong sense of the database underlying the conclusions. Often they look upon the report as special pleading. Evaluators are now learning how to present qualitative reports in ways that gain the trust of users.

As for the program sphere, what Wildavsky and May called "the policy space" has become more crowded.[13] Where once a new program entered an open arena, now there are likely to be dozens of other programs dealing with the same problem already on the scene. Each is jostling for turf and support. Similarly, where once a new program was the only externally mandated program with which an agency—say, a school system—had to deal, now the agency is already running a battery of other federally and state-mandated programs. The new program interacts with all the existing programs. Some clients have to be shifted from one to another, some get duplicate services, there may be financial advantages in changing diagnoses (e.g., from "disadvantaged" to "learning disabled") in order to enroll students under better-funded titles, new staff and space have to be found and fit into the system, and more complex lines of coordination and accountability have to be developed. Furthermore, the new program puts greater stress on the organization's capacity for management.

The crowded policy space has ramifications not only for programming but also for evaluation. Evaluations have to be sensitive to the interactions among agencies, interactions among managers, staff, and program recipients associated with different services within an agency, and the longer-term consequences of multiple programs. For example, by looking at program interactions, Lewis found that cutbacks in Aid to Families with Dependent Children (AFDC) reduced expenditures in AFDC but diverted demand for day care to the Social Security program, which cost the federal government more than had the allowances for day care under AFDC.[14]

The Future of Evaluation Research

The last part of the 1973 paper wrestled with the question of whether evaluation research was helping in the improvement of social programming. I was much concerned that most of the evaluations of the period were bringing bad news. Since the programs that were being studied at the time were largely programs for the poor and disadvantaged under the War on Poverty, the bad-news tidings could potentially be used to gut the reform effort. (I use the word "reform," although many of us at the time thought we were part of something much less tepid and far more important than reform.) I considered what evaluators could do when they found that a well-meaning program was ineffective. I suggested, for example, that they take a critical look at the standards they were using to judge effectiveness. Sometimes evaluators were accepting the inflated promises of program advocates as goals and holding the program to unrealistic expectations. More modest expectations would be reasonable. Another suggestion was to evaluate a particularly strong version of the program, well-funded and well-staffed, run with all the stops pulled out. Such an evaluation would tell whether the program, *at its best*, could have the desired effects. If it did, then lower-cost versions could be tested to see if the effects would be sustained. Should the low-budget versions fizzle, it would be clear that more intensive service was called for. If even the high-budget, industrial-strength program did not achieve desired results, then it was likely that the theory underlying the program was faulty, and the lesson would be: Back to the drawing board. Still, there was a tone of disenchantment in the 1973 paper, a yearning for more direct ways of improving public policy than through evaluation.

At this point I am more sanguine about evaluation. The change in my point of view comes less from what evaluation is newly doing than from my increased awareness of how resistant social problems are and how difficult it is to bring about social change. Even modest progress should be cherished. So I am more impressed with the utility of the findings that evaluation has provided. Perhaps they have not led to massive improvements in programming, but they have increased people's understanding of how programs operate. Evaluators have helped program directors, program designers, and program staff understand the kinds of effects that programs have and the consequences of different program strategies. In many agencies and many countries, officials have heeded the lessons. Incremental improvements have been made, and cumulative increments can add up to pretty significant change after all.

I am also heartened by the widespread recognition today among evaluators, as well as policy researchers and social scientists more generally, that research has a political dimension. Researchers are likely to recognize the influence of their own values and choices on the work they do. They are not so ready to expect that policymakers and program managers yield instantly to the truth and beauty of their studies. There is something becoming about this type of modesty. But of course it should not deter all of us from doing the best evaluations of which we are capable and then working hard and sensitively to see that the results are widely communicated.

The current political climate is one of center and right-of-center ideology and severe constraints on government budgets. In this climate, evaluations have tended to become cautious. Rather than being allied with left-liberal reform and expansionist services, they are more concerned with efficiency and cost savings, feasibility, and adherence to prescribed rules. They seem to pay less attention to the effectiveness of government action in terms that are responsive to clients and consumers. That is a large generalization and there are many exceptions, but the trend is in that direction. I have some regrets that sights are set low; on the other hand, I think that the evenhandedness with which evaluation is being used probably has something to recommend it.

There was a time in the early 1980s, shortly after President Reagan took office, when it looked as though conservatives were going to jettison social science research and evaluation. David Stockman at the Office of Management and Budget (OMB) was cutting every pocket of money allotted to social science research, analysis, and evaluation throughout government.[15] Republicans seemed to be on a rampage against social science research in any guise, presumably because the social sciences had been associated with Democratic programs and policies. The future of research and evaluation funding looked bleak. Flather has provided a parallel account of British cuts under Prime Minister Thatcher.[16]

Today evaluation funds have risen again although they are still below the 1980 level.[17] Fewer large external evaluations are being funded but more small internal studies. Evaluations are being done in health care, environmental protection, agriculture, policing, personnel management, transportation, international development, executive training, land use, dispute resolution, military recruitment, and many other fields beyond those traditionally the province of evaluation.

More evaluations are being sponsored by states and localities and by not-for-profit and private organizations. Expectations have been tempered for the benefits they will produce, but it is clear that evaluation has become an aid to officials across the political spectrum. Even the Heritage Foundation has come out in support.[18] In the long run it is probably all to the good that people of many political persuasions recognize benefits in program and policy evaluation. If evaluation is identified with only one political position, it runs the risk of being wiped out—offices dismantled, people "terminated"—when that position is out of favor.

What is needed now, as it has been all along, is support for independent *critical* evaluation. Funds should be available for some small segment of evaluation studies that take a critical look at programs, irrespective of the views of agency managers and their political superiors. An important contribution that evaluators can make is to question the goals, the activities, and the outcomes of programming supported by the constituted authorities, whether they are right, left, or green, and bring different views to bear. I am suggesting support for multiple evaluations from multiple perspectives.[19] To some extent this function is being served at the present time by the analytic agencies responsible to the Congress—the Congressional Research Service, the General Accounting Office, the Congressional Budget Office, and the Office of Technology Assessment. Because the Congress includes representatives of a wide range of political views, its members and its committees do not limit their evaluative requests to the prevailing political orthodoxies. In addition, it would be a great idea to have independent bodies support systematic critical evaluations of government policies from a variety of perspectives.

A collateral suggestion is that evaluation results should be reported more widely. Not only policymakers, officials, and program staff need to learn the findings, but so, too, do clients, interest groups, professional groups, journalists, and the public at large. Evaluators who work at it may well find that journalists will report the results of evaluations of newsworthy programs to a mass audience.[20] Lindblom's as yet unpublished book on "the probing society" has reinforced my conviction that it is essential to communicate analytic findings not only to stakeholders but to "informed publics" and the public at large. Even if many members of the public are not yet interested in the information, evaluators should accept a responsibility to get the word out—in order to inform people about what was, what is, and what could be. In a democratic polity, all people have a say about the kind of society they want, and evaluators can use their knowledge to try to help members of society participate more wisely.

Footnotes

1. Carol H. Weiss, "Where Politics and Evaluation Research Meet," in *The Politics of Program Evaluation*, ed. Dennis Palumbo (Newbury Park, CA: Sage, 1987). Originally published in *Evaluation* 1, no. 3 (1973). Reprinted as "Evaluation Research in the Political Context" in *Handbook of Evaluation Research*, ed. Elmer Struening and Marcia Guttentag, vol. 1 (Beverly Hills, CA: Sage, 1975), pp. 13-26.

2. Carol H. Weiss, "The Politicization of Evaluation Research," *Journal of Social Issues* 26, no. 4 (1970): 57-68.

3. Thomas D. Cook and Donald T. Campbell, *Quasi-Experimentation: Design and Analysis Issues for Field Settings* (Boston: Houghton Mifflin, 1979).

4. Eleanor Farrar and Ernest R. House, "The Evaluation of PUSH/Excel: A Case Study," in *New Directions in Educational Evaluation*, ed. Ernest R. House (London: Falmer Press, 1986), pp. 158-185.

5. Robert E. Stake, *Quieting Reform: Social Science and Social Action in an Urban Youth Program* (Urbana, IL: University of Illinois Press, 1986).

6. Carol H. Weiss, with M. J. Bucuvalas, *Social Science Research and Decision-Making* (New York: Columbia University Press, 1980).

7. Weiss, "Evaluation Research in the Political Context," in *Handbook of Evaluation Research*, ed. Struening and Guttentag, vol. 1, p. 19.

8. Carol H. Weiss, "Knowledge Creep and Decision Accretion," *Knowledge: Creation, Diffusion, Utilization* 1 (March 1980): 381-404.

9. Carol H. Weiss, "Congressional Committees as Users of Analysis," *Journal of Policy Analysis and Management* 8 (Summer 1989): 411-431.

10. Charles L. Schultze, *The Politics and Economics of Public Spending* (Washington, DC: Brookings Institution, 1968).

11. Henry J. Aaron, *Politics and the Professors: The Great Society in Perspective* (Washington, DC: Brookings Institution, 1978).

12. Edie N. Goldenberg, "The Three Faces of Evaluation," *Journal of Policy Analysis and Management* 2, no. 4 (1983): 515-525.

13. Aaron B. Wildavsky and Judith V. May, eds., *The Policy Cycle* (Beverly Hills: Sage, 1978).

14. G. H. Lewis, "The Day Care Tangle: Unexpected Outcomes when Programs Interact," *Journal of Policy Analysis and Management* 2 (1983): 531-547.

15. Roberta Balstad Miller, "Social Science under Siege: The Political Response, 1981-1984," in *Social Science Research and Government*, ed. Martin Bulmer (Cambridge: Cambridge University Press, 1987), pp. 373-391.

16. Paul Flather, " 'Pulling Through': Conspiracies, Counterplots and How the SSRC Escaped the Axe in 1982," in *Social Science Research and Government*, ed. Martin Bulmer (Cambridge: Cambridge University Press, 1987), pp. 353-372.

17. General Accounting Office, *Federal Evaluation: Fewer Units, Reduced Resources, Different Studies from 1980* (Washington, DC: General Accounting Office, 1987).

18. Stuart M. Butler, Michael Sanera, and W. B. Weinrod, *Mandate for Leadership II: Continuing the Conservative Revolution* (Washington, DC: Heritage Foundation, 1984).

19. See also Lee Cronbach and Associates, *Toward Reform of Program Evaluation* (San Francisco: Jossey-Bass, 1980).

20. Carol H. Weiss and Eleanor Singer, with Phyllis Endreny, *Reporting of Social Science in the National Media* (New York: Russell Sage Foundation, 1988).

Justice in Evaluation

By the early 1970s it had become clear that the field of evaluation was multidisciplinary, in the sense that contributions from many of the traditional academic disciplines could be useful in illuminating the complex issues of the domain. There were, of course, the traditional issues of sampling, data collection, and overall research design; but there also were political and economic issues. It was not long before it was recognized that there were philosophical and epistemological dimensions to evaluation as well. How we can claim to *know* about social and educational life, and make judgments, were matters that received increasing attention (witness the work of Lincoln and Guba, Eisner, Stake, Hamilton, House, and others).

Ernest House, then at CIRCE in the University of Illinois at Urbana-Champaign, realized that evaluations can influence the distribution of "social goods"—after all, programs deliver services to segments of society, and evaluations can influence the fate of programs. Issues of fair distribution have been the "bread and butter" for the domain of ethics. So in 1976 House published a paper, "Justice in Evaluation," that approached evaluation from the point of view of the latest views in the domain of ethics, in particular in terms of the ideas of the influential philosopher John Rawls, whose book *A Theory of Justice* (1971) is regarded as one of the major philosophical works of the twentieth century. Following Rawls, House traced out the consequences for evaluation of the view that just social and educational programs should not harm any individual (unless the program was in the interests of everybody, including the harmed person), and should benefit most those individuals who needed the most assistance. House stressed that this approach was in marked opposition to the utilitarian approach that assessed programs by simply averaging the benefits of each, and then recommended the particular program that had the greatest average benefit. (Average benefit, Rawlsians hold, neglects the issue of the distribution of the benefit.)

CHAPTER X

Evaluation and Social Justice: Where Are We?

ERNEST R. HOUSE

The Liberal Consensus

At the end of World War II the United States achieved a position of unparalleled power, influence, and wealth in the world. To many countries, and certainly to itself, its social, political, and economic system seemed far superior to anything else the world had ever seen, a model for emulation. Americans were united in what one British historian has called "the ideology of the liberal consensus," which included the following beliefs:

1. The American free-enterprise system is different from the old capitalism. It is democratic. It creates abundance. It has a revolutionary potential for social justice.

2. The key to this potential is production: specifically, increased production, or economic growth. This makes it possible to meet people's needs out of incremental resources. Social conflict over resources between classes . . . therefore becomes obsolete.

3. Thus there is a natural harmony of interests in society. American society is getting more equal. It is in the process of abolishing . . . social class.

4. Social problems can be solved like industrial problems: The problem is first identified; programs are designed to solve it, by government enlightened by social science; money and other resources . . . are then applied to the problem as "inputs"; the outputs are predictable: the problems will be solved.

5. The main threat to this beneficent system comes from the deluded adherents of Marxism.[1]

The key to this revolutionary social system was economic growth. Democratic capitalism seemed to work. The massive unemployment and social turmoil of the Great Depression had ended, and everyone was better off. Continued economic expansion provided more for everybody, so there was no need for social class conflict or indeed for social classes. Everyone could be middle class. Social problems would be solved with the increasing economic resources without taking anything away from anyone.

"Production has eliminated the more acute tensions associated with inequality. Increasing aggregate output is an alternative to redistribution," Galbraith wrote in *The Affluent Society* in 1957.[2] Furthermore, both economic growth and the solutions to social problems could be engineered by the federal government. These ideas guided not only the Truman and Eisenhower administrations, but those of Kennedy ("In short, our primary challenge is not how to divide the economic pie, but how to enlarge it"),[3] and Johnson ("So long as the economic pie continues to grow, Johnson argued, there will be few disputes about its distributions among labor, business, and other groups").[4] The size of the economic pie was the critical factor, and new economic indicators such as the gross national product were available to measure the pie.

Where did the social sciences and the emerging field of evaluation fit into this framework? Economists were to determine how to fuel the economy, while other social scientists and evaluators were to discover which programs would solve the remaining social problems most effectively. The social science literature of this period reveals supreme confidence in social science's applied capabilities. To put the situation bluntly, "Alternatives were not what the government wanted. It wanted solutions. It expected to get them from men who displayed a maximum of technical ingenuity with a minimum of dissent."[5]

When Johnson's Great Society ushered in large federal educational programs in 1965, evaluators assessed such things as education for the disadvantaged, Head Start, Follow Through, Job Corps, Sesame Street, Community Action, income maintenance, and social welfare. The practice of evaluation fit the dominant public philosophy. As Campbell said, "[Quasi-experiments and true experiments] stand together in contrast with a morass of obfuscation and self-deception. . . . We must provide political stances that permit true experiments, or good quasi-experiments."[6]

Seminal works presented the basic methodology: "This chapter is committed to the experiment: as the only means for settling disputes regarding educational practice, as the only way of verifying educational improvements, and as the only way of establishing a cumulative tradition in which improvements can be introduced without the danger of a faddish discard of old wisdom in favor of inferior novelties."[7] And from sociology, "The most identifying feature of evaluative research is the presence of some goal or objective whose measure of attainment constitutes the main focus of the research problem. . . . Characterized this way, one may formulate an evaluation project in terms of a series of hypotheses which state that 'Activities A, B, C will produce results X, Y, and Z'."[8]

This rationale was carried forward in federal policy by government officials such as Alice Rivlin, former Assistant Secretary of HEW and Director of the Congressional Budget Office: "In other words, the conditions of scientific experiments should be realized as nearly as possible. . . . Individual project leaders have to agree to follow the plan and to use common measures of what is done and what is accomplished so that the results can be compared. . . . Information necessary to improve the effectiveness of social services is impossible to obtain any other way. . . . Effective functioning of the system depends on measures of achievement."[9]

An evaluation practice so conceived led to what Scriven calls the doctrines of managerialism and positivism.[10] That is, studies were conducted for the benefit of managers of programs, and evaluators acted as value neutral scientists who relied upon the methods of the social sciences to protect against bias. In evaluation these research methods were primarily experimental or survey, utilizing quantitative outcome measures as befit the demand for maximizing the surrogates of economic growth, such as test scores, years of schooling, and income.

This framework was justified formally by the utilitarian theory of justice. Utilitarianism is a moral theory which holds that policies are morally right when they promote the greatest sum total of good or happiness from among the alternatives. Quantitative measures often serve as surrogates for total happiness in utilitarian calculations, and the logic of many evaluation studies was to find the best alternative, i.e., that which maximized the outcomes. Equality is a fundamental notion only insofar as each individual is to count equally in such calculations. This conception of equality does not entail egalitarianism nor even that gross inequality of results be reduced. If it turned out that spending disproportionate sums on education of the advantaged would produce a higher sum total of good for society than spending disproportionate sums on the disadvantaged, then utilitarianism would dictate spending more on the advantaged; and it would do so without violating its own conception of justice.[11]

In this way justice is a derivative principle. That is, whether reducing unequal shares of wealth and power ought to be attempted depends on whether equal shares contribute to maximizing the good. For utilitarians, it usually makes sense to advocate equal educational opportunity by removing obstacles that stand in the way of developing natural talents, but only to the extent that such policies contribute to the overall good. Utilitarians would be hard pressed to support policies that exacted a cost in terms of the sum total of good.

For utilitarians there is no necessary conflict between equality of persons and the unequal shares of goods that exist in liberal societies. As long as each person's good is weighed equally and the sum total of all these goods is maximized, the social arrangement is just. Utilitarianism is based upon considering individuals, not groups, in utilitarian calculations. Hence, one does not have to deal with social classes or other groups, since it is presumed that the common measures represent the common good for all.

Stakeholders and the Fractured Consensus

Between 1960 and 1972, the liberal consensus came apart. In 1958, Martin Luther King, Jr., began his quest for racial equality as a devout affirmation of the American dream and his life ended in bitter disillusionment and assassination in 1968. The civil rights movement shattered the social harmony and gave way to black power, feminism, gay liberation, and ecology. Students, professors, mothers, and laborers marched in the streets to protest the Vietnam War. Civil disobedience became a routine affair.

The national economy suffered double digit inflation. The gross national product continued to expand but mostly through new workers entering the labor force. Median family income peaked in 1973, decreased 6 percent by 1984, and became more unequal in distribution.[12] Something was wrong, even with the economic pie. Social programs were frozen in place. These traumas and the emergence of special interest groups vying for power and advantage did not fit the prevailing ideology. American society needed a new political framework, and social scientists supplied the pluralist-elitist-equilibrium theory of democracy:

Mainstream current American pluralism . . . disclaims any normative judgments (though they are there, not far below the surface). It is held that the current system of competing parties and pressure groups does perform, as well as is possible, the democratic function of equilibrating the diverse and shifting demands for political goods with the available supply, and producing the set of political decisions most agreeable to, or least disagreeable to, the whole set of individual demands. This empirical pluralism is based on an economic market model: the party leaders are the entrepreneurs, the voters are the consumers. The voters' function is not to decide on policies but merely to choose one set of politicians who are authorized to decide the policies.[13]

According to this theory, individual demands are fed into groups, and group leaders articulate these demands to government officials who adjudicate them as best they can. Hence, the entire system is kept in equilibrium by group elites bargaining for their constituencies and government elites reaching accommodations. There is little need for direct participation by members of the basic groups other than to express their demands to their leaders. Leaders are made accountable through consumer sovereignty. Unlike the previous liberal technocratic conception, this model of pluralist democracy recognizes the different interests of diverse groups, accounts for social conflict and the lack of social harmony, while still preserving the primary goal of economic growth to satisfy demands.

Among the first evaluators to recognize diverse values and interests were those such as Edwards and Guttentag,[14] who tried to incorporate them into a utilitarian calculus using procedures such as multiattribute utility scaling, and those such as Stake and MacDonald, who advocated qualitative methodologies for registering such views.[15] Most evaluators continued to practice evaluation based upon the old technocratic presumptions, but eventually the changed social context forced these pluralist notions into mainstream evaluation, as manifested in concepts such as "stakeholders," "contexts of command and accommodation," and the "policy shaping community."[16]

On the surface, this theory allows evaluators to maintain their value neutrality by merely describing the interests of various individuals and groups, who are seen to exist in a sort of plural equilibrium from which legitimate decisions emerge. As Cook and Shadish state the position,

Evaluators may also be unwilling to endorse particular prescriptive ethics because few data have been advanced thus far to support particular philosophers' claims that a better society will result if one ethic is followed rather than another and because the American political system has traditionally preferred to foster a pluralism of values. Promoting a single prescriptive ethic is therefore inconsistent with the political context in which evaluation occurs. . . . A descriptive approach to value is better suited to the political context in which evaluators function, since decision making depends more on the values held by relevant legislators, managers, voters, lobbyists, etc., than on any single prescriptive calculus of value. Hence, knowledge of stakeholder values can be used to help select criteria so that no criteria are overlooked that are of crucial importance to particular groups.[17]

Neither the government nor the evaluator is supposed to intervene to support any particular interests but rather only to provide information which is interest-neutral and value-neutral. The interests of various groups somehow dissolve into the values of decision makers and stakeholders. This view of democracy, originally advanced by the economist Joseph Schumpeter and developed by political scientists such as Robert Dahl, is based upon a model of the economic marketplace in which various interests are registered to work their way out automatically.[18] Sometimes this marketplace derivation is explicit:

The evaluator engages to produce something—information—that has value to consumers and for which they are willing to pay. Deciding what product to deliver is an economic decision; both sides of the supply-demand equation contribute to it. The sponsor, as procurer of information, should not have to take sole responsibility for specifying the product. In industry, suppliers perform a part of their economic function by offering options to customers. In a similar way, the sponsor of an evaluation should be a broker for the many interest communities. And, by anticipating the wishes of those who are in the market for social information, the evaluator assists the sponsor (thus increasing, in a quite legitimate manner, the demand for the evaluator's services).[19]

One result of this new sensibility was that "stakeholders" became a common concept in evaluation. As Weiss put it, "The stakeholder concept represents an appreciation that each program affects many groups, which have divergent and even incompatible concerns. It realizes—and legitimizes—the diversity of interests at play in the program world. It recognizes the multiple perspectives that these interests bring to judgment and understanding. . . . Realization of the legitimacy of competing interests and the multiplicity of perspectives and willingness to place evaluation at the service of diverse groups are important intellectual advances. . . . No longer is the federal agency to have a monopoly on control. The concept enfranchises a diverse array of groups, each of which is to have a voice in the planning and conduct of studies."[20]

Norman Gold and colleagues at the National Institute of Education developed a stakeholder model that focused upon the information needs of stakeholders for evaluating two highly visible programs, Cities-in-Schools and Jesse Jackson's PUSH-Excel program.[21] In both cases the evaluations diminished the success of these programs for the disadvantaged because the evaluators did not attend to the needs of either the program developers or recipients; in truth, the NIE stakeholder model was never implemented.[22] Charles Murray, the evaluator in both cases, substituted a more technocratic model of evaluation and expressed his disdain for the stakeholder concept in his article, "Stakeholders as Deck Chairs."[23] In a more considered assessment, Weiss concluded that the approach holds modest promise for improving the fairness of the evaluation, for marginally improving the range of information collected, for giving more say to local groups, and for democratizing access to information, but that it does not produce harmony or resolve conflicts among diverse groups.[24]

Although the stakeholder concept seems firmly entrenched, there is disagreement about how to implement it. According to Weiss, "Many other evaluators simply paid no attention. Their primary commitment was to the canons of social science. Whether they satisfied program people was of secondary concern. They had been trained in proper methodology, and they were not willing to sacrifice their standards in order to satisfy the whims of people who knew little about validity and causality and who cared less."[25] Some evaluators limited stakeholder involvement to ascertaining values, while others solicited stakeholders as audiences, and yet others wanted stakeholders actively involved in the conduct of the study. But generally, evaluators accepted the pluralist ideas of multiple perspectives, multiple audiences, multiple measures, and multiple methods.

Attempts at Further Reform

Although from the standpoint of social justice the stakeholder approach is decidedly superior to what went before, the pluralist-elitist model is no more value neutral than is the economic marketplace, and the state of methodological grace claimed by evaluators for themselves does not exist. One problem is that all the relevant interests are not represented in the planning and negotiations that determine policies and programs. The powerless and the poor are excluded from inner bargaining processes, and typically their interests are ignored. Evaluation agreements negotiated between the sponsor and evaluator consider powerful interests because of their political potency but not the powerless. Furthermore, on those rare occasions when powerless groups are included, there is the question of whether their leaders properly represent their interests. For the pluralist elitist model to work, all groups must be included, and the leaders must represent their members' interests faithfully.

Another problem is that many critical issues never arise for study or decision. That is, fundamental issues involving conflicts of interests often do not evolve into public issues because they are not formulated. Powerful groups and ideological screens prevent such issues from being considered. For example, in the PUSH/Excel evaluation, the fact that some individual sites had evidence of success was never discussed. Rather, lack of standardization among program sites was interpreted as there being no program. In essence, the pluralist model confuses conflicts of interests with conflicts of power. It can balance only those interests that are represented—typically those of the powerful. The pluralist elitist equilibrium model suffers the same problems of abuse and inequality that the free market does. Free markets are not usually free, at least not for long.

There have been attempts to redress this lack of justice in evaluation. Scriven seems to accept the marketplace analogy and proposes that evaluators defend the interests of consumers against those of producers, a definite nonneutral stance. For example, he has argued that basing evaluations upon program goals biases the study towards producers, since producers define the goals, thus defining the content of the evaluation. Scriven's position often appears to bewilder an evaluation community whose practice is based largely upon assessing sponsor goals. Perhaps his position would be clearer if one thought of the producer and sponsor of an evaluation as being General Motors. Would justice be done if Consumers Union assessed General Motors' goals without taking sides and neutrally allowed the various interests involved to work things out, rather than representing the interests of the consumers?

While supporting stakeholder approaches as a decided improvement, in 1976 I urged evaluators to attend to the plight of the disadvantaged, and employed Rawls's theory of justice as a rationale.[26] Rawls's theory has two basic principles that supplant the principle of utility: (1) each person is to have an equal right to the most extensive basic liberty compatible with a similar liberty for others; (2) social and economic inequalities are to be arranged so that they are both (a) to the greatest benefit to the least advantaged (the "difference principle"), and (b) attached to offices and positions open to all under conditions of fair equality of opportunity.

The difference principle distinguishes Rawls from strict egalitarians. Like utilitarians, Rawls does permit unequal distributions of goods, but he is much more restrictive regarding what kinds of inequalities are permissible. Unlike utilitarians, Rawls would distribute educational resources toward the least advantaged *and* sometimes at the expense of the total good, until the point was reached at which the disadvantaged would receive a greater benefit by distributing more toward the advantaged (e.g., a point might be reached where the disadvantaged could benefit more from expenditures to reduce a shortage of doctors than from expenditures to improve the quality of school facilities).

Thus, although Rawls's principles permit equality of persons and unequal distributions to exist side-by-side, they do so in a way that differs from utilitarianism. His conception of equality is identified with "equal respect" rather than the utilitarian "equal treatment." To treat an individual with equal respect requires responding to needs and thus sometimes requires unequal treatment (e.g., policies that require special educational services for handicapped children). And inequalities in the distribution of goods must meet a stricter test. Maximizing the sum total of good is permissible only so long as it does not violate the kinds of distributions sanctioned by the "difference principle."

Finally, establishing conditions of "fair equality of opportunity" requires active steps to mitigate the effects of the "natural lottery," and thus to level out class differences, including those that students encounter in education. Individuals do not deserve what it is their good or bad fortune to inherit in the "natural lottery"—levels of intelligence, wealth, social advantages—since they can in no way be credited or blamed for being born with such things. Equal opportunity becomes a mechanism for evening out class barriers, instilling in persons a secure sense of self-worth, and empowering them to participate effectively in the democratic process.

I suggested that this conception could be implemented within evaluation by a "fair evaluation agreement" that would include the interests of the disadvantaged, an agreement having to meet certain conditions to be considered fair.[27] This justice-as-fairness position elicited considerable reaction, with some critics contending I was biased towards the interests of the disadvantaged. It seems to me that

making certain the interests of the disadvantaged are represented and
seriously considered is not being biased, though it is certainly more
egalitarian than most current practice.

Social Class and the Postwar Consensus

Why is there so much resistance to including the interests of the
poor and powerless in evaluations? First, both professional and
personal ties lead evaluators to believe that the programs being
evaluated already incorporate the best interests of the poor and
powerless, and that it is not the evaluators' job to question this.
Evaluators belong to the same professional and social strata as the
people who construct and run social programs. These are well-
intentioned people with whom we share both careers and friendships.
We depend on these people for contracts. Questioning whether their
programs incorporate such interests is a potential breach of the
relationship, and possibly a dangerous one for the evaluator.

Second, our conceptual models tell us that these interests are
included already. The liberal technocratic view assumes that such
interests are part of the larger common interests of society, and that
these interests are represented adequately in gross outcome measures.
The pluralist model of democracy assumes that poor and powerless
groups already participate in democratic government, demanding and
negotiating their interests along with other groups. Is it not the case,
for example, that Jesse Jackson was influential enough to obtain
funding for his educational program from the Carter administration?
And, indeed, sometimes these interests are represented, although not
typically.

But I believe there is a deeper resistance too, which relates to the
postwar consensus and the ideological background against which we
conduct evaluations. I believe that we associate the interests of the
poor and powerless with the lower social classes and that we are
extremely reluctant to recognize social classes as enduring causal
entities which greatly influence life chances in American society. The
pervasive influences of gender, ethnicity, regionality, and religion
have been recognized as equally or more important than social class,
which is given no particular emphasis in our studies, except
occasionally as a background variable. And, for that matter, only
recently have race and gender been accorded much importance.

By now most tenets of the postwar ideological consensus have
been shattered or seriously weakened, including the idea that social

science can provide technocratic solutions to social problems. Japanese capitalism has replaced American capitalism as the wonder of the economic world, and fear of Soviet marxism is waning to some degree. Yet two steadfast tenets remain—the belief in economic growth and the belief that the United States has eliminated social classes or soon will. Social classes are not recognized as enduring entities like gender and race. Yet they continue to operate as primary causal factors, restricting opportunity for some and enhancing it for others.

And these two beliefs are interconnected. The pluralist-elitist-equilibrium model depends on "the extreme pluralist assumption that the politically important demands of each individual are diverse, and are shared with varied and shifting combinations of other individuals, none of which combinations can be expected to be a numerical majority of the electorate. . . . Where the economy provides, or promises a share of affluence, class interest will not outrank all other divisions of interest."[28] An expanding economy which meets expectations is crucial in preventing individuals from acting politically as members of a social class, or so it is believed. To defend the interests of the poor and powerless risks questioning one of the fundamental tenets of contemporary American society.

In evaluation the reluctance to recognize social class as a primary causal factor is reflected in assigning failures of educational and social programs to other causes, particularly to traits of individual persons, group subcultures, genetics, lack of knowledge, and the intractability of social problems, and also including program management, ambiguous goal statements, unrealistic expectations, lack of coordination, poor planning, inadequate training, not enough time, and other contingencies too numerous to catalogue. Often the topic is simply avoided. The National Assessment of Educational Progress does not even collect social class data such as parents' occupation, though it does collect data on race and parental education. And in an examination of all articles in four major educational research journals between 1973 and 1983, Grant and Sleeter found only seventy-one articles dealing with race, gender, and social class, or 1.775 per journal per year. Of these, only fifteen dealt primarily with social class, or .375 per major journal per year.[29] These were not evaluation journals but the frequency would not be higher for those journals.

Another way of ignoring conflicting social class interests is to treat matters of conflicting interests as matters of diverse value, as if these differences are matters of personal opinion, like preferences for religion or life style. Stakeholder approaches to evaluation often proceed by ascertaining the values of individuals in the program, e.g., sponsors, managers, and participants, and deriving criteria for the evaluation from these values. As important as these values may be, they are not likely to represent the interests of the poor and powerless. An interest is anything conducive to the achievement of an individual's wants, needs, or purposes, and a need is anything necessary to the survival or well-being of an individual.[30] To be free is to know one's interests, to possess the ability and resources, i.e., power and opportunity to act towards them, and to be disposed to do so.

Social justice requires that the interests of all individuals and groups in society be served. Whose interests are served and how interests are registered are critical issues for evaluation studies. Whether the social class structure acts as a major impediment to the fulfillment of interests for large groups of people is an empirical question; I believe the evidence is quite strong that it does and that this topic is avoided in evaluation. In any case, the influence of social class is an important topic for investigation in evaluations of educational programs if we are to improve the way in which evaluation advances social justice.

Social Justice and Evaluation in Liberal Democracies

Social justice has been a historically emergent feature of liberal democracies. These societies were liberal long before they were democratic. In the beginning political choice in government was for only the privileged. Only through long struggle did the mercantile classes, the middle classes, the working classes, slaves, and eventually women receive the right to vote and some measure of political control in Western countries. Democratic justice came long after liberal choice and was always hard fought.[31]

Justice in evaluation is also historically emergent. I interpret the establishment of evaluation as an open procedure for arriving at judgments about public programs to be a move toward increased democratic control, though evaluation can be turned to antidemocratic ends as well. In taking educational programs as objects of public decision, evaluation should further democratic control as opposed to hidden control. Such a practice of public evaluation entails that evaluation be socially just as well as true, that it attend to the interests of everyone in society and not solely the privileged.

Justice in evaluation is also historically emergent in that the dominant conception of justice changes with social context. However, because justice is relative to the social context does not mean that it is relative morally. We inherit a set of ideas from which we construct our conceptions of justice, and what seems just depends in part on our ideas and the social structure in which we live. What seemed morally correct during the postwar consensus may not seem so now. Society has changed and so have our beliefs about it. Some of our beliefs may have been false. But there is usually a moral choice to be made, an alternative that under the circumstances is morally correct, one that is more just within the social context. Indeed, choice of the correct conception of social justice is not only a problem for evaluation but of evaluation.

During this past twenty-five years of institutionalized evaluation, we have moved from a conception of justice in which it was assumed that increasing the economic productivity of the nation and the outcome measures of a program would benefit everyone alike to a conception of justice in which we see that social programs may have differential effects for different people and groups. During this time injustices regarding race, gender, and ethnicity have been recognized by evaluators, though not always remedied. To that degree the justice of evaluation has improved. The same cannot be said of inequalities of social class, which among all these groupings is most strongly identified with lower educational achievement, opportunity, and income.

Here is a test for our conception of justice in evaluation. If this were 1920 and female suffrage were being debated, should evaluators remain neutral, not taking sides on this issue but rather leaving it to the balance of active interest groups, such as legislators, lobbyists, and program managers, to work things out among themselves? Or should evaluators represent within their evaluations the interests and needs of those unjustly ignored, in this case women, and give weight to those interests? I believe that the latter position is morally correct and will be seen so historically. Evaluators cannot be value neutral in these matters. Our conceptions and even our methodologies are value laden. Evaluators do not live in a state of methodological grace.[32]

FOOTNOTES

1. Geoffry Hodgson, *America in Our Times* (New York: Vintage, 1978), p.76.

2. John Kenneth Galbraith, *The Affluent Society* (Boston: Houghton Mifflin, 1958), p. 97.

3. Hobart Rowen, *The Free Enterprisers: Kennedy, Johnson, and the Business Establishment* (New York: Putnam, 1964), p. 114.

4. Doris Kearns, *LBJ and the American Dream* (New York: Harper and Row, 1976), p. 145.

5. Hodgson, *America in Our Times*, p. 97.

6. Donald T. Campbell, "Reforms as Experiments," *American Psychologist* 24 (1969): 409-429. This paper was highly influential years earlier in mimeographed form.

7. Donald T. Campbell and Julian C. Stanley, "Experimental and Quasi-experimental Designs for Research on Teaching," in *Handbook of Research on Teaching*, ed. N. L. Gage (Chicago: Rand McNally, 1963), p. 172.

8. Edward A. Suchman, *Evaluative Research* (New York: Russell Sage, 1967), pp. 37-38.

9. Alice M. Rivlin, *Systematic Thinking for Social Action* (Washington, DC: Brookings Institution, 1971), pp. 91, 108, 140.

10. Michael Scriven, "Evaluation Ideologies," in *Evaluation Models*, ed. George F. Madaus, Michael Scriven, and Daniel L. Stufflebeam (Boston: Kluwer-Nijoff, 1983), pp. 229-260.

11. Ernest R. House and Kenneth Howe, "Second Chance as Education Policy," in *Second Chance in Education*, ed. Daniel Inbar (London: Falmer Press, forthcoming).

12. Frank Levy, *Dollars and Dreams: The Changing American Income Distribution* (New York: Russell Sage Foundation, 1987).

13. C. B. MacPherson, *The Rise and Fall of Economic Justice* (Oxford: Oxford University Press, 1987), pp. 94-95.

14. Ward Edwards, "Social Utilities," *Engineering Economist* 6 (Summer Symposium 1971); Marcia Guttentag, "Subjectivity and Its Use in Evaluation Research," *Evaluation* 1, no. 2 (1973): 60-65.

15. Robert E. Stake, "The Case Study Method in Social Inquiry," *Educational Researcher* 7, no. 2 (1978): 5-7; Barry MacDonald, "A Political Classification of Evaluation Studies," in *Beyond the Numbers Game*, ed. David Hamilton, D. Jenkins, C. King, Barry MacDonald, and M. Parlett (London: Macmillan, 1977), pp. 224-227.

16. Lee J. Cronbach and Associates, *Toward Reform of Program Evaluation* (San Francisco: Jossey-Bass, 1980).

17. Thomas D. Cook and William R. Shadish, Jr., "Program Evaluation: The Worldly Science," *Annual Review of Psychology* 37 (1986): 210.

18. Joseph A. Schumpeter, *Capitalism, Socialism, and Democracy* (New York: Harper and Row, 1942); Robert A. Dahl, *A Preface to Democratic Theory* (Chicago: University of Chicago Press, 1956).

19. Lee J. Cronbach, *Designing Evaluations of Educational and Social Programs* (San Francisco: Jossey-Bass, 1983), p. 211.

20. Carol H. Weiss, "The Stakeholder Approach to Evaluation: Origins and Promise," in *Stakeholder Based Evaluation*, New Directions for Program Evaluation, no. 17, ed. Anthony S. Bryk (San Francisco: Jossey-Bass, 1983), p. 11.

21. Norman Gold, "Stakeholder and Program Evaluation: Characterizations and Reflections," in *Stakeholder Based Evaluation*, ed. Bryk, pp. 63-72.

22. Robert E. Stake, *Quieting Reform: Social Science and Social Action in an Urban Youth Reform* (Champaign, IL: University of Illinois Press, 1986); Eleanor Farrar and Ernest R. House, "The Evaluation of PUSH/Excel: A Case Study," in *Stakeholder Based Evaluation*, ed. Bryk, pp. 31-57; Ernest R. House, *Jesse Jackson and the Politics of Charisma: The Rise and Fall of the PUSH/Excel Program* (Boulder, CO: Westview Press, 1988).

23. Charles A. Murray, "Stakeholders as Deck Chairs," in *Stakeholder Based Evaluation*, ed. Bryk, pp. 59-61.

24. Carol H. Weiss, "Toward the Future of Stakeholder Approaches in Evaluation," in *Stakeholder Based Evaluation*, ed. Bryk, pp. 83-95.

25. Carol H. Weiss, "The Stakeholder Approach to Evaluation: Origins and Promise," in *Stakeholder Based Evaluation*, ed. Bryk, p. 6.

26. John Rawls, *A Theory of Justice* (Cambridge, MA: Harvard University Press, 1971); Ernest R. House, "Justice in Evaluation," in *Evaluation Studies Review Annual* 1, ed. Gene V Glass (Beverly Hills, CA: Sage Publications, 1976), p. 100.

27. Ernest R. House, *Evaluating with Validity* (Beverly Hills, CA: Sage, 1980).

28. C. B. MacPherson, *Democratic Theory: Essays in Retrieval* (Oxford: Oxford University Press, 1973), p. 180.

29. Carl A. Grant and Christine E. Sleeter, "Race, Class, Gender in Education Research: An Argument for Integrative Analysis," *Review of Educational Research* 56, no. 2 (Summer 1986): 195-211.

30. Roy Bhaskar, *Scientific Realism and Human Emancipation* (London: Verso Press, 1986), p. 170.

31. C. B. MacPherson, *The Life and Times of Liberal Democracy* (Oxford: Oxford University Press, 1977).

32. For an analysis of how ideology and values affect the details of evaluation methodology itself, see Ernest R. House, "Methodology and Justice," in *Evaluation and Social Justice: Issues in Public Education*, New Directions for Program Evaluation, no. 45, ed. Kenneth Sirotnik (San Francisco: Jossey-Bass, 1990).

Professional Standards

In the early years of modern program evaluation, many factors stimulated movement toward development of a set of professional standards. Most, if not all, of those who practiced as evaluators had not been specifically trained for this field; they more or less drifted into it from a wide variety of social sciences or other fields. The authors represented in the present volume constitute a fair sample: they come from educational measurement, educational psychology, curriculum theory, philosophy of science, political science, education and art, economics. There were no agreed-upon canons to guide practice, and in 1964 Lee Cronbach, then president of the American Educational Research Association, called for the development of a guiding set of professional standards. However, a subcommittee concluded that the time was not yet ripe—more thinking and exploring of methods were required before codification should take place.

In the following years the need for standards was underscored as concern grew that many evaluations were being incompetently performed, that much money was being wasted on evaluations that would never be used, and that standardized tests and experimental designs were being misapplied. There was also an expectation that as program evaluations became more common, and more prestigious, decisions would be influenced; but as a result, evaluators might be sued by stakeholders who became disgruntled when evaluation-based decisions went against them. Finally, a body of opinion existed that consumers of evaluations needed some authoritative guidance for distinguishing good from bad evaluation work.

By 1981 the time *was* ripe, and a volume of standards was produced by a joint committee whose seventeen members were drawn from twelve cooperating professional associations. The volume was very thorough. Each standard was carefully discussed, and then illustrated with a detailed case; caveats to the use of each standard also were mentioned. Drafts of the standards had been widely examined within the relevant professional communities, and they had even been field tested. This complex project was headed by Daniel Stufflebeam, an experienced evaluator from Western Michigan University, who was widely known for developing a "decision oriented" approach to evaluation known as the "CIPP model."

CHAPTER XI

Professional Standards and Ethics for Evaluators

DANIEL L. STUFFLEBEAM

Professional educators throughout the world must evaluate their work in order to obtain direction for improving it and to record and assess educational outcomes. They must evaluate the performance of students, programs, personnel, and institutions. Such evaluations occur at many levels: classroom, school, school district, state or province, and national system. And they vary widely in the objects assessed, the questions addressed, the methods used, the audiences served, the funds expended, the values invoked, and, to the point of this chapter, their merit and worth.

In evaluations, as in any professional endeavor, many things can and do go wrong. They are subject to bias, misinterpretation, and misapplication. They might be motivated and conducted unethically, they might address the wrong questions and/or provide erroneous information, or they might simply waste time and resources. Clearly, evaluations themselves should be evaluated in order to help assure that clients receive sound information and ethical service.

During the past thirty years, there have been substantial efforts in the United States to professionalize educational evaluation services. In addition to creating professional evaluation societies and developing preparation programs and a substantial professional literature, the field of education has developed professional standards for educational evaluation.

The seminal standards-setting effort in educational evaluation focused on a particular evaluation method. In the middle 1950s, the American Psychological Association (APA) joined with the American Educational Research Association and the National Council on Measurements Used in Education to develop standards for educational and psychological tests.[1] Updated versions of the "Test Standards" have been published by APA in 1966, 1974, and 1985,[2] and they have been widely used—in the courts as well as in

249

professional settings—to evaluate tests and the uses of test scores. In 1981, the Joint Committee on Standards for Educational Evaluation, whose original seventeen members were appointed by twelve professional societies, issued the *Standards for Evaluations of Educational Programs, Projects, and Materials* (which originally was commissioned to serve as a companion volume to the "Test Standards"). In 1982, the Evaluation Research Society[3] released a parallel set of program evaluation standards (intended to deal with program evaluations both outside and inside education). In 1988, the Joint Committee on Standards for Educational Evaluation completed the *Personnel Evaluation Standards*, a companion volume to their program evaluation standards. In 1989, the National Center for Education Statistics, in cooperation with the states, launched a project to develop Cooperative Education Data Collection and Reporting Standards.

The different sets of standards are noteworthy because they provide: (1) operational definitions of student evaluation, program evaluation, personnel evaluation, and (in the future) national and state education system evaluation; (2) evidence about the extent of agreement concerning the meaning and appropriate methods of educational evaluation, (3) general principles for dealing with a variety of evaluation problems, (4) practical guidelines for planning evaluations, (5) widely accepted criteria for judging evaluation plans and reports, (6) conceptual frameworks by which to study evaluation, (7) status reports on progress, in the United States, toward professionalizing evaluation, (8) content for evaluation training, and (9) a basis for synthesizing an overall view of the different types of evaluation.

Many evaluators, psychologists, and others concerned with the evaluation of education are likely aware of the "Test Standards" but might not know about the program evaluation standards or the personnel evaluation standards. The purpose of this chapter is to review and discuss the significance and limitations of the *Standards for Evaluations of Educational Programs, Projects, and Materials* (hereafter called the "Program Evaluation Standards") and the more recent work of its authors, the *Personnel Evaluation Standards*.[4] I also examine the relevance of the standards for assuring that evaluation practices are ethical as well as accurate, practical, and useful.

The chapter is divided into four parts: (1) an introduction to the "Program Evaluation Standards," (2) an overview of the *Personnel Evaluation Standards*, (3) a discussion of the relevance of the standards for addressing ethics issues in evaluation, and (4) in response to an explicit request from the editors of this yearbook, a retrospective examination of critical issues and practical limitations of standards for improving educational evaluations.

The Program Evaluation Standards

In developing the "Program Evaluation Standards," the Joint Committee devised thirty standards that pertain to four attributes of an evaluation: Utility, Feasibility, Propriety, and Accuracy. The *Utility* standards reflect a general consensus that emerged in the educational evaluation literature during the late 1960s requiring program evaluations to respond to the information needs of their clients, and not merely to address the interests of the evaluators. The *Feasibility* standards are consistent with the growing realization that evaluation procedures must be cost-effective and workable in real-world, politically charged settings; partly, these standards are a countermeasure to the penchant for applying the procedures of laboratory research to real-world settings regardless of the fit. The *Propriety* standards—particularly American—reflect ethical issues, constitutional concerns, and litigation concerning such matters as rights of human subjects, freedom of information, contracting, and conflict of interest. The *Accuracy* standards build on those that have long been accepted for judging the technical merit of information, especially validity, reliability, and objectivity.

The "Program Evaluation Standards" reflect certain definitions of key concepts. Evaluation means the systematic investigation of the worth or merit of some object. The object of an evaluation is what one is examining (or studying) in an evaluation: a program, a project, instructional materials, personnel qualifications and performance, or student needs and performance. Standards are principles widely accepted for determining the value or the quality of an evaluation.

To ensure that the "Program Evaluation Standards" would reflect the best current knowledge and practice, the Joint Committee sought contributions from many sources. They collected and reviewed a wide range of literature. They devised a list of possible topics for standards, lists of guidelines and pitfalls thought to be associated with each standard, and illustrative cases showing an application of each standard. They engaged a group of thirty experts independently to expand the topics and write alternative versions for each standard. With the help of consultants, the Committee rated the alternative standards, devised their preferred set, and compiled the first draft of the "Program Evaluation Standards." They then had their first draft critiqued by a nationwide panel of fifty experts who were nominated by the twelve sponsoring organizations. Based upon the critiques, the Committee debated the identified issues and prepared a version that was subjected to national hearings and field tests. The results of this five-year period of development and assessments led, in 1981, to the published version of the "Program Evaluation Standards." Presently, the Joint Committee is collecting feedback on the use of the "Program Evaluation Standards" to help in preparing the next edition.

An important feature of the standards-setting process is the breadth of perspectives represented in their development. The twelve organizations that originally sponsored the Joint Committee included the perspectives of the consumers as well as those who conduct program evaluations. The perspectives represented on the Joint Committee and among the approximately 200 other persons who contributed include, among others, statistician and administrator, psychologist and teacher, researcher and counselor, psychometrician and curriculum developer, evaluator and philosopher, and school board member and sociologist. There is perhaps no feature about the Joint Committee that is as important as its representative nature, since by definition a standard is a principle agreed to by persons involved in evaluation of education. The diversity on the Committee made reaching agreements very difficult, but once reached the agreed-upon standards and presentation material proved to be credible to a wide group concerned with education, to be relatively free of specialized jargon, and, in general, to be readable by a wide range of users.

The depth of content in each standard is apparent in the common format for all the standards. This format starts with a descriptor—for instance, "Formal Obligation." The descriptor is followed by a statement of the standard, e.g., "Obligations of the formal parties to an evaluation (what is to be done, how, by whom, when) should be agreed to in writing, so that these parties are obligated to adhere to all conditions of the agreement or formally to renegotiate it," and by an overview that includes a rationale for the standard and definitions of its key terms. Also included, for each standard, are lists of pertinent guidelines, pitfalls, and caveats. The guidelines are procedures that often would prove useful in meeting the standard; the pitfalls are common mistakes to be avoided; and the caveats are warnings about being overzealous in applying given standards, lest such effort detract from meeting other standards. The presentation of each standard is concluded with an illustration of how it might be applied in an

educational evaluation. The illustration includes a situation in which
the standard is violated, and a discussion of corrective actions that
would result in better adherence to the standard. Usually, the
illustrations are based on real situations, and they encompass a wide
range of different types of evaluations, e.g., small and large, formative
and summative, and internal and external. One easy step to extending
the applicability of the "Program Evaluation Standards" to
evaluations in fields outside education would be to develop additional
illustrative cases drawn directly from experiences in evaluating
programs outside education. Such a step would also assist in adapting
the "Program Evaluation Standards" for use in countries outside the
United States.

CONTENT OF THE STANDARDS

Utility standards. In general, the Utility standards are intended to
guide evaluations so that they will be informative, timely, and
influential. These standards require evaluators to acquaint themselves
with their audiences, earn their confidence, ascertain the audiences'
information needs, gear evaluations to respond to these needs, and
report the relevant information clearly and when it is needed. The
topics of the standards included in this category are Audience Identification, Evaluator Credibility, Information Scope and Selection,
Valuational Interpretation, Report Clarity, Report Dissemination,
Report Timeliness, and Evaluation Impact. Overall, the standards of
utility are concerned with whether an evaluation serves the practical
information needs of a given audience.

Feasibility standards. The Feasibility standards recognize that an
evaluation usually must be conducted in a "natural," as opposed to a
"laboratory," setting, and require that no more materials and
personnel time than necessary be consumed. The three topics of the
Feasibility standards are Practical Procedures, Political Viability, and
Cost Effectiveness. Overall, the Feasibility standards call for
evaluations to be realistic, prudent, diplomatic, and frugal.

Propriety standards. The Propriety standards reflect the fact that
evaluations affect many people in different ways. These standards are
aimed at ensuring that the rights of persons affected by an evaluation
will be protected. The topics covered by the Propriety standards are
Formal Obligation, Conflict of Interest, Full and Frank Disclosure,
Public's Right to Know, Rights of Human Subjects, Human
Interactions, Balanced Reporting, and Fiscal Responsibility. These
standards require that those conducting evaluations learn about and

abide by laws concerning such matters as privacy, freedom of information, and protection of human subjects. The standards charge those who conduct evaluations to respect the rights of others and to live up to the highest principles and ideals of their professional reference groups. Taken as a group, the Propriety standards require that evaluations be conducted legally, ethically, and with due regard for the welfare of those involved in the evaluation, as well as those affected by the results.

Accuracy standards. Accuracy, the fourth group, includes those standards that determine whether an evaluation has produced sound information. These standards require that the obtained information be technically adequate and that conclusions be linked logically to the data. The topics developed in this group are Object Identification, Context Analysis, Defensible Information Sources, Described Purposes and Procedures, Valid Measurement, Reliable Measurement, Systematic Data Control, Analysis of Quantitative Information, Analysis of Qualitative Information, Justified Conclusions, and Objective Reporting. The overall rating of an evaluation against the Accuracy standards gives a good idea of the evaluation's overall truth value.

The following summary of the "Program Evaluation Standards" is included here with the permission of the Joint Committee on Standards for Educational Evaluation:

A. *Utility standards.* These standards are intended to ensure that an evaluation will serve the practical information needs of given audiences.

A1. Audience identification. Audiences involved in or affected by the evaluation should be identified, so that their needs can be addressed.

A2. Evaluator credibility. The persons conducting the evaluation should be trustworthy and competent to perform the evaluation, so that their findings achieve maximum credibility and acceptance.

A3. Information scope and selection. Information collected should be of such scope and selected in such ways as to address pertinent questions about the object of the evaluation and be responsive to the needs and interests of specified audiences.

A4. Valuational interpretation. The perspectives, procedures, and rationale used to interpret the findings should be carefully described, so that the bases for value judgments are clear.

A5. Report clarity. The evaluation report should describe the object being evaluated and its context, and the purposes, procedures, and findings of the evaluation, so that the audiences will readily understand what was done, why it was done, what information was obtained, what conclusions were drawn, and what recommendations were made.

A6. Report dissemination. Evaluation findings should be disseminated to clients and other right-to-know audiences, so that they can assess and use the findings.

A7. Report timeliness. Release of reports should be timely, so that audiences can best use the reported information.

A8. Evaluation impact. Evaluations should be planned and conducted in ways that encourage follow-through by members of the audiences.

B. *Feasibility standards.* These standards are intended to ensure that an evaluation will be realistic, prudent, diplomatic, and frugal.

B1. Practical procedures. The evaluation procedures should be practical, so that disruption is kept to a minimum, and that needed information can be obtained.

B2. Political viability. The evaluation should be planned and conducted with anticipation of the different positions of various interest groups, so that their cooperation may be obtained, and so that possible attempts by any of these groups to curtail evaluation operations or to bias or misapply the results can be averted or counteracted.

B3. Cost effectiveness. The evaluation should produce information of sufficient value to justify the resources expended.

C. *Propriety standards.* These standards are intended to ensure that an evaluation will be conducted legally, ethically, and with due regard for the welfare of those involved in the evaluation, as well as those affected by its results.

C1. Formal obligation. Obligations of the formal parties to an evaluation (what is to be done, how, by whom, when) should be agreed to in writing, so that these parties are obligated to adhere to all conditions of the agreement or formally to renegotiate it.

C2. Conflict of interest. Conflict of interest, frequently unavoidable, should be dealt with openly and honestly, so that it does not compromise the evaluation processes and results.

C3. Full and frank disclosure. Oral and written evaluation reports should be open, direct, and honest in their disclosure of pertinent findings, including the limitations of the evaluation.

C4. Public's right to know. The formal parties to an evaluation should respect and assure the public's right to know, within the limits of other related principles and statutes, such as those dealing with public safety and the right to privacy.

C5. Rights of human subjects. Evaluations should be designed and conducted so that the rights and welfare of the human subjects are respected and protected.

C6. Human interactions. Evaluators should respect human dignity and worth in their interactions with other persons associated with an evaluation.

C7. Balanced reporting. The evaluation should be complete and fair in its presentation of strengths and weaknesses of the object under investigation, so that strengths can be built upon and problem areas addressed.

C8. Fiscal responsibility. The evaluator's allocation and expenditure of resources should reflect sound accountability procedures and otherwise be prudent and ethically responsible.

D. *Accuracy standards.* These standards are intended to ensure that an evaluation will reveal and convey technically adequate information about the features of the object being studied that determine its worth or merit.

D1. Object identification. The object of the evaluation (program, project, material) should be sufficiently examined, so that the form(s) of the object being considered in the evaluation can be clearly identified.

D2. Context analysis. The context in which the program, project, or material exists should be examined in enough detail, so that its likely influences on the object can be identified.

D3. Described purposes and procedures. The purposes and procedures of the evaluation should be monitored and described in enough detail, so that they can be identified and assessed.

D4. Defensible information sources. The sources of information should be described in enough detail, so that the adequacy of the information can be assessed.

D5. Valid measurement. The information-gathering instruments and procedures should be chosen or developed and then implemented in ways that will assure that the interpretation arrived at is valid for the given use.

D6. Reliable measurement. The information-gathering instruments and procedures should be chosen or developed and then implemented in ways that will assure that the information obtained is sufficiently reliable for the intended use.

D7. Systematic data control. The data collected, processed, and reported in an evaluation should be reviewed and corrected, so that the results of the evaluation will not be flawed.

D8. Analysis of quantitative information. Quantitative information in an evaluation should be appropriately and systematically analyzed to ensure supportable interpretations.

D9. Analysis of qualitative information. Qualitative information in an evaluation should be appropriately and systematically analyzed to ensure supportable interpretations.

D10. Justified conclusions. The conclusions reached in an evaluation should be explicitly justified, so that the audiences can assess them.

D11. Objective reporting. The evaluation procedures should provide safeguards to protect the evaluation findings and reports against distortions by the personal feelings and biases of any party to the evaluation.

The "Program Evaluation Standards" do not exclusively endorse any one approach to evaluation. Instead, the Joint Committee has written standards that encourage the sound use of a variety of evaluation methods. These include surveys, observations, document reviews, jury trials for projects, case studies, advocacy teams to generate and assess competing plans, adversary and advocacy teams to expose the strengths and weaknesses of projects, testing programs, simulation studies, time series studies, check lists, goal-free evaluations, secondary data analysis, and quasi-experimental design. Evaluators should employ whatever methods are best suited to answering the questions posed by their clients, yet sufficient to assess the program's effectiveness, costs, feasibility, and worth. Usually, it is desirable to employ multiple methods, qualitative as well as quantitative.

The Joint Committee deliberately limited the "Program Evaluation Standards" to evaluations of educational programs, projects, and materials. They decided not to deal with evaluations of educational institutions and personnel nor with evaluations outside education. They set these boundaries for reasons of feasibility and political viability of the project.

Given these constraints, the Joint Committee attempted to define principles that apply to the full range of different types of program evaluation studies. These include, for example, a small-scale, informal study by a school committee to assist in planning and operating one or more workshops. As another example, they include large-scale, formal studies such as a special evaluation team might conduct to assess and report publicly on the worth and merit of a statewide or national instructional program. Other types of evaluations to which the "Program Evaluation Standards" apply include pilot studies, needs assessments, process evaluations, outcome studies, cost-effectiveness studies, and meta analyses. In general, the Joint Committee says the "Program Evaluation Standards" are intended for use with studies that are internal and external, small and large, informal and formal, and for those that are formative (designed to improve a program while it is still being developed) and summative (designed to support conclusions about the worth or merit of an object and to provide recommendations about whether it should be retained, revised, or eliminated).

TRADE-OFFS AMONG THE STANDARDS

A particular difficulty in applying the "Program Evaluation Standards" concerns how to deal with conflicts between individual standards. Inevitably, efforts to meet certain standards will detract from efforts to meet others, and trade-off decisions will be required. For example, efforts to produce valid and reliable information and to develop firm conclusions often impede the production of timely reports. Trade-off problems vary across different types and sizes of studies, and within a given study the trade-offs are different depending on the stage of the study (e.g., deciding whether to evaluate, designing the evaluation, collecting the data, analyzing the data, reporting the results, or assessing the study). Evaluators need to recognize and deal as judiciously as they can with such conflicts.

Some general advice for dealing with trade-off problems can be offered. At a macro level, the Joint Committee decided to present the four groups of standards in a particular order. For the "Program Evaluation Standards," the order is Utility, Feasibility, Propriety, and Accuracy. The rationale for this sequence might be stated as "a program evaluation not worth doing is not worth doing well." In deciding whether to evaluate, it is more important to begin with assurances that the findings, if obtained, would be useful than to start with assurances only that the information would be technically sound. If the report would not be used, there is no need to work out an elegant design for data collection. If the report would be used, the evaluator and client would next consider whether it is feasible to move ahead. Are sufficient resources available to obtain and report the needed information in time for its use? Can the needed cooperation and political support be mustered? And, would the projected information gains, in the judgment of the client, be worth the required investment of time and resources? If such feasibility questions cannot be answered affirmatively, then the evaluation planning effort should be discontinued with no further consideration of the other standards. Otherwise, the evaluator would next consider whether the evaluation could be carried through within appropriate bounds of propriety. Once the evaluator and client decide that a proposed evaluation could meet conditions of utility, feasibility, and propriety, they would subsequently consider the accuracy standards. By following the sequence described above, resources for evaluating programs would be allocated to those studies worth doing and the studies would then proceed in accordance with the standards.

In the *Personnel Evaluation Standards* project, the Joint Committee concluded that a different sequence of the categories of standards is appropriate: Propriety, Utility, Feasibility, and Accuracy. In general, there is not an option of whether or not to evaluate the qualifications and performance of educators. School board policies and collective bargaining agreements in virtually all United States school districts and in many colleges and universities require the institution to evaluate its professional staff. Thus, the Joint Committee decided that the first step should be to ensure that evaluations are conducted so that the best interests of students are served. Given adequate attention to this and other propriety concerns, the evaluation designers should subsequently assure that personnel evaluations will also be useful, feasible, and accurate.

The recommended sequences do not indicate that any of the categories of standards are relatively unimportant. The Joint Committee concluded that, in general, all four categories are very important in judging evaluation plans, activities, and reports. Recommending certain orders for considering categories of standards was done to help make evaluation planning functional in the case of the "Program Evaluation Standards" and to give emphasis to service to students in the *Personnel Evaluation Standards*.

There are also problems with trade-offs among the individual standards. The Committee decided against assigning a priority rating to each standard because the trade-off issues vary from evaluation to evaluation and within a given evaluation at different stages. Instead, the Committee provided a Functional Table of Contents for each set of standards. The one for the "Program Evaluation Standards" is summarized in table 1. This matrix summarizes the Committee's judgments about which standards are most applicable to each of a range of common evaluation tasks. The standards are identified down the side of the matrix. Across the top are ten tasks that are commonly involved in any evaluation. The "x" marks in the cells denote which standards should be heeded most carefully in addressing a given evaluation task. All the standards are potentially applicable in all evaluations. However, the Functional Table of Contents is an aid to identifying quickly those standards that are most relevant to certain tasks in given evaluations.

To assist evaluators and their clients to record their decisions about

TABLE 1
Functional Table of Contents for Program Evaluation Standards

Standards (Descriptors)	1. Decide Whether To Do a Study	2. Define the Study	3. Design the Study	4. Budget the Study	5. Contract the Study	6. Staff the Study	7. Manage the Study	8. Collect Data	9. Analyze Data	10. Report Findings
A1 Audience Identification	X	X	X		X		X	X		X
A2 Evaluator Credibility	X				X	X	X	X		X
A3 Information Scope and Selection			X	X	X			X	X	X
A4 Valuational Interpretation			X							X
A5 Report Clarity					X		X			X
A6 Report Dissemination					X		X			X
A7 Report Timeliness										X
A8 Evaluation Impact	X								X	
B1 Practical Procedures	X		X		X	X	X	X		
B2 Political Viability	X			X			X	X		
B3 Cost Effectiveness	X			X		X	X	X		
C1 Formal Obligation	X		X		X	X				
C2 Conflict of Interest					X					X
C3 Full & Frank Disclosure					X					X
C4 Public's Right to Know					X			X		
C5 Rights of Human Subjects					X		X	X		
C6 Human Interactions							X	X		
C7 Balanced Reporting			X				X	X		X
C8 Fiscal Responsibility		X		X	X		X	X	X	X
D1 Object Identification	X	X	X		X					X
D2 Context Analysis	X	X	X	X	X					X
D3 Described Purposes and Procedures			X		X		X	X		X
D4 Defensible Information Sources			X					X		
D5 Valid Measurement			X					X		
D6 Reliable Measurement			X					X		
D7 Systematic Data Control							X			
D8 Quantitative Analysis									X	
D9 Qualitative Analysis									X	
D10 Justified Conclusions			X						X	X
D11 Objective Reporting			X			X			X	X

applying given standards and their judgments about the extent to which each one was taken into account, the Committee provided a citation form (figure 1). This form is intended to be completed, signed, and appended to evaluation plans and reports. Like an auditor's statement, the signed citation form should assist audiences to assess the merits of given evaluations. Of course, the completed citation form should often be backed up by more extensive documentation, especially with regard to the judgments given about the extent that each standard was met. In the absence of such documentation, the completed citation form can be used as an agenda for discussions between evaluators and their audiences about the adequacy of evaluation plans and reports.

VALIDITY OF THE PROGRAM EVALUATION STANDARDS

Since the "Program Evaluation Standards" were published, a considerable amount of information that bears on their validity has been presented. In general, this evidence supports the position that the "Program Evaluation Standards" are needed, have been carefully developed, have involved an open search for participation and critique, have good credibility in the United States, and have been used. While not intended to be used outside the geographic and substantive boundaries set by the Joint Committee, the "Program Evaluation Standards" have been shown to have some applicability outside education, outside program evaluation, and outside the United States. Despite the overall positive feedback, the assessments of the "Program Evaluation Standards" also point out some limitations and areas for improvement.

Four papers presented at the 1982 meeting of the National Council on Measurement in Education[5] examined the congruence between the "Program Evaluation Standards" and the principles of measurement that are embodied in the 1974 revision of *Standards for Educational and Psychological Tests.* The authors independently concluded that great consistency exists between these two sets of standards with regard to measurement. Jeri Ridings closely studied standard setting in the accounting and auditing fields and developed a check list by which to assess the Joint Committee effort against key checkpoints in the more mature standard-setting programs in accounting and auditing.[6] In general, she concluded that the Joint Committee had adequately dealt with four key issues: rationale, the standard-setting structure, content, and uses. Wildemuth issued an annotated bibliography with about five sources identified for each standard. These references help to confirm

The *Standards for Evaluations of Educational Programs, Projects, and Materials* guided the development of this (check one)

   request for evaluation plan design proposal
   evaluation plan design proposal
   evaluation contract
   evaluation report
   other

To interpret the information provided on this form, the reader needs to refer to the full text of the standards as they appear in Joint Committee on Standards for Educational Evaluation. *Standards for Evaluations of Educational Programs, Projects, and Materials* (New York: McGraw-Hill, 1981).

The *Standards* were consulted and used as indicated in the table below (check as appropriate):

DESCRIPTOR	THE STANDARD WAS DEEMED APPLICABLE AND TO THE EXTENT FEASIBLE WAS TAKEN INTO ACCOUNT	THE STANDARD WAS DEEMED APPLICABLE BUT COULD NOT BE TAKEN INTO ACCOUNT	THE STANDARD WAS NOT DEEMED APPLICABLE	EXCEPTION WAS TAKEN TO THE STANDARD
A1 Audience Identification				
A2 Evaluator Credibility				
A3 Information Scope and Selection				
A4 Valuational Interpretation				
A5 Report Clarity				
A6 Report Dissemination				
A7 Report Timeliness				
A8 Evaluation Impact				
B1 Practical Procedures				
B2 Political Viability				
B3 Cost Effectiveness				
C1 Formal Obligation				
C2 Conflict of Interest				
C3 Full and Frank Disclosure				
C4 Public's Right to Know				
C5 Rights of Human Subjects				
C6 Human Interactions				
C7 Balanced Reporting				
C8 Fiscal Responsibility				
D1 Object Identification				
D2 Context Analysis				
D3 Described Purposes and Procedures				
D4 Defensible Information Sources				
D5 Valid Measurement				
D6 Reliable Measurement				
D7 Systematic Data Control				
D8 Analysis of Quantitative Information				
D9 Analysis of Qualitative Information				
D10 Justified Conclusions				
D11 Objective Reporting				

Name: _____   Date: _____
              (typed)

         _____
              (signature)

Position or Title: _____

Agency: _____

Address: _____

Relation to Document: _____
                        (e.g., author of document, evaluation team leader, external auditor, internal auditor)

Figure 1. Citation Form

the theoretical validity of the "Program Evaluation Standards," and
they provide a convenient guide to users for pursuing in-depth
study of the involved principles.[7] Linn reported the results of
twenty-five field trials conducted during the development of the
"Program Evaluation Standards." These trials confirmed that the
"Program Evaluation Standards" were useful but not sufficient
guides in such applications as designing evaluations, assessing evaluation proposals, judging evaluation reports, and training evaluators.[8] Additionally, they provided direction for revising the "Program Evaluation Standards" prior to publication. Stake observed
that the Joint Committee had made a strong case in favor of
evaluation standards, but he urged a careful look at the case against
standards.[9] He offered analysis in this vein and questioned whether
the evaluation field has matured sufficiently to warrant the
development and use of standards.

A number of writers have examined the applicability of the
"Program Evaluation Standards" to specialized situations. Wargo
concluded that the "Program Evaluation Standards" represent a sound
consensus of good evaluation practice, but he called for more
specificity regarding large-scale, government-sponsored studies and
for more representation from this sector on the Committee.[10]
(Ironically, federal agencies had been invited to appoint representatives to the Joint Committee but declined due to potential conflicts of
interest regarding their involvement in funding the effort.) Marcia
Linn concluded that the "Program Evaluation Standards" contain
sound advice for evaluators in out-of-school learning environments,
but she observed that the "Program Evaluation Standards" are not
suitable for dealing with trade-offs between standards or settling
disputes between and among stakeholders.[11] While the "Program
Evaluation Standards" explicitly are not intended for personnel
evaluations, Carey examined the extent to which a draft of these
standards was congruent with state policies for evaluating teachers.
She concluded that only one standard (D11, Objective Reporting)
was deemed inappropriate for judging teacher evaluations.[12]

Burkett and Denson surveyed participants at a conference on
evaluation in the health professions to obtain their judgments of the
"Program Evaluation Standards."[13] While the respondents generally
agreed that "the *Standards* represent a useful framework for designing
evaluations and offer substantial potential for application to the
evaluation of continuing education programs for the health professions" (p. 54), they also issued the following criticisms:

1. Crucial elements of certain standards lie outside the evaluator's professional area of control.

2. The *Standards* assume more flexibility, e.g., in the choice of methods of assessment, than sometimes may exist in institutional settings.

3. The *Standards* deal better with external evaluations than with internal, self-evaluations.

4. The *Standards* need to be made more useful by ordering them in the same sequence as an evaluation typically unfolds, providing more specific guidelines and examples, and adding bibliographic references (pp. 54-55).

Marsh, Newman, and Boyer used the "Program Evaluation Standards" to study the practice of educational evaluation in California and concluded the following: "(1) the standards were perceived as important ideals for the orientation of the process and practice of evaluation; (2) the current practice of evaluation in California was perceived by professional evaluators as being, at most, of average quality; and (3) the practice of low-quality evaluation was attributed to a combination of restriction of time, of political and bureaucratic coercions, and of incompetence of the evaluator."[14] Newman found that many of the standards were frequently violated.[15] Newman and Brown also found that perceptions of seriousness of the violations depended on one's experience with evaluation.[16] Newman and Brown used the "Program Evaluation Standards" to study ethical issues in evaluation, finding that professional evaluators and educators could relate the standards to five ethical principles: autonomy, nonmaleficence, beneficence, justice, and fidelity.[17]

Several evaluators from other countries have examined the "Program Evaluation Standards" for their applicability outside the United States. Nevo[18] and Straton,[19] respectively from Israel and Australia, both concluded that while the "Program Evaluation Standards" embody sound advice, they assume an American situation—regarding level of effort and citizens' rights, for example—that is different from their own national contexts. Rodrigues, Hoffman, Barros, Arruda, and Santos published a summary and critique of the "Program Evaluation Standards" in Portuguese in the hope that their contribution would "positively influence the quality of the evaluations conducted in Brazil, help in the training of educational evaluators, and help those who recommend evaluations to improve their value."[20] Lewy, from Israel, concluded that the "Program Evaluation Standards" provide "useful guidelines for evaluators in

Israel as well as the USA," but raised questions about the adequacy of their theoretical rationale and criticized their lack of specificity.[21]

Lewy, like Dockrell,[22] saw great possibilities for unhealthy collusion between evaluators and sponsors and disagreed with the position reflected in the "Program Evaluation Standards" that evaluators should communicate continuously with their clients and report interim findings. Dockrell also observed that evaluation in Scotland and other European countries is much more qualitatively oriented than is evaluation practice in the United States and that the "Program Evaluation Standards" do not and probably could not provide much guidance for the perceptiveness and originality required of excellent qualitative research. Scheerens and van Seventer saw in the "Program Evaluation Standards" a useful contribution to the important need in the Netherlands to upgrade and professionalize evaluation practice. To promote utility in their country, however, they said the standards would need to be translated and illustrated at the national research policy level, as opposed to their present concentration on the individual evaluation project.[23] Even so, they questioned whether such standards could be enforced in Holland, given the susceptibility of national research policy there to frequently changing political forces and priorities. Marklund concluded that the "Program Evaluation Standards" provides a "good check list of prerequisites for a reliable and valid evaluation," but that "due to differences in values of program outcomes, such standards do not guarantee that the result of the evaluation will be indisputable."[24] Overall, the main value of the "Program Evaluation Standards" outside the United States appears to be as a reference for discussing evaluation concepts and practices.

Six studies were conducted to examine the extent to which the "Program Evaluation Standards" are congruent with the set of program evaluation standards issued by the Evaluation Research Society.[25] The studies all found that the two sets of standards are largely overlapping.

Overall, the literature on the "Program Evaluation Standards" indicates considerable support for these standards. They are seen to fill a need. They are judged to contain sound and clear content. They have been shown to be applicable in a wide range of American settings. They have been applied successfully. They are consistent with the principles in other sets of standards. And they are subject to an open and systematic process of review and revision. But, by no means are they a panacea. Their utility is limited, especially outside the United States, and in the case of large-scale, government-sponsored studies. Other criticisms were that the standards deal inadequately with the trade-offs and disputes in evaluations, in some cases hold evaluators responsible for decisions not under their control, may not be needed (because the field of practice is not well defined and because it is not clear that standards in this field would safeguard the public), are not sufficiently detailed to guide specific evaluation design decisions, and deal inadequately with internal self-evaluations. Also, several editorial issues were identified for consideration in subsequent revision cycles, such as the need for a bibliography.

The Personnel Evaluation Standards

An initial decision in developing the "Program Evaluation Standards" was to exclude the area of personnel evaluation. One reason was that developing standards for program evaluation presented a sufficiently large challenge. Another reason was that members of the Committee believed that teachers' organizations would not support development of standards for evaluations of personnel. Also, in 1975 when the Joint Committee was formed, there was little concern for increasing or improving evaluations of educators.

In 1984, a number of factors led to the Joint Committee's decision to develop standards for evaluations of educational personnel. The Committee had successfully developed the "Program Evaluation Standards" and felt capable of addressing the personnel evaluation standards issue. They were also convinced that personnel evaluation in education was greatly in need of improvement. They saw this need as urgent because of the great increase in the development of systems for evaluating teachers and because of the great turmoil and litigation that accompanied the expansion of teacher evaluation. Moreover, they believed that the major teachers' organizations would support the development of professional standards that could be used to expose unsound teacher evaluation plans and programs.

In the course of deciding to develop the educational personnel evaluation standards, the Committee also decided to expand its membership to ensure that its members reflected relevant perspectives on evaluations of educational personnel as well as evaluations of educational programs. Additions to the Committee included representatives from the American Association of School Personnel Administrators, the American Federation of Teachers, and the American Association of Secondary School Principals, as well as individual members-at-large with expertise in litigation in personnel evaluation and research on teacher evaluation. New appointments by sponsoring organizations also included the perspectives of industrial/ organizational psychology and traditionally underrepresented groups. The Committee continued to include a balance between the perspectives of educational practitioners and evaluation specialists. The members of the Joint Committee and their organizational affiliations, as of September 1988, were as follows:

Daniel L. Stufflebeam, Chair (Western Michigan University)
James Adams (Indianapolis Public Schools), representing the American Association of School Administrators
Ralph Alexander (University of Akron), representing the American Psychological Association
Marvin Alkin (University of California, Los Angeles), representing the American Educational Research Association
Esther Diamond (Educational and Psychological Consultant), representing the Association for Measurement and Evaluation in Counseling and Development
A. Keith Esch (Wichita Public Schools), representing the American Association of School Personnel Administrators
Ronald K. Hambleton (University of Massachusetts), representing the National Council on Measurement in Education
Philip L. Hosford (New Mexico State University), representing the Association for Supervision and Curriculum Development
William Mays, Jr. (Michigan Elementary and Middle School Principals Association), representing the National Association of Elementary School Principals
Diana Pullin (Boston College), member-at-large
Marilyn Rauth (American Federation of Teachers), representing the American Federation of Teachers
James R. Sanders (Western Michigan University), representing the American Evaluation Association
Sheila Simmons (National Education Association), representing the National Education Association
Scott D. Thomson (National Association of Secondary School Principals), representing the National Association of Secondary School Principals
JoAnn Wimmer (Logan, Utah), representing the National School Boards Association

An independent validation panel provided further perspective and checks and balances on the development of the *Personnel Evaluation Standards*. This group was led by Dr. Robert Linn and included persons representing the following perspectives: law, research on teaching, personnel psychology, international education, psychometrics, philosophy, teaching, school district superintendency, and school principalship. The Validation Panel's main clients are those groups that might for a variety of reasons want independent assessments of the appropriateness, quality, and potential utility of the *Standards*. The panel monitored and evaluated the work of the Committee and ultimately published an independent evaluation of the *Personnel Evaluation Standards*,[26] which is summarized later in this chapter.

It is appropriate for the Joint Committee to deal with personnel evaluation as well as program evaluation. Both types of evaluation are prevalent in education, and both are vitally important for assuring the quality of educational services. For practical and political reasons, these two types of evaluation are usually conducted independently. But logically, they are inseparable.

Practice and literature had lodged responsibility for personnel evaluation with supervisors and administrators and have created expectations that program evaluators will not evaluate individuals. Program evaluators might help plan personnel evaluations and might evaluate personnel evaluation systems; but they have avoided direct evaluation of individuals. To do otherwise would stimulate fear about the power and motives of program evaluators, and would undoubtedly generate much resistance on the part of principals and teachers, leading in turn to lack of cooperation in program evaluations. Program evaluators have emphasized the constructive contributions of program evaluation and often have promised anonymity and confidentiality to program personnel. On the whole, efforts to separate personnel and program evaluation in school districts have remained in vogue.

But a basic problem remains: it is fundamentally impossible to remove personnel evaluation from sound program evaluation. A useful program evaluation must determine whether a program shows a desirable impact on the rightful target population. If the data reveal otherwise, the assessment must discern those aspects of a program that require change to yield the desired results. Inescapably, program evaluators must check the adequacy of all relevant instrumental variables, including the personnel. The rights of teachers and administrators must be respected, but evaluators must also protect the rights of students to be taught well and of communities to have their schools effectively administered.

However, personnel evaluation is too important and difficult a task to be left exclusively to the program evaluators. Many personnel evaluations are conducted by supervisors who rarely conduct formal program evaluations. Also, state education departments and school districts are heavily involved, apart from their program evaluation efforts, in evaluating teachers and other educators for certification, licensing, selection, placement, promotion, tenure, merit, staff development, and termination.

Undesirably, the literatures and methodologies of program evaluation and personnel evaluation are distinct. The work of the Joint Committee in both areas affords an opportunity to start synthesizing these fields and coordinating the efforts of program evaluators and personnel evaluators.

To develop standards for personnel evaluations, the Joint Committee employed the approach it found successful in the development of the "Program Evaluation Standards." They also engaged the Validation Panel to monitor and report on their work, both during and after the period of development.

CONTENTS OF THE STANDARDS

After reviewing a great deal of material on personnel evaluation, the Joint Committee decided that the four basic concerns of Utility, Feasibility, Propriety, and Accuracy are as relevant to personnel evaluation as they are to program evaluation. Some of the topics for individual standards are likewise the same, e.g., valid measurement and reliable measurement. However, there are important differences in the two sets of topics. For example, Full and Frank Disclosure, a program evaluation standard, is not in the personnel evaluation standards; and Service Orientation, a key entry in the personnel evaluation standards (requiring that evaluators show concern for the rights of students to be taught well), is not among the "Program Evaluation Standards." The following summary of the twenty-one personnel evaluation standards is included here with the permission of the Joint Committee on Standards for Educational Evaluation:

Propriety standards. These standards require that evaluations be conducted legally, ethically, and with due regard for the welfare of evaluatees and clients of the evaluations.

P-1. Service orientation. Evaluations of educators should promote sound education principles, fulfillment of institutional missions, and effective performance of job responsibilities, so that the educational needs of students, community, and society are met.

P-2. Formal evaluation guidelines. Guidelines for personnel evaluations should be recorded in statements of policy, negotiated agreements, and/

or personnel evaluation manuals, so that evaluations are consistent, equitable, and in accordance with pertinent laws and ethical codes.

P-3. Conflict of interest. Conflicts of interest should be identified and dealt with openly and honestly, so that they do not compromise the evaluation process and results.

P-4. Access to personnel evaluation reports. Access to reports of personnel evaluation should be limited to individuals with a legitimate need to review and use the reports, so that appropriate use of the information is assured.

P-5. Interactions with evaluatees. The evaluation should address evaluatees in a professional, considerate, and courteous manner so that their self-esteem, motivation, professional reputations, performance, and attitude toward personnel evaluation are enhanced or, at least, not needlessly damaged.

Utility standards. These standards are intended to guide evaluations so that they will be informative, timely, and influential.

U-1. Constructive orientation. Evaluations should be constructive, so that they help institutions to develop human resources and encourage and assist those evaluated to provide excellent service.

U-2. Defined uses. The users and the intended uses of a personnel evaluation should be identified, so that the evaluation can address appropriate questions.

U-3. Evaluator credibility. The evaluation system should be managed and executed by persons with the necessary qualifications, skills, and authority, and evaluators should conduct themselves professionally, so that evaluation reports are respected and used.

U-4. Functional reporting. Reports should be clear, timely, accurate, and germane, so that they are of practical value to the evaluatee and other appropriate audiences.

U-5. Follow-up and impact. Evaluations should be followed up, so that clients and evaluatees are aided to understand the results and take appropriate actions.

Feasibility standards. These standards call for evaluation systems that are as easy to implement as possible, efficient in their use of time and resources, adequately funded, and viable from a number of other standpoints.

F-1. Practical procedures. Personnel evaluations should be planned and conducted so that they produce the needed information while minimizing disruption and cost.

F-2. Political viability. The personnel evaluation system should be developed and monitored collaboratively, so that all concerned parties are constructively involved in making the system work.

F-3. Fiscal viability. Adequate time and resources should be provided for personnel evaluation activities, so that evaluation plans can be effectively and efficiently implemented.

Accuracy standards. These standards require that the obtained information be technically accurate and that conclusions be linked logically to the data.

A-1. Defined role. The role, responsibilities, performance objectives, and needed qualifications of the evaluatee should be clearly defined, so that the evaluator can determine valid assessment criteria.

A-2. Work environment. The context in which the evaluatee works should be identified, described, and recorded, so that environmental influences and constraints on performance can be considered in the evaluation.

A-3. Documentation of procedures. The evaluation procedures actually followed should be documented, so that the evaluatees and other users can assess the actual, in relation to intended, procedures.

A-4. Valid measurement. The measurement procedures should be chosen or developed and implemented on the basis of the described role and the intended use, so that the inferences concerning the evaluatee are valid and accurate.

A-5. Reliable measurement. Measurement procedures should be chosen or developed to assure reliability, so that the information obtained will provide consistent indications of the performance of the evaluatee.

A-6. Systematic data control. The information used in the evaluation should be kept secure, and should be carefully processed and maintained, so as to ensure that the data maintained and analyzed are the same as the data collected.

A-7. Bias control. The evaluation process should provide safeguards against bias, so that the evaluatee's qualifications or performance are assessed fairly.

A-8. Monitoring evaluation systems. The personnel evaluation system should be reviewed periodically and systematically, so that appropriate revisions can be made.

EVALUATIONS OF THE PERSONNEL EVALUATION STANDARDS

In 1989, the Validation Panel issued its final evaluation of the *Personnel Evaluation Standards*.[27] The panel's main conclusions were:

1. Assumptions underlying the *Personnel Evaluation Standards* (that personnel evaluation can contribute both to serving students and society and constructively help evaluatees improve their services) may sometimes be in conflict or need to be weighted differently.

2. The standards development process was highly systematic,

employed input and criticism from a wide variety of perspectives, and likely resulted in "standards that are consistent with the dominant state of the art and current assumptions. The major omissions in regard to formally represented perspectives are those of client groups, e.g., students, parents, and the business community."

3. The *Standards* are most applicable in the public elementary and secondary schools. "They are also likely to be useful in postsecondary institutions or in private schools, and, in a more limited way, in international settings and in business or military education."

4. "The fact that such a diverse set of associations was able to work together to produce a mutually agreeable document is a major accomplishment. The careful and systematic way in which the Joint Committee developed and refined the *Standards* gives them a good deal of credibility and should enhance their acceptance." Nevertheless, "the degree to which the standards will contribute to the improvement of personnel evaluations in education and, in doing so, will help to [enhance] . . . the quality of services provided to students and society will only be determined by careful observation in the future."

Orris investigated the industrial applicability of the *Personnel Evaluation Standards* by engaging a jury of five judges to assess the strengths and weaknesses of the performance development section of the Specific Corporate Evaluation Process (SCEP), as employed by a division of General Motors, and by studying the resulting meta-evaluation.[28] He concluded that the *Personnel Evaluation Standards* are generally applicable in industrial settings; that all 21 standards were applicable and sufficient in the specific industrial case; that SCEP fully satisfied 10 of the standards and partially satisfied the other 11; that 177 of the 199 guidelines associated with the 21 standards were applicable; that "the jury found it feasible to use the *Standards* for critiquing an SCEP and made 45 recommendations to improve the SCEP, . . ." along with 20 recommendations to improve the *Standards*; and that the panel required 24 working hours to apply the *Standards*, not including time for training and preliminary description of SCEP. Based on these conclusions, Orris recommended that the Joint Committee consider generalizing their guidelines, so that they would be clearly applicable in settings beyond education.

Montoya used a draft of the *Personnel Evaluation Standards* to examine the effects of a 1985 Illinois act requiring school boards to obtain state approval for and implement programs to evaluate certified employees.[29] She concluded that the Illinois mandate is congruent with the *Personnel Evaluation Standards*, that about half of the district evaluation plans examined met at least 16 of the 21 standards, and that nearly half of the plans failed to meet 11 or more of the standards.

At this writing, the State of Texas is using the *Personnel Evaluation Standards* to design a statewide system to aid its more than 1,000 public school districts to evaluate district and school administrators. This is a consequence of using these standards to assess an earlier plan and finding that it violated or failed to meet a majority of the standards.

The Standards and Professional Ethics

As seen in the preceding sections, the standards for evaluations of both programs and personnel offer parties to an evaluation some protections concerning the propriety of the evaluation work. In this section I discuss further the need for propriety standards, describe five relevant issues, and assess the potential contributions and limitations of professional standards vis-à-vis professional ethics for evaluators.

Because evaluation is a specialized field of practice, and because it is often imposed as a condition for funding or holding a job, many persons and organizations have little choice but to use (or be subjected to) its services. Consequently, they are at risk to the extent that the evaluators are incompetent, careless, lazy, or not well intentioned.

Charges and confirmed cases of unethical practices in evaluation work exist. These include falsifying results; maliciously defaming a person or organization; violating a person's right to privacy; accepting an assignment to advocate or attack something according to the interests of the client; covering up negative findings; overstating a criticism in order to gain national attention; consuming program funds without returning a valuable service; and exposing subjects, without their knowledge or consent, to possible harm through involvement in an evaluation. Clearly, professional standards should address such ethics issues. However, incorporation of ethics considerations into professional standards for evaluators has not been easy or extensive, as the history of evaluation reveals.

Among the first systematic presentations of criteria for judging evaluation studies were those of internal validity and external validity, as articulated by Campbell and Stanley.[30] In limiting the criteria for judging evaluations to technical matters, they drew interest away from other issues in evaluation work, especially propriety and utility. Subsequent treatments expanded the suggested criteria to include utility and efficiency as well as technical adequacy. This expansion was seen in a 1971 book by the Phi Delta Kappa Study Committee on Evaluation.[31] Their recommendations cast evaluation in more of an instrumental role than had the recommendations by Campbell and Stanley. However, the Phi Delta Kappa committee's recommendations did not address such ethics concerns as protection of human subjects, freedom of information, equality of opportunity, censorship of reports, and due process. Evaluators did not write seriously about ethical requirements for evaluations until the middle 1970s, well after relevant laws had been passed and enforced.

The status of the evaluation field in dealing with ethics concerns is partially reflected in the Joint Committee's "Program Evaluation Standards" and its *Personnel Evaluation Standards*, which include, respectively, eight and five propriety standards. They define principles of good practice, give examples of malpractice, denote common errors to be avoided, offer practical guidelines, guide clients in scrutinizing evaluations, and include content for training evaluators.

Recommendations in the standards related to ethics include:

- collect and report findings so as to serve the best interests of students and other clients;
- provide feedback to help educators advance their skills and deliver high-quality, effective service;
- identify all groups that are entitled to the findings and provide them with access to the reports;
- search out and openly address conflicts of interest;
- safeguard the rights of those who will be affected by the study;
- report both strengths and weaknesses and provide direction for improvement;
- treat participants in evaluations with respect and dignity;
- evaluate performance by educators in terms of clearly defined roles and the work environment;
- and, as a last example, negotiate contracts to govern the evaluation work and to help assure that the advance understandings and agreements are remembered and implemented.

Although these recommendations may seem obvious, evaluators often get into difficulty by ignoring them. By applying the standards, evaluators can better earn the respect and trust of their clients.

But, despite the progress in defining professional standards, evaluation includes many unresolved ethics issues. The complexity of such issues is seen in five general problems.

First, many conflicts of interest occur naturally in evaluations. The client often seeks an expedient approach to goal achievement. The evaluator wants to get paid and hopes to be rehired. While many persons might informally express concerns about a program or educator, they often refuse to file their complaints. Also, some evaluators zealously support particular evaluation methods. Clearly, vested interests can lead to biased or otherwise faulty evaluations. The Joint Committee seeks to ameliorate conflicts of interest by highlighting the issue, describing its characteristics, and suggesting steps to combat it. But, conflicts of interest in evaluation are inevitable, and standards alone will not forestall or correct their harmful effects.

A second source of ethical and moral difficulty in evaluation is the suboptimization that occurs. Especially, the subfields of student evaluation, program evaluation, and personnel evaluation are not well integrated. An ends-justifies-the-means mentality has helped to compartmentalize these subfields. When student test scores are judged good, program and personnel are seldom examined, even though they may be deficient and harmful. If one does evaluate a program, staff are frequently granted immunity from scrutiny in order to obtain their good will and cooperation. On the other side, personnel are frequently evaluated against the minimum requirements in a union contract and a job description, but in isolation from their roles in particular programs or assessed needs of students. Because evaluations of personnel, programs, and students are typically done separately, evaluators often fail to address the full range of potential improprieties. Clearly, suboptimizations make work more manageable, but they also can obscure harmful or unjust practices. The evaluation field must find better ways to integrate evaluations of programs, personnel, and students, and the standards in these areas should help.

A third source of difficulty in assuring ethical evaluations is an attitude among evaluators of no harm, no foul. According to this position, evaluators need not consider professional standards if they and others do not see that clients are being harmed. This attitude probably contributed to evaluators' failure to confront problems in evaluations of due process, human rights, and censorship until after the enactment of relevant legislation. By waiting for government to identify and address such injustices and ethical issues, evaluators abrogate their professional responsibility. As professionals they must exercise leadership in providing the best and most ethical service possible. The Joint Committee and its standards-setting process has helped the evaluation field to become more proactive in identifying and addressing ethics issues.

The fourth area of concern is that professional standards are vulnerable to misuse. The Joint Committee standards are general. They exclude specific rules for resolving conflicts among the standards, and do not stipulate penalties for violations of the standards. Considering these limitations, the effectiveness of the standards depends largely on the good intentions of evaluators and the thoughtful deliberations and wise judgments of those clients, auditors, and evaluators who apply the standards. In a recent application of the "Program Evaluation Standards," a federal defense agency decided not to consider any of the propriety standards. Unfortunately, evaluators can apply the standards superficially or selectively, or even use them to cover up poor service or malpractice.

The final difficulty follows from the fourth one. Standards are insufficient by themselves to ward off or confront ethics issues in evaluation and are only one of the professional initiatives needed to assure that evaluations are ethical. Considering the experiences of more mature professions, the evaluation field needs to examine several means of enforcing its principles of practice. For example, it could accredit worthy training programs and set up examinations and other mechanisms for certifying and/or licensing evaluators. Such steps would aid clients to identify evaluators who are appropriately qualified. In addition, a group such as the American Evaluation Association might define sanctions for malpractice, set up a practice review board to hear charges, adopt procedures for executing the decisions of the review board, and subsequently use the sanctions to help shape up, censure, or decertify ineffective or unethical evaluators. Probably the young evaluation profession is not close to introducing professional sanctions, since it does not license or certify evaluators; but it might someday pursue such steps. In the meantime, the evaluation field can and should use its professional standards to conduct third-party meta-evaluations.

Professional standards provide one mechanism for promoting ethical practice in evaluation. Their greatest potential impact is on those evaluators who have a keen sense of moral responsibility and desire to improve their services. Professional standards can aid evaluators to police their ranks and can aid clients to assess whether or not an evaluation proposal or report is sound. However, the Joint Committee standards are not, and never will be, the final word on what constitutes good and ethical evaluation service. They will always be only a dated approximation of ideals for the field, a negotiated set of general agreements. They must be periodically reviewed and updated. Also, to ward off or deal with unethical practices, standards must be supplemented with measures such as certification, practice review boards, and defined sanctions.

Personal Reflections on the Standards Work

The editors of this yearbook requested a retrospective examination of critical issues and limitations of professional standards in improving educational evaluation.

I chaired the Joint Committee work for thirteen years; and obviously, I do not believe that my colleagues and I who served on the Committee throughout that period wasted our time. Two sets of standards were produced and are being used. Field tests demonstrated that these standards can lead to improvements in both program evaluation and personnel evaluation. The Joint Committee is a mechanism of thirteen sponsoring organizations, collectively with about three million members. This effort may be the first time that groups so diverse as the American Psychological Association, the American Educational Research Association, the National Education Association, the American Association of School Administrators, and the National School Boards Association have collaborated productively in such a sensitive area as evaluation.

The Joint Committee is incorporated and serves the ongoing function of reviewing and updating the standards, plus developing additional sets as needs for them are determined. In 1989, the Joint Committee became the first group in education to be accredited by the American National Standards Institute (ANSI). ANSI accreditation signifies that the Joint Committee is the sole body in the United States recognized as duly constituted and authorized to develop professional standards for educational evaluations. To meet the ANSI accreditation requirements, the Committee had to demonstrate that it follows systematic standard-setting procedures; employs an open, participatory process; is representative of the constituencies it serves; is the only United States group authorized and constituted to set standards for educational evaluation; is capable of developing consensus standards; and periodically reviews and revises its standards.

At this writing, the Joint Committee has launched a third project: to develop standards for evaluations of student needs and performance, especially those evaluations that are planned and conducted by classroom teachers. The new project recognizes that evaluations in classrooms are important and that standards for tests are too limited to help classroom teachers diagnose student needs and assess student outcomes. The Committee has also started to revise and update the "Program Evaluation Standards."

The Committee has stuck to its mission to serve education in the United States and has avoided delusions of grandeur. The Committee has consistently rejected periodic recommendations that it generalize its standards and declare them to be applicable to evaluations in a wide range of fields and in countries outside the United States. While the Committee is glad to collaborate with educators in other countries and to aid other fields—such as business and industry, social work, and economic development—to examine their standards, it has no special qualifications to set and recommend standards for countries outside the United States and for fields other than education. Overall, the decisions to establish the Joint Committee and develop standards by which to improve evaluations in education have been quite thoroughly implemented, have resulted in an important and functioning coalition of groups concerned with education, and have led to credible and practical recommendations for planning and assessing evaluations.

But, having the Joint Committee and the standards has not eliminated bad evaluations. And these steps, though important, will not eliminate poor evaluation services any more than standards bodies and standards in the field of medicine have eliminated malpractice by doctors. Realistically, I think we can mainly expect from standards that they provide an authoritative reference to help well-intentioned professionals to make more systematic their ongoing quest to improve their services. Also, the standards advise clients what they should expect of evaluators.

On the issue of generality, for quite good reasons the Joint Committee has avoided writing highly specific standards. The state of the art in educational evaluation does not warrant great specificity. In many cases alternative approaches are equally defensible, and creative approaches might improve on the extant evaluation methodology.

Did the Joint Committee make long-standing serious mistakes? I do not think so. Along the way, they wrote some bad drafts of standards, but these got corrected. The Committee's standard-setting process is rigorous and includes many checkpoints so that errors can be detected and corrected. Also, the fact that the Committee is a standing, incorporated body and every five years reviews, and, if needed, revises its standards helps to assure that flawed standards will be corrected and that the total set periodically will be updated. Also, because the Validation Panel for the Personnel Evaluation Standards Project said the Committee lacked representation from client groups, including students, parents, and the business community, the Joint Committee is expanding its membership to improve its representativeness.

Another indication of the Committee's self-correcting mechanism is in how it dealt with the issue of applying the standards. The "Program Evaluation Standards" did not directly address this area, and the Committee agreed the omission is a deficiency. Consequently, they included a chapter on applying the standards in the *Personnel Evaluation Standards* and plan to do so in the next revision of the "Program Evaluation Standards."

But, while I am pleased that the standard-setting work did not fail, that it went rather well, and that it is ongoing and viable, I am not entirely satisfied with the experience. Dissemination of the standards has not been spectacular, and the sponsoring organizations, while generally supportive, have not initiated effective efforts to get their members to use the standards. The Joint Committee has many ideas and plans concerned with disseminating the standards, but almost no funds to carry them out. If funding agencies and the sponsoring organizations would fund dissemination of the standards, the Joint Committee would do much more training, development of illustrative cases and other supplementary materials, and promotion of the standards.

Also, more thought and work is needed in regard to trade-offs among different standards. The Committee will not label some standards as "essential" and others as "desirable," because we have found that such classifications do not hold across different steps in the evaluation process and different evaluation purposes. A simplistic solution is not the answer. Research into the trade-off issue, with the aim of specifying how conflicts between certain standards should be handled in well-defined evaluation situations, is needed. The rule book for baseball umpires does not cover every decision an umpire might face and is supplemented with a casebook which examines and gives adjudication for actual instances not covered by the rule book. Likewise, if the evaluation profession is to deal effectively and consistently with certain classes of trade-offs (e.g., between service to students and constructive assistance to teachers), it might need to develop and adopt its own casebook. For example, the *Personnel*

Evaluation Standards do not address the following important questions: What steps should the evaluator recommend when a teacher has had a history of poor teaching, negative evaluations, and no improvement? What would the evaluator have to do to make a recommendation of termination stick? Research and development into actual cases dealing with such questions could lead to supplementary materials designed to help evaluators, school boards, and other clients better apply the standards.

Summary

Increasingly, evaluation is becoming a formalized field of practice. Its services are complex and costly and it has the potential to do harm as well as to promote progress. Since 1975, evaluators and educators have pursued a concerted effort to define standards of sound practice—initially with respect to program evaluations, more recently in the area of personnel evaluations, and soon to expand into the area of student evaluation. The standards have been defined through the efforts of the Joint Committee on Standards for Educational Evaluation, whose members were appointed by the major national professional societies concerned with education, and which was recently accredited by ANSI as the United States body recognized to set standards for educational evaluations. In this chapter I have reviewed the work of the Committee, discussed the relevance of its standards for addressing ethical issues in evaluation, and reflected on the significance of the experience. The Joint Committee is an important and viable mechanism in American education and its standards are a significant but not sufficient means of making educational evaluations useful, feasible, accurate, and ethical. The objectives of the Joint Committee will be achieved only when educators, evaluators, school districts, other educational institutions, and professional societies take the standards seriously and effectively disseminate and apply them. Moreover, there is a need for research, development, and dissemination aimed at increasing the contributions of the Joint Committee and its standards.

FOOTNOTES

1. American Psychological Association, *Technical Recommendations for Psychological Tests and Diagnostic Techniques* (Washington, DC: American Psychological Association, 1954); American Educational Research Association and National Council on Measurements Used in Education, *Technical Recommendations for Achievement Tests* (Washington, DC: National Education Association, 1955).

2. American Psychological Association, *Standards for Educational and Psychological Tests and Manuals* (Washington, DC: American Psychological Association, 1966); idem, *Standards for Educational and Psychological Tests*, rev. ed. (Washington, DC: American Psychological Association, 1974); American Educational Research Association, American Psychological Association, and National Council on Measurement in Education, *Standards for Educational and Psychological Testing* (Washington, DC: American Psychological Association, 1985).

3. Peter H. Rossi, ed., *Standards for Evaluation Practice* (San Francisco: Jossey-Bass, 1982).

4. Joint Committee on Standards for Educational Evaluation, *Standards for Evaluations of Educational Programs, Projects, and Materials* (New York: McGraw-Hill, 1981); idem, *The Personnel Evaluation Standards* (Newbury Park, CA: Sage Publications, 1988).

5. See four papers presented at the 1982 meeting of the National Council on Measurement in Education in New York: Mary Anne Bunda, "Concerns and Techniques in Feasibility"; James C. Impara, "Measurement and the Utility Standards"; Jack C. Merwin, "Measurement and Propriety Standards"; and James L. Wardrop, "Measurement and Accuracy Standards."

6. Jeri M. Ridings, "Standard Setting in Accounting and Auditing: Considerations for Educational Evaluation" (Doct. diss., Western Michigan University, 1980).

7. Barbara M. Wildemuth, *A Bibliography to Accompany the Joint Committee's Standards on Educational Evaluation*, ERIC/TM, Report 81 (Princeton, NJ: Educational Testing Service, 1981).

8. Robert L. Linn, "A Preliminary Look at the Applicability of the Educational Evaluation Standards," *Educational Evaluation and Policy Analysis* 3 (1981): 87-91.

9. Robert E. Stake, "Setting Standards for Educational Evaluators," *Evaluation News* 2, no. 2 (1981): 148-152.

10. Michael J. Wargo, "The Standards: A Federal Level Perspective," *Evaluation News* 2, no. 2 (1981): 157-162.

11. Marcia Linn, "Standards for Evaluating Out-of-School Learning," *Evaluation News* 2, no. 2 (1981): 171-176.

12. Lou Carey, "State-Level Teacher Performance Evaluation Policies," *Inservice Centerfold* (New York: National Council on State and Inservice Education, 1979).

13. Deborah Burkett and Teri Denson, "Another View of the Standards," in *Evaluation of Continuing Education in the Health Professions*, ed. Stephen Abrahamson (Boston: Kluwer-Nijhoff Publishing, 1985).

14. David D. Marsh, Warren B. Newman, and William F. Boyer, "Comparing Ideal and Real: A Study of Evaluation Practice in California Using the Joint Committee's Evaluation Standards" (Paper presented at the Annual Meeting of the American Educational Research Association, Los Angeles, 1981).

15. Dianna L. Newman, "Evaluation Standards: Are They Related to Ethical Principles and Evaluator Roles?" (Paper presented at the Canadian Evaluation Society Annual Meeting, Banff, 1986).

16. Dianna L. Newman and Robert D. Brown, "Violations of Evaluation Standards: Frequency and Seriousness of Occurrence" (Paper presented at the Annual Meeting of the American Educational Research Association, Washington, DC, 1987).

17. Dianna L. Newman and Robert D. Brown, "Ethical Reasoning and the Standards for Evaluation: Do the Guidelines Represent Ethical Principles?" (Paper presented at the Annual Conference of the American Evaluation Association, Boston, 1987).

18. David Nevo, "Applying the Evaluation Standards in a Different Social

Context" (Paper presented at the 20th Congress of the International Association of Applied Psychology, Edinburgh, Scotland, 1982).

19. Ralph B. Straton, "Appropriateness and Potential Impact of the Programme Evaluation Standards in Australia" (Paper presented at the 20th International Congress of Applied Psychology, Edinburgh, Scotland, 1982).

20. Terezinha Rodrigues de Oliveira, Jussara Maria Lerch Hoffman, Raimundo Faco Barros, Nilce Fatima Correa Arruda, and Raulo-Ruas Santos, "Standards for Evaluations of Educational Programs, Projects, and Materials" (Unpublished paper, Department of Education, Federal University of Rio de Janeiro [UFRJ], 1981).

21. Arieh Lewy, "Evaluation Standards: Comments from Israel" (Presentation at the Annual Meeting of the American Educational Research Association, Montreal, 1983).

22. William B. Dockrell, "Applicability of Standards for Evaluations of Educational Programs, Projects, and Materials" (Presentation at the Annual Meeting of the American Educational Research Association, Montreal, 1983).

23. J. Scheerens and C. W. van Seventer, "Political and Organizational Preconditions for Application of the Standards for Educational Evaluation" (Presentation at the Annual Meeting of the American Educational Research Association, Montreal, 1983).

24. Sixten Marklund, "Applicability of *Standards for Evaluations of Educational Programs, Projects, and Materials* in an International Setting" (Presentation at the Annual Meeting of the American Educational Research Association, Montreal, 1983).

25. See Rossi, *Standards for Evaluation Practice*; David Cordray, "An Assessment of the Utility of the ERS Standards," in *Standards for Evaluation Practice*, New Directions for Program Evaluation, no. 15, ed. Peter H. Rossi (San Francisco: Jossey-Bass, 1982); Larry A. Braskamp and Paul W. Mayberry, "A Comparison of Two Sets of Standards" (Paper presented at the joint annual meeting of the Evaluation Network and the Evaluation Research Society, Baltimore, MD, 1982); Daniel L. Stufflebeam, "An Examination of the Overlap between ERS and Joint Committee Standards" (Paper presented at the annual meeting of the Evaluation Network, Baltimore, 1982); Jack McKillip and Roger Garbert, "A Further Examination of the Overlap between ERS and Joint Committee Evaluation Standards," unpublished paper (Carbondale, IL: Department of Psychology, Southern Illinois University, 1983); Stacey H. Stockdill, "The Appropriateness of the Evaluation Standards for Business Evaluations" (Presentation at the Evaluation Network/Evaluation Research Society joint meeting, San Francisco, 1984).

26. Robert L. Linn et al., "The Development, Validation, and Applicability of the Personnel Evaluation Standards," *Journal of Personnel Evaluation in Education* 2, no. 3 (1989): 199-214.

27. Ibid.

28. Michael J. Orris, "Industrial Applicability of the Joint Committee's Personnel Evaluation Standards" (Doct. diss., Western Michigan University, 1989).

29. C. Rebecca Montoya, "A Study of a Sample of Evaluation Plans for Elementary and High School Certified Personnel in the State of Illinois" (Doct. diss., Northern Illinois University, 1988).

30. Donald Campbell and Julian C. Stanley, "Experimental and Quasi-experimental Designs for Research on Teaching," in *Handbook of Research on Teaching*, ed. N. L. Gage (Chicago: Rand McNally, 1963).

31. Daniel L. Stufflebeam, William J. Foley, William J. Gephart, Egon G. Guba, Robert L. Hammond, Howard O. Merriman, and Malcolm M. Provus, *Educational Evaluation and Decision Making* (Itasca, IL: F. E. Peacock, Publishers, 1971).

Name Index

Subject Index

Secondary analysis, use of, in cost-effectiveness studies, 201-2

Social classes, reluctance of evaluation to recognize, as factors influencing life chances, 243-44

Social programs, purposes for evaluation of, 3-4

Social science research, study of uses of, 219-21

Society for the Psychological Study of Social Issues, 195

Stakeholders: concept of, in evaluation, 238-39, 244; roles of, in evaluation, 100-1

Standards for Evaluation of Educational Programs, Projects, and Materials ("Program Evaluation Standards"): applicability of, outside U.S., 264-65; citation form for use in application of, 260-61, fig., 262; content of, 253-57; format used in, 252-53; functional table of contents for, 259, table, 260; problems associated with trade-offs among, 258-59; process used in formulating, 251-

52; propriety standards in, 274; studies of validity of, 261-66

Student behavior, criteria for appraising samples of, 10-11

Summative evaluation: definition of, 20; power of, 25-26

Teacher selection, cost-effectiveness study of, 193-94

Teachers, evaluation of, 39-40, 49-50, 52, 53-54

Thematics, as dimension of educational criticism, 177-79

U.S. Department of Defense, 189

U.S. Department of Education, 147, 148, 149, 150, 153, 155, 201

U.S. Department of Labor, 154

Utilitarianism: concept of equality in, 325-36; theory of justice derived from, 235-36

Youth Employment Development Program Act, 150, 154

INFORMATION ABOUT MEMBERSHIP IN THE SOCIETY

Membership in the National Society for the Study of Education is open to all who desire to receive its publications.

There are two categories of membership, Regular and Comprehensive. The Regular Membership (annual dues in 1991, $25) entitles the member to receive both volumes of the yearbook. The Comprehensive Membership (annual dues in 1991, $45) entitles the member to receive the two-volume yearbook and the two current volumes in the Series on Contemporary Educational Issues. For their first year of membership, full-time graduate students pay reduced dues in 1991 as follows: Regular, $20; Comprehensive, $40.

Membership in the Society is for the calendar year. Dues are payable on or before January 1 of each year.

New members are required to pay an entrance fee of $1, in addition to annual dues for the year in which they join.

Members of the Society include professors, researchers, graduate students, and administrators in colleges and universities; teachers, supervisors, curriculum specialists, and administrators in elementary and secondary schools; and a considerable number of persons not formally connected with educational institutions.

All members participate in the nomination and election of the six-member Board of Directors, which is responsible for managing the affairs of the Society, including the authorization of volumes to appear in the yearbook series. All members whose dues are paid for the current year are eligible for election to the Board of Directors.

Each year the Society arranges for meetings to be held in conjunction with the annual conferences of one or more of the major national educational organizations. All members are urged to attend these sessions. Members are also encouraged to submit proposals for future yearbooks or for volumes in the series on Contemporary Educational Issues.

Further information about the Society may be secured by writing to the Secretary-Treasurer, NSSE, 5835 Kimbark Avenue, Chicago, IL 60637.

RECENT PUBLICATIONS OF THE NATIONAL SOCIETY FOR THE STUDY OF EDUCATION

1. The Yearbooks

Ninetieth Yearbook (1991)

Part 1. *The Care and Education of America's Young Children: Obstacles and Opportunities.* Sharon L. Kagan, editor. Cloth.

Part 2. *Evaluation and Education: At Quarter Century.* Milbrey W. McLaughlin and D. C. Phillips, editors. Cloth.

Eighty-ninth Yearbook (1990)

Part 1. *Textbooks and Schooling in the United States.* David L. Elliott and Arthur Woodward, editors. Cloth.

Part 2. *Educational Leadership and Changing Contexts of Families, Communities, and Schools.* Brad Mitchell and Luvern L. Cunningham, editors. Cloth.

Eighty-eighth Yearbook (1989)

Part 1. *From Socrates to Software: The Teacher as Text and the Text as Teacher.* Philip W. Jackson and Sophie Haroutunian-Gordon, editors. Cloth.

Part 2. *Schooling and Disability.* Douglas Biklen, Dianne Ferguson, and Alison Ford, editors. Cloth.

Eighty-seventh Yearbook (1988)

Part 1. *Critical Issues in Curriculum.* Laurel N. Tanner, editor. Cloth.

Part 2. *Cultural Literacy and the Idea of General Education.* Ian Westbury and Alan C. Purves, editors. Cloth.

Eighty-sixth Yearbook (1987)

Part 1. *The Ecology of School Renewal.* John I. Goodlad, editor. Cloth.

Part 2. *Society as Educator in an Age of Transition.* Kenneth D. Benne and Steven Tozer, editors. Cloth.

Eighty-fifth Yearbook (1986)

Part 1. *Microcomputers and Education.* Jack A. Culbertson and Luvern L. Cunningham, editors. Cloth.

Part 2. *The Teaching of Writing.* Anthony R. Petrosky and David Bartholomae, editors. Paper.

Eighty-fourth Yearbook (1985)

Part 1. *Education in School and Nonschool Settings.* Mario D. Fantini and Robert Sinclair, editors. Cloth.

Part 2. *Learning and Teaching the Ways of Knowing.* Elliot Eisner, editor. Paper.

Eighty-third Yearbook (1984)

Part 1. *Becoming Readers in a Complex Society.* Alan C. Purves and Olive S. Niles, editors. Cloth.

Part 2. *The Humanities in Precollegiate Education.* Benjamin Ladner, editor. Paper.

Eighty-second Yearbook (1983)

Part 1. *Individual Differences and the Common Curriculum.* Gary D Fenstermacher and John I. Goodlad, editors. Paper.

Eighty-first Yearbook (1982)

Part 1. *Policy Making in Education.* Ann Lieberman and Milbrey W. McLaughlin, editors. Cloth.

Part 2. *Education and Work.* Harry F. Silberman, editor. Cloth.

Eightieth Yearbook (1981)

Part 1. *Philosophy and Education.* Jonas P. Soltis, editor. Cloth.

Part 2. *The Social Studies.* Howard D. Mehlinger and O. L. Davis, Jr., editors. Cloth.

Seventy-ninth Yearbook (1980)

Part 1. *Toward Adolescence: The Middle School Years.* Mauritz Johnson, editor. Paper.

Seventy-eighth Yearbook (1979)

Part 1. *The Gifted and the Talented: Their Education and Development.* A. Harry Passow, editor. Paper.

Part 2. *Classroom Management.* Daniel L. Duke, editor. Paper.

Seventy-seventh Yearbook (1978)

Part 1. *The Courts and Education.* Clifford B. Hooker, editor. Cloth.

Seventy-sixth Yearbook (1977)

Part 1. *The Teaching of English.* James R. Squire, editor. Cloth.

The above titles in the Society's Yearbook series may be ordered from the University of Chicago Press, Book Order Department, 11030 Langley Ave., Chicago, IL 60628. For a list of earlier titles in the yearbook series still available, write to the Secretary, NSSE, 5835 Kimbark Ave., Chicago, IL 60637.

2. The Series on Contemporary Educational Issues

The following volumes in the Society's Series on Contemporary Educational Issues may be ordered from the McCutchan Publishing Corporation, P.O. Box 774, Berkeley, CA 94702.

Boyd, William Lowe, and Walberg, Herbert J., editors. *Choice in Education: Potential and Problems.* 1990.

Case, Charles W., and Matthes, William A., editors. *Colleges of Education: Perspectives on Their Future.* 1985.

Eisner, Elliot, and Vallance, Elizabeth, editors. *Conflicting Conceptions of Curriculum.* 1974.

Erickson, Donald A., and Reller, Theodore L., editors. *The Principal in Metropolitan Schools.* 1979.

Farley, Frank H., and Gordon, Neal J., editors. *Psychology and Education: The State of the Union.* 1981.

Fennema, Elizabeth, and Ayer, M. Jane, editors. *Women and Education: Equity or Equality.* 1984.

Griffiths, Daniel E., Stout, Robert T., and Forsyth, Patrick, editors. *Leaders for America's Schools: The Report and Papers of the National Commission on Excellence in Educational Administration.* 1988.

Jackson, Philip W., editor. *Contributing to Educational Change: Perspectives on Research and Practice.* 1988.

Lane, John J., and Walberg, Herbert J., editors. *Effective School Leadership: Policy and Process.* 1987.

Levine, Daniel U., and Havighurst, Robert J., editors. *The Future of Big City Schools: Desegregation Policies and Magnet Alternatives.* 1977.

Lindquist, Mary M., editor. *Selected Issues in Mathematics Education.* 1981.

Murphy, Joseph, editor. *The Educational Reform Movement of the 1980s: Perspectives and Cases.* 1990.

Nucci, Larry P., editor. *Moral Development and Character Education.* 1989.

Peterson, Penelope L., and Walberg, Herbert J., editors. *Research on Teaching: Concepts, Findings, and Implications.* 1979.

Pflaum-Connor, Susanna, editor. *Aspects of Reading Education.* 1978.

Purves, Alan, and Levine, Daniel U., editors. *Educational Policy and International Assessment: Implications of the IEA Assessment of Achievement.* 1975.

Sinclair, Robert L., and Ghory, Ward. *Reaching Marginal Students: A Prime Concern for School Renewal.* 1987.

Spodek, Bernard, and Walberg, Herbert J., editors. *Early Childhood Education: Issues and Insights.* 1977.

Talmage, Harriet, editor. *Systems of Individualized Education.* 1975.

Tomlinson, Tommy M., and Walberg, Herbert J., editors. *Academic Work and Educational Excellence: Raising Student Productivity.* 1986.

Tyler, Ralph W., editor. *From Youth to Constructive Adult Life: The Role of the Public School.* 1978.

Tyler, Ralph W., and Wolf, Richard M., editors. *Crucial Issues in Testing.* 1974.

Walberg, Herbert J., editor. *Educational Environments and Effects: Evaluation, Policy, and Productivity.* 1979.

Walberg, Herbert J., editor. *Improving Educational Standards and Productivity: The Research Basis for Policy.* 1982.

Wang, Margaret C., and Walberg, Herbert J., editors. *Adapting Instruction to Student Differences.* 1985.

Warren, Donald R., editor. *History, Education, and Public Policy: Recovering the American Educational Past.* 1978.

Waxman, Hersholt C., and Walberg, Herbert J., editors. *Effective Teaching: Current Research.* 1991.